A-Z STOKE-ON-TRENT

CONTE...

C000283208

Key to Map Pages	2-3
Large Scale Centres	4-7
Map Pages	8-49

REFEREN...

Motorway	**M6**	Map Continuation 12	Large Scale Centres 4
A Road	A50	Car Park (Selected)	P
Under Construction		Church or Chapel	†
B Road	B5040	Fire Station	■
Dual Carriageway		Hospital	H
One Way Street	→	House Numbers A and B Roads only	128 460
Traffic flow on A Roads is also indicated by a heavy line on the driver's left.	→	Information Centre	🆔
Restricted Access		National Grid Reference	³50
Pedestrianized Road		Police Station	▲
Track		Post Office	★
Footpath		Toilet	▽
		with facilities for the Disabled	▽
Residential Walkway		Educational Establishment	
Railway	Station / Tunnel / Level Crossing / Heritage Station	Hospital, Hospice or Health Centre	
Built-up Area	GLOVER ST.	Industrial Building	
		Leisure & Recreational Facility	
Local Authority Boundary		Place of Interest	
Posttown Boundary		Public Building	
Postcode Boundary within Posttown		Shopping Centre or Market	
		Other Selected Buildings	

SCALE

Map Pages 8-49	Map Pages 4-7
1:19,000 3⅓ inches (8.47 cm) to 1 mile, 5.26 cm to 1km	1:7920 8 inches (20.32 cm) to 1 mile, 12.63 cm to 1km

0	¼	½ Mile	0	⅛	¼ Mile
0	250	500	750 Metres	0	100	200	300	400 Metres

Copyright of Geographers' A-Z Map Company Limited

Head Office:
Fairfield Road, Borough Green, Sevenoaks, Kent TN15 8PP
Telephone: 01732 781000 (Enquiries & Trade Sales)
01732 783422 (Retail Sales)
www.a-zmaps.co.uk
Copyright © Geographers' A-Z Map Co. Ltd.

Ordnance Survey® This product includes mapping data licensed from Ordnance Survey® with the permission of the Controller of Her Majesty's Stationery Office.
© Crown Copyright 2002. All rights reserved. Licence number 100017302
Edition 4 2002   Edition 4a 2005 (Part Revision)

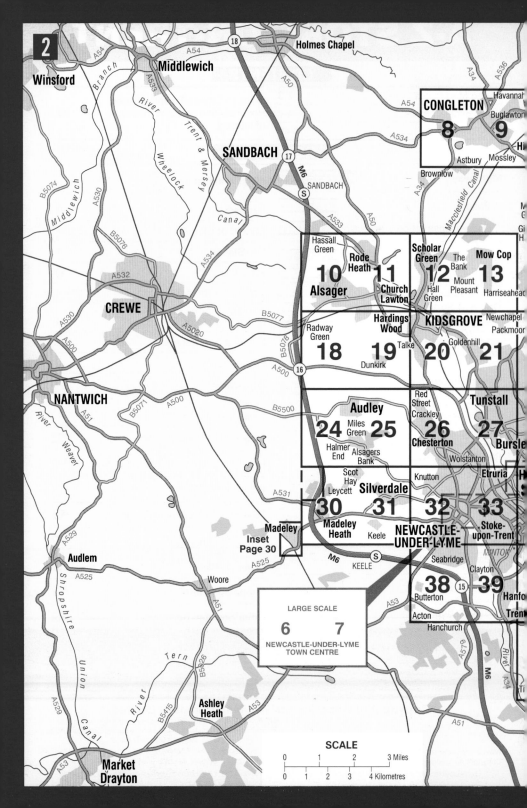

2

Winsford
Middlewich
Holmes Chapel
A54
A54
A533
Branch
River
Trent & Mersey
SANDBACH
17
A50
A533
A50
Wheelock
Middlewich
B5074
A530
B5076
A534
Canal

CONGLETON
8 **9**
Havannah
Buglawton
H.
Astbury Mossley
Brownlow
A534
A34
A536
Macclesfield Canal

SANDBACH
S
M6

Hassall Green
Rode Heath
10 **11**
Alsager
Church Lawton

Scholar Green
The Bank
Mow Cop
12 **13**
Hall Green
Mount Pleasant
Harriseahead

CREWE
A532
B5077
B5078
A500
16

Radway Green
Hardings Wood
Talke
18 **19**
Dunkirk

KIDSGROVE
Newchapel
Packmoor
20 **21**
Goldenhill

NANTWICH
A51
B5071
A500
B5500

Audley
Miles Green
24 **25**
Halmer End
Alsagers Bank

Red Street
Crackley
26
Chesterton
Wolstanton

Tunstall
27
Bursle

River Weaver

A531

Scot Hay
Leycett
Silverdale
30 **31**
Madeley Heath
Keele

Knutton
32 **33**
Stoke-upon-Trent

Etruria
H.
MINTON

Audlem
A529

Madeley
Inset
Page 30

M6
S
KEELE

Seabridge
Clayton
38 **39**
Butterton
Acton
Hanchurch

Hanfo
Tren

Shropshire Union Canal

A525
Woore
A51

LARGE SCALE
6 **7**
NEWCASTLE-UNDER-LYME
TOWN CENTRE

NEWCASTLE-UNDER-LYME

A53
A576
M6
A34

Tern
River
B5026

Ashley Heath
A53

Market Drayton
A529
B5415
A53

SCALE

0   1   2   3 Miles
0   1   2   3   4 Kilometres

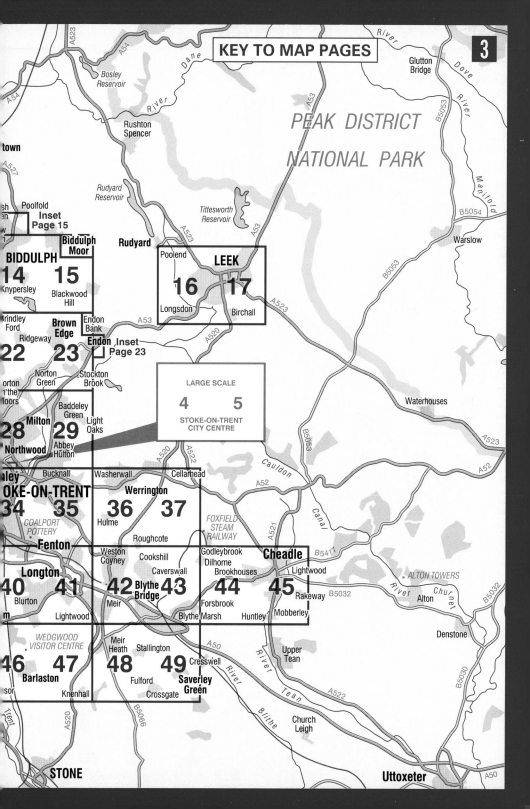

PEAK DISTRICT

NATIONAL PARK

Glutton Bridge

Warslow

Bosley Reservoir

Rushton Spencer

town

Poolfold

Inset Page 15

Rudyard Reservoir

Tittesworth Reservoir

Biddulph Moor

BIDDULPH

Rudyard

14 **15**

Knypersley

Blackwood Hill

Poolend

LEEK

16 **17**

Longsdon   Birchall

Brindley Ford   Ridgeway

Brown Edge

22 **23**

Endon Bank

Endon Inset Page 23

Norton Green   Stockton Brook

Waterhouses

Norton i'the Moors

Baddeley Green

Milton

28 **29**

Northwood

Light Oaks

Abbey Hulton

LARGE SCALE

4   **5**

STOKE-ON-TRENT CITY CENTRE

Bucknall   Washerwall   Cellarhead

OKE-ON-TRENT

34 **35**

Werrington

36 **37**

Hulme

COALPORT POTTERY

Fenton

FOXFIELD STEAM RAILWAY

Roughcote

Cheadle

ALTON TOWERS

Weston Coyney

Cookshill

Godleybrook Dilhorne   Lightwood

Longton

40 **41**   **42** **43**   **44** **45**

Blurton

Meir

Blythe Bridge

Caverswall

Brookhouses

Rakeway

Alton

Lightwood

Blythe Marsh

Forsbrook

Huntley   Mobberley

Denstone

WEDGWOOD VISITOR CENTRE

Meir Heath

Stallington

Cresswell

Upper Tean

46 **47**   **48** **49**

Barlaston

Fulford

Saverley Green

Knenhall   Crossgate

Church Leigh

STONE

Uttoxeter

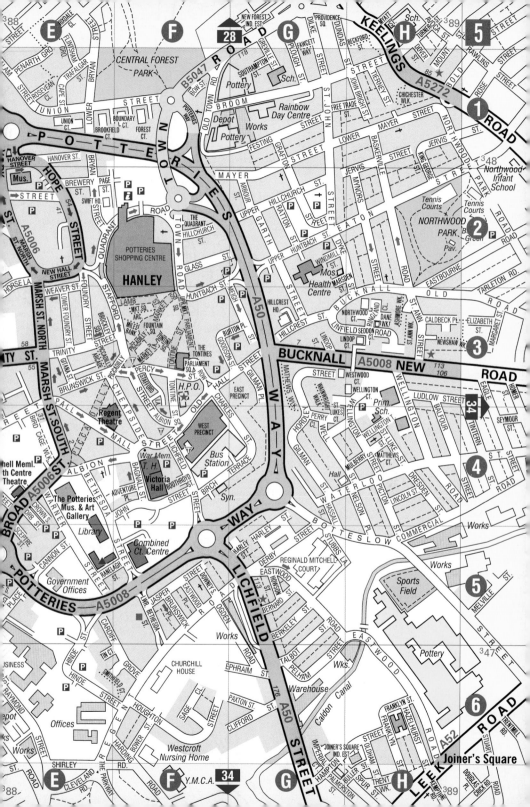

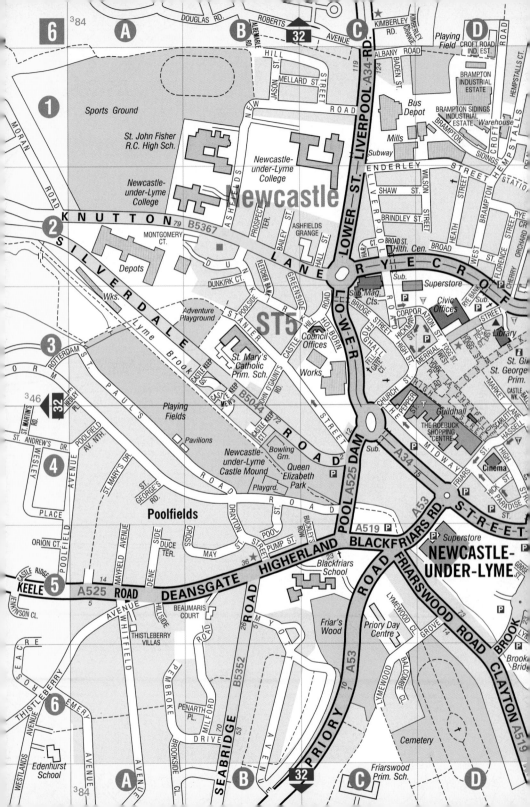

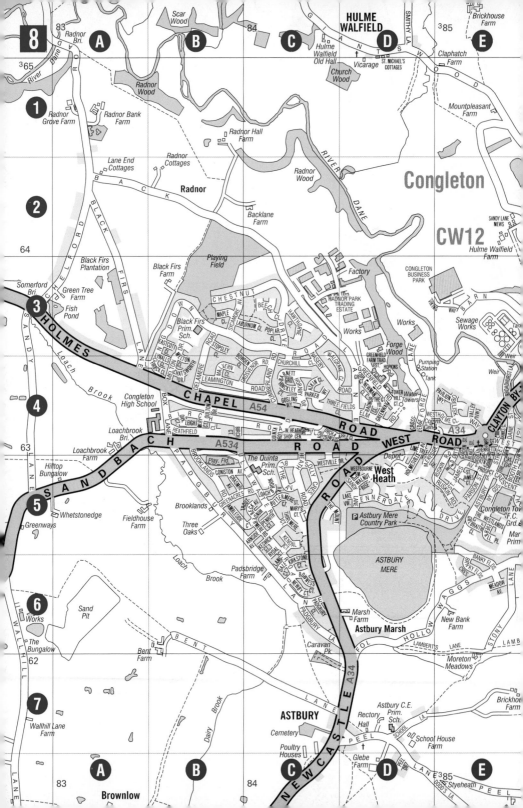

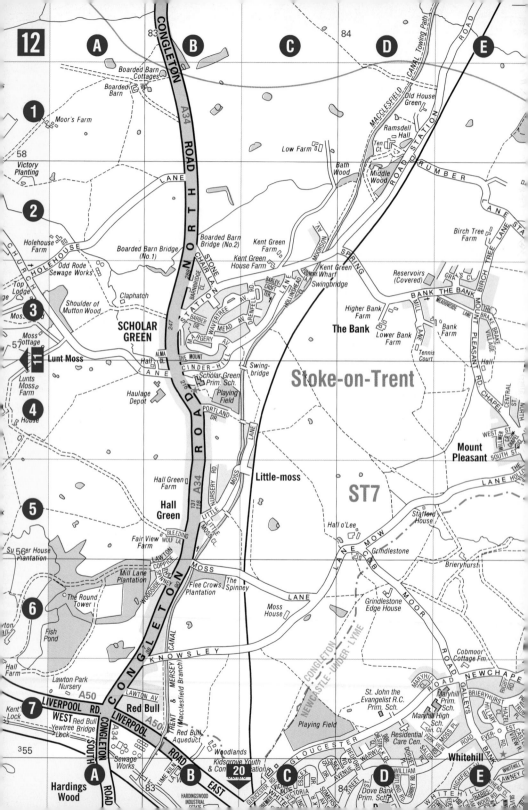

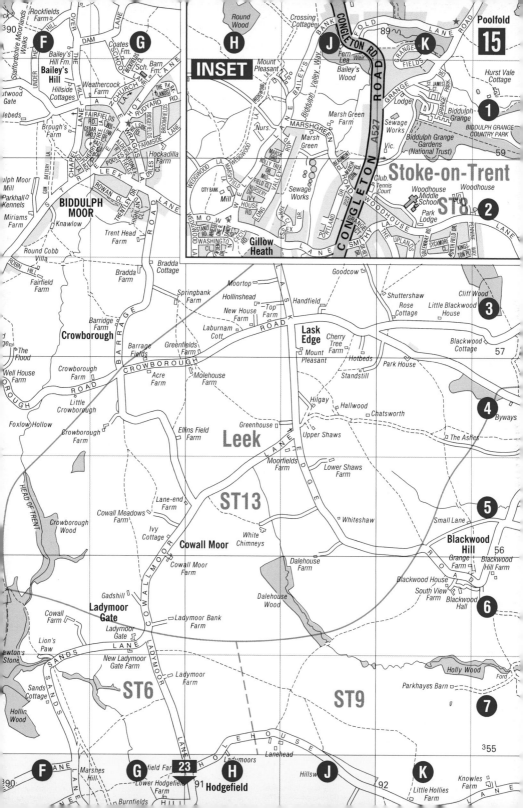

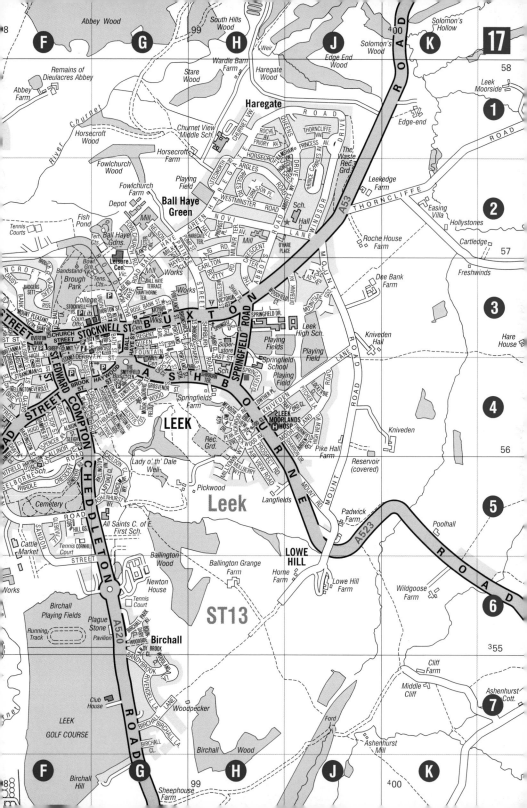

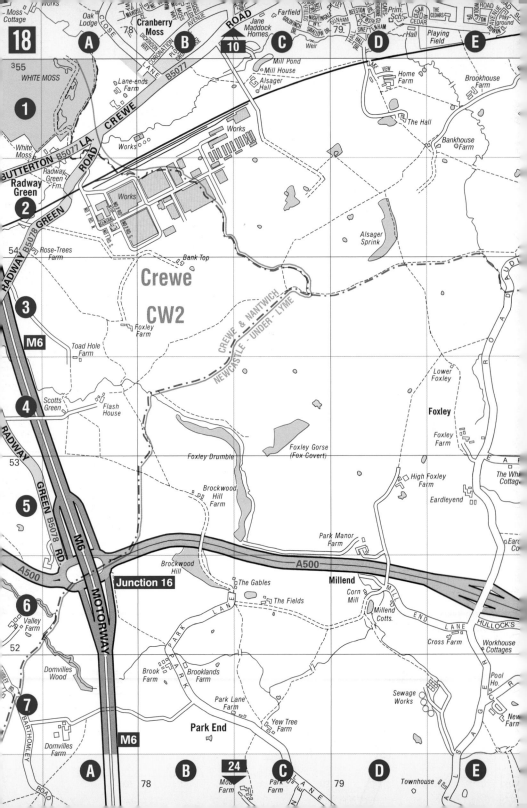

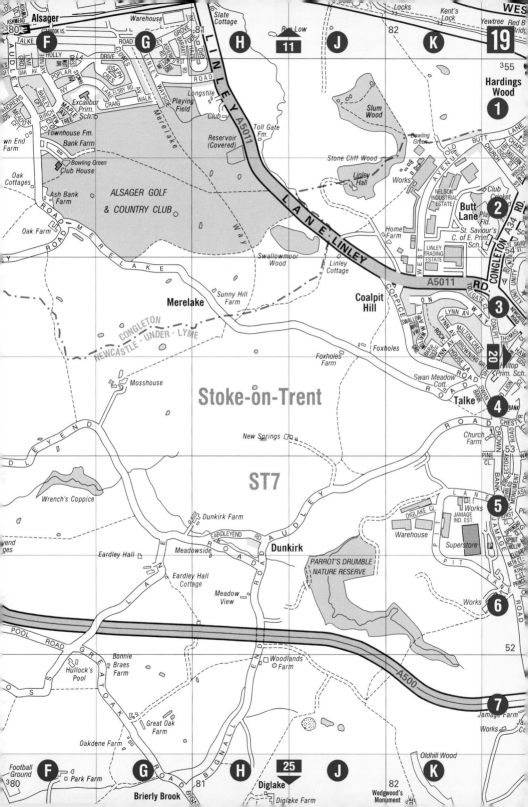

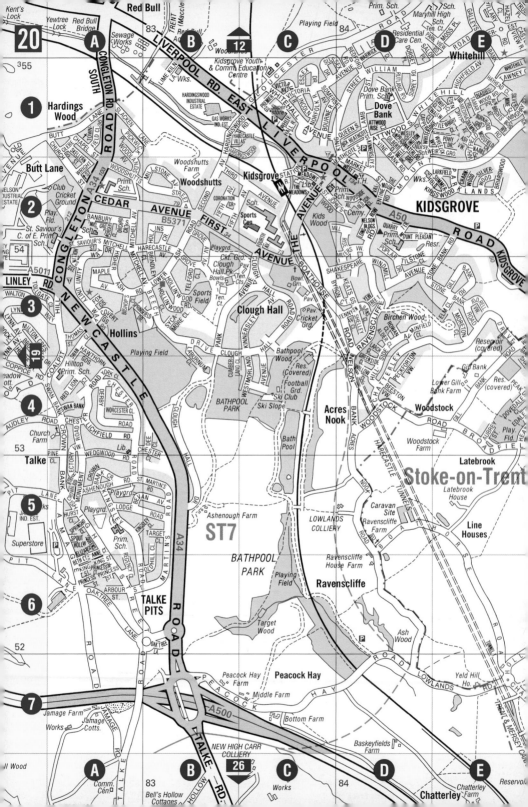

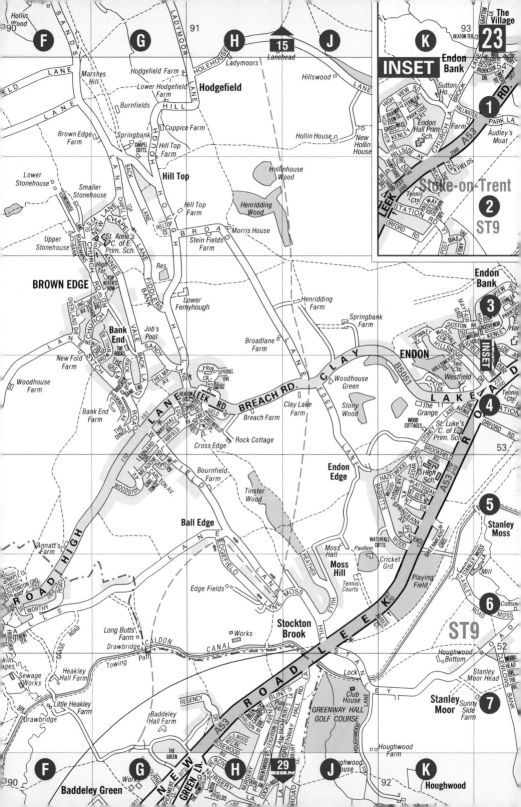

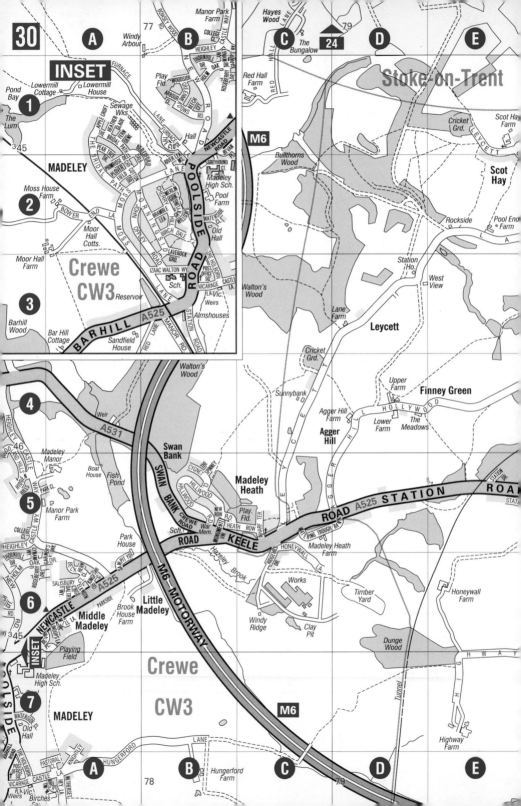

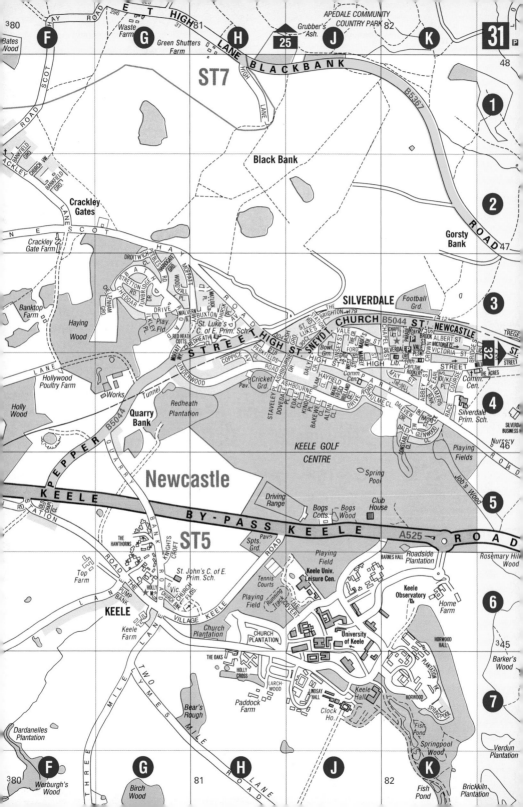

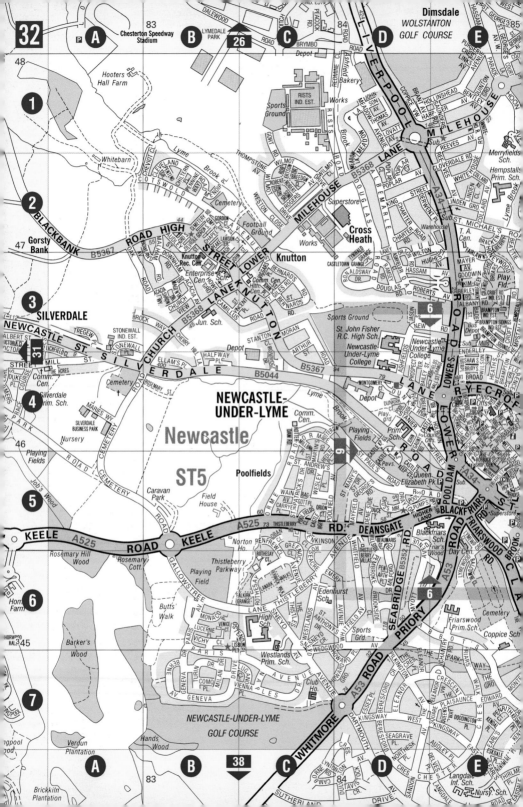

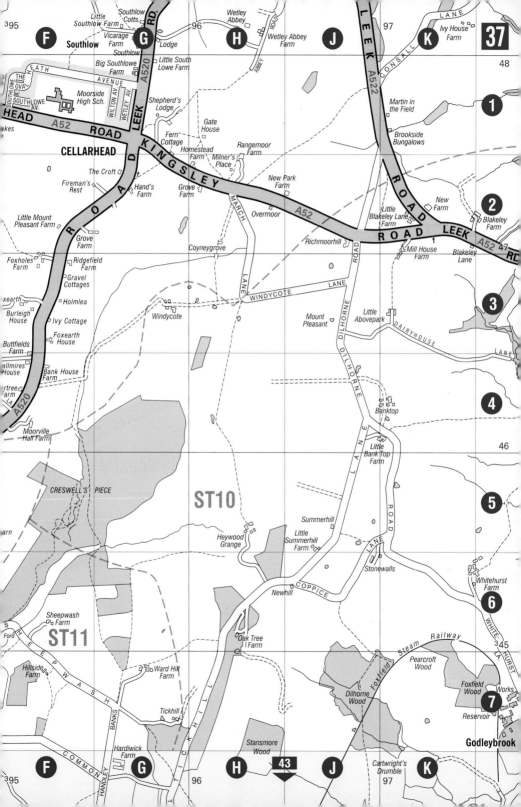

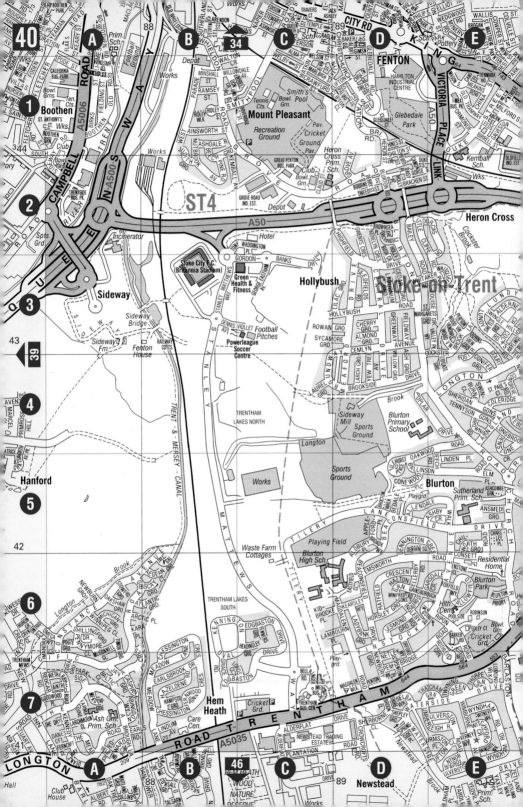

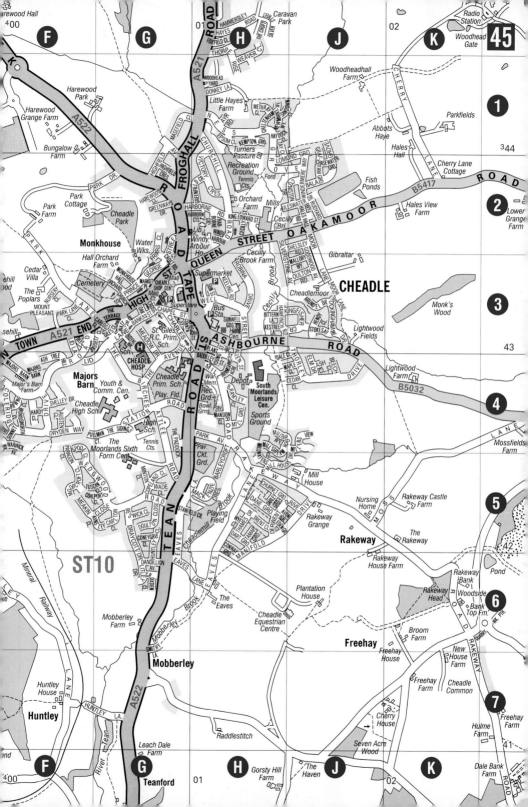

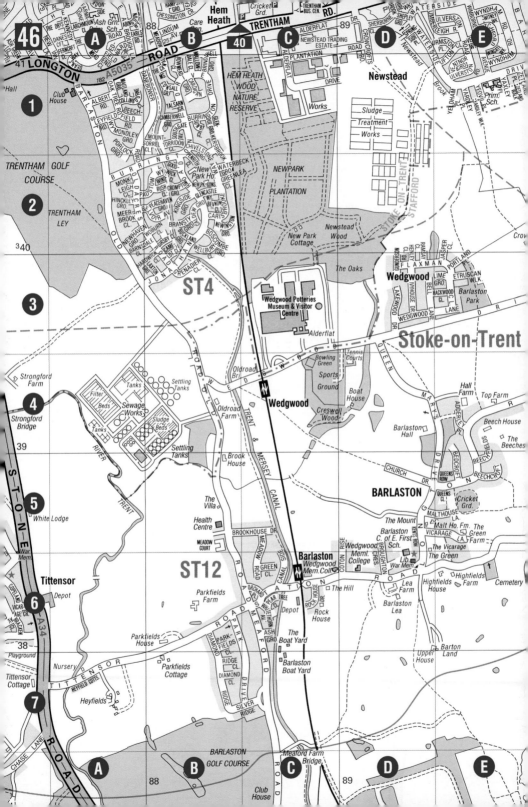

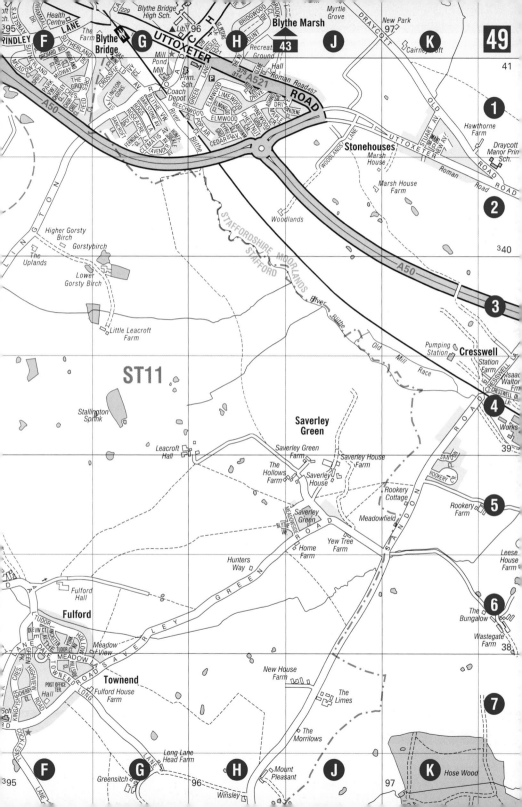

INDEX

Including Streets, Places & Areas, Hospitals & Hospices, Industrial Estates,
Selected Flats & Walkways, Stations and Selected Places of Interest.

HOW TO USE THIS INDEX

1. Each street name is followed by its Posttown or Postal Locality and then by its map reference; e.g. Abbey Grn. Rd. *Leek* ....1E **16** is in the Leek Posttown and is to be found in square 1E on page **16**. The page number being shown in bold type.

2. A strict alphabetical order is followed in which Av., Rd., St., etc. (though abbreviated) are read in full and as part of the street name; e.g. Alanley Clo. appears after Alan Dale but before Alan Rd.

3. Streets and a selection of flats and walkways too small to be shown on the maps, appear in the index in *Italics* with the thoroughfare to which it is connected shown in brackets; e.g. Axbridge Wlk. *Stoke* ....3B **28** *(off Kinver St.)*

4. Places and areas are shown in the index in **blue type** and the map reference is to the actual map square in which the town centre or area is located and not to the place name shown on the map; e.g. **Alsager.** 6E **10**

5. An example of a selected place of interest is **Apedale Heritage Cen.** 7K **25**

6. An example of a hospital or hospice is **BRADWELL HOSPITAL.** 5D **26**

7. An example of a station is **ALSAGER STATION. RAIL** 7F **11**

8. Map references shown in brackets; e.g. Adventure Pl. *Stoke* ....2B **34** (4F **5**) refer to entries that also appear on the large scale pages **4-7**.

GENERAL ABBREVIATIONS

All : Alley	Ct : Court	Lit : Little	Rd : Road
App : Approach	Cres : Crescent	Lwr : Lower	Shop : Shopping
Arc : Arcade	Cft : Croft	Mc : Mac	S : South
Av : Avenue	Dri : Drive	Mnr : Manor	Sq : Square
Bk : Back	E : East	Mans : Mansions	Sta : Station
Boulevd : Boulevard	Embkmt : Embankment	Mkt : Market	St : Street
Bri : Bridge	Est : Estate	Mdw : Meadow	Ter : Terrace
B'way : Broadway	Fld : Field	M : Mews	Trad : Trading
Bldgs : Buildings	Gdns : Gardens	Mt : Mount	Up : Upper
Bus : Business	Gth : Garth	Mus : Museum	Va : Vale
Cvn : Caravan	Ga : Gate	N : North	Vw : View
Cen : Centre	Gt : Great	Pal : Palace	Vs : Villas
Chu : Church	Grn : Green	Pde : Parade	Vis : Visitors
Chyd : Churchyard	Gro : Grove	Pk : Park	Wlk : Walk
Circ : Circle	Ho : House	Pas : Passage	W : West
Cir : Circus	Ind : Industrial	Pl : Place	Yd : Yard
Clo : Close	Info : Information	Quad : Quadrant	
Comn : Common	Junct : Junction	Res : Residential	
Cotts : Cottages	La : Lane	Ri : Rise	

POSTTOWN AND POSTAL LOCALITY ABBREVIATIONS

Act : Acton	*Cong* : Congleton	*Knut* : Knutton	*Row I* : Rowhurst Ind. Est.
Als : Alsager	*C'wll* : Cresswell	*Knyp* : Knypersley	*Rud* : Rudyard
Als B : Alsagers Bank	*Dil* : Dilhorne	*Lask E* : Lask Edge	*Sand* : Sandyford
Ash B : Ash Bank	*Dray* : Draycott	*Leek* : Leek	*Sav G* : Saverley Green
A'bry : Astbury	*Dres* : Dresden	*Ley* : Leycett	*Sch G* : Scholar Green
A'ly : Audley	*Eat T* : Eaton Bank Trad. Est.	*L Oaks* : Light Oaks	*S Hay* : Scot Hay
Bad G : Baddeley Green	*End* : Endon	*Long H* : Longbridge Hayes	*Sil* : Silverdale
Bag : Bagnall	*Fen I* : Fenton Ind. Est.	*Long* : Longsdon	*Smal* : Smallthorne
B'stn : Barlaston	*For* : Forsbrook	*L'tn* : Longton	*S Grn* : Sneyd Green
B'ly : Barthomley	*Ful* : Fulford	*Lyme B* : Lymedale Bus. Pk.	*Som* : Somerford
B'ton : Betchton	*Gil H* : Gillow Heath	*Mad* : Madeley	*Spot A* : Spot Acre
Bet : Betley	*Halm* : Halmerend	*Mad H* : Madeley Heath	*Stoc B* : Stockton Brook
Bid : Biddulph	*Han* : Hanchurch	*Meir H* : Meir Heath	*Stoke* : Stoke-on-Trent
Bid M : Biddulph Moor	*Har* : Harriseahead	*Mor* : Moreton	*Stone* : Stone
Big E : Bignall End	*Has G* : Hassall Green	*Mow C* : Mow Cop	*Tal* : Talke
B Bri : Blythe Bridge	*Hav* : Havannah	*New* : Newcastle	*Tal P* : Talke Pits
B Frd : Brindley Ford	*Hem H* : Hem Heath	*N'cpl* : Newchapel	*Thor* : Thorncliffe
Brn E : Brown Edge	*High B* : High Carr Bus. Pk.	*Pac* : Packmoor	*T'sor* : Tittensor
Brn L : Brown Lees	*Hot I* : Hot Lane Ind. Est.	*P East* : Parkhouse Ind. Est. E.	*Tren* : Trentham
B'lw : Brownlow	*Hul* : Hulme	*P West* : Parkhouse Ind. Est. W.	*T Vale* : Trent Vale
Bug : Buglawton	*Hul W* : Hulme Walfield	*Park* : Parklands	*Tun* : Tunstall
Bur : Burslem	*Join I* : Joiners Square Ind. Est.	*Port* : Porthill	*Werr* : Werrington
But : Butterton	*K'le* : Keele	*Rad G* : Radway Green	*W Coy* : Weston Coyney
Cav : Caverswall	*Ker* : Kermincham	*Red S* : Red Street	*Wet R* : Wetley Rocks
C'dle : Cheadle	*Kid* : Kidsgrove	*Rode H* : Rode Heath	*Wol* : Wolstanton
Ches : Chesterton	*King* : Kingsley	*Rook* : Rookery	
Chu L : Church Lawton	*Knen* : Knenhall	*R'gh C* : Rough Close	

A		

	Abbey Ct. *Stoke* 7G **29**	Abbey Rd. *Wet R* 1H **37**	Abbot's Way. *New* 6D **32**
	Abbey Grn. Rd. *Leek* 1E **16**	Abbey St. *New* 4K **31**	Abbott's Clo. *Cong* 7K **9**
	Abbey Hulton. 6H **29**	Abbey St. *Stoke* 6F **29**	Abbotts Ct. *Stoke* 5G **29**
Aarons Dri. *Big E* 2G **25**	Abbey La. *Stoke* 1F **35**	Abbots Pl. *Stoke* 6G **29**	Abbotts Dri. *Stoke* 4D **28**
Abberley Ho. *New* 5F **27**	Abbey Rd. *Stoke* 6F **29**	Abbots Rd. *Stoke* 5G **29**	Abbott's Rd. *Leek* 3H **17**

Abercorn St.—Ayr Rd.

Abercorn St. Stoke 1E 40
Aberford Gro. Stoke 7D 28
Abingdon Way. Stoke 7A 40
Acacia Av. New 3B 32
Acacia Gdns. Kid 7F 13
Acacia Gro. New 3B 32
Achilles Way. Stoke 4E 34
Acorn Ri. Stoke 6J 41
Acres Nook. 4D 20
Acres Nook Rd. Stoke 4D 20
Acres, The. New 4A 32
Acreswood Rd. Stoke 2A 28
Acton. 6A 38
Acton La. Act 7A 38
Acton St. Stoke 6C 28
Acton Way. Chu L 4E 10
Adams Av. Stoke 6G 21
Adams Gro. Leek 5C 16
Adams St. New 1F 33
Adams St. Stoke 3G 29
Adamthwaite Clo. B Bri 7E 42
Adamthwaite Dri. B Bri 6E 42
Adderley Green. 7J 35
Adderley Pl. B'stn 4E 46
Adderley Rd. Stoke 1D 28
Addington Way. Stoke 1J 41
Addison St. Stoke 6C 28
Adelaide St. Stoke 5K 27
Adkins St. Stoke 5B 28
Adrian St. Stoke 7D 34
Adventure Pl. Stoke 2B 34 (4F 5)
Aegean Clo. Stoke 6B 40
Agger Hill. 4C 30
Agger Hill. Ley 5C 30
Ainsdale Clo. Stoke 5J 41
Ainsley Clo. Stoke 6G 29
Ainsworth St. Stoke 1B 40
Aintree Clo. Stoke 7A 40
Aitken St. Stoke 4H 27
Ajax Way. Stoke 4E 34
Akesmoor La. Gil H 3J 13
Alanbrooke Gro. Stoke 5K 41
Alan Dale. Werr 1C 36
Alanley Clo. Stoke 3C 28
Alan Rd. Stoke 2H 35
Alastair Rd. Stoke 2J 39
Albany Gro. Stoke 5G 33 (5H 7)
Albany Rd. New 3E 32 (1C 6)
Albany Rd. Stoke 5G 33 (5H 7)
Albany St. Stoke 4F 21
Albemarle Rd. New 2D 32 (1B 6)
Alberta St. Stoke 4H 41
Albert Av. Stoke 3K 41
Albert Pl. Cong 3H 9
(Havannah St.)
Albert Pl. Cong 5G 9
(High St.)
Albert Pl. Stoke 5G 41
Albert Rd. Stoke 1A 46
Albert Sq. Stoke 7D 34
Albert St. Bid 2B 14
Albert St. Big E 1F 25
Albert St. Ches 5B 26
Albert St. Leek 3F 17
Albert St. New 4G 33 (2G 7)
Albert St. Sil 3K 31
Albert St. Stoke 1H 41
Albert Ter. New 7F 27
Albion Sq. Stoke 2B 34 (4F 5)
Albion St. Leek 4F 17
Albion St. Stoke 2B 34 (4E 5)
Alcester Clo. Stoke 5A 22
Aldbury Pl. Stoke 5D 40
Aldeburgh Dri. New 4E 38
Alder Clo. Kid 3D 20
Alderflat Dri. Stoke 7C 40
Alder Gro. New 4A 26
Alderhay La. Rook 6F 13
Alderney Clo. New 2B 38
Alderney Cres. Stoke 3E 40
Aldersea Clo. Stoke 3H 27
Alders Rd. Bid M 1G 15
Alderton Gro. Stoke 1C 48
Alder Wlk. Stoke 2H 39
Aldrin Clo. Stoke 7D 42
Alexandra Rd. New 7F 27
Alexandra Rd. Stoke 4K 41
Alford Dri. Stoke 2B 36
Alfred St. Stoke 6D 34
Alfreton Rd. Stoke 7F 35
Algar Rd. Stoke 7H 33
Alicia Way. Stoke 1F 29
Allenby Sq. Stoke 2H 39
Allendale Wlk. Stoke 5D 40
Allensmore Av. Stoke 1G 41
Allen St. C'dle 4H 45
Allen St. Stoke 5H 33
Allensway. New 2B 38
Allerton Rd. Stoke 7J 39
All Saints Rd. Stoke 1K 39
Alma Clo. Sch G 3B 12
Almar Pl. Stoke 6K 21
Alma St. Leek 3E 16
Alma St. Stoke 7C 34
Almond Gro. Stoke 3D 40
Almond Pl. New 3A 26
Alsager. 6E 10
Alsager Leisure Cen. 6C 10
Alsager Rd. A'ly 5E 18
Alsager Rd. Has G 2A 10
Alsagers Bank. 7G 25
ALSAGER STATION. RAIL . . .7F 11
Alsop St. Leek 4F 17
Alstonfield Av. Stoke 6H 29
Althorpe Pl. New 3C 38
Althrop Gro. Stoke 3J 41
Alton Clo. New 4J 31
Alton Gro. Stoke 6J 35
Alwyn Cres. Stoke 4C 28
Amber Ct. Stoc B 6K 23
Amberfield Clo. Stoke 2K 41
Amblecote Dri. Stoke 2K 41
Ambleside Ct. Cong 5B 8
Ambleside Pl. Stoke 1K 27
Ambrose Pl. Stoke 4J 21
Amelia Clo. Bad G 2F 29
America St. Stoke 1G 27
Amicable St. Stoke 5J 27
Amison St. Stoke 2J 41
Ampthill Pl. Stoke 5J 39
Ancaster St. Stoke 4G 21
Anchor Ind. Est.
Stoke 2H 41
Anchor Pl. Stoke 2H 41
Anchor Rd. Stoke 2H 41
Anchor Ter. Stoke 2H 41
Anderson Pl. Stoke 1D 28
Andover Clo. Stoke 7H 35
Andrew Mulligan Clo.
Stoke 6F 21
Andrew Pl. New 4F 33 (3G 7)
Andrew St. Stoke 4F 21
Anglesey Dri. Stoke 3F 41
Angle St. Leek 3E 16
Angus Clo. Stoke 2H 35
Annan Clo. Cong 6J 9
Anna Wlk. Stoke 5J 27
Anne Ct. Tal P 5A 20
Anne St. Stoke 4F 21
Annette Rd. Stoke 7G 35
Ansmede Gro. Stoke 5E 40
Anson Rd. Stoke 6A 42
Anthony Gro. Stoke 3A 48
Anthony Pl. Stoke 2J 41
Antrobus St. Cong 4F 9
Apedale. 5J 25
Apedale Community Country Pk.
. . . . .7J 25
Apedale Heritage Cen. 7K 25
Apedale Rd. Big E 4G 25
Apedale Rd. New & Ches 5J 25
Apley Pl. Stoke 6J 39
Apollo Wlk. Stoke 3B 28
Apple Clo. Cong 4D 8
Applecroft. Mad 1A 30
Applecroft. New 3B 26
Appledore Gro. Stoke 3H 21
Appleford Pl. Stoke 5D 40
Applegarth Clo. Stoke 7G 35
Appleton Clo. Bid 4D 14
Appleton Clo. Cong 7G 9
Applewood Cres. Stoke 6D 42
Aqueduct St. Stoke 6A 34
Aquinas St. Stoke 6K 33
Arbour Clo. Mad 1B 30
Arbourfield Dri. Stoke 3F 35
Arbour St. Stoke 1C 34 (2G 5)
Arbour St. Tal P 6A 20
Arclid Ct. Cong 4H 9
Arclid Way. Stoke 3G 35
Arctic Pl. Stoke 6A 40
Arden Clo. Leek 4J 17
Arden Ct. Cong 7K 9
Argles Rd. Leek 2H 17
Argosy Clo. Stoke 7C 42
Argyle St. Stoke 3A 34 (6C 4)
Argyll Clo. B Bri 1F 49
Argyll Rd. Stoke 4J 41
Aries Clo. Stoke 5J 21
Arkwright Gro. Stoke 4E 28
Arley Clo. Als 7D 10
Arlington Way. Stoke 7B 42
Armshead. 1C 36
Armshead Rd. Werr 1C 36
Armstrong Grn. Stoke 5B 28
Arnold Gro. New 4E 26
Arnside Av. Cong 5C 8
Arran Dri. Pac 3J 21
Arrowsmith Dri. Als 7C 10
Arthur Cotton Ct. Stoke 3K 27
Arthur St. Leek 3G 17
Arthur St. New 3C 32
Arthur St. Stoke 1H 27
Arundel Dri. C'dle 3J 45
Arundel Way. Stoke 7H 35
Ascot Clo. Cong 3F 9
Ash Bank. 2A 36
Ash Bank Rd. Stoke & Werr . . .2K 35
Ashbourne Dri. New 4H 31
Ashbourne Gro. Stoke 7B 28
Ashbourne Rd. C'dle 3H 45
Ashbourne Rd. Leek 4G 17
Ashburton St. Stoke 5A 28
Ashby Cres. Stoke 5E 40
Ash Clo. C'dle 4J 45
Ashcombe Grn. Stoke 5E 40
Ashcombe Way. Leek 5G 17
Ashcott Wlk. Stoke 4H 35
Ashcroft Av. Stoke 3H 39
Ashcroft Clo. New 6D 26
Ashcroft Gro. New 6E 26
Ashcroft Oval. New 6E 26
Ashcroft Pl. New 6E 26
Ashcroft Rd. New 6D 26
Ashdale Clo. Als 5D 10
Ashdale Ri. New 3E 38
Ashdale Rd. Leek 3J 17
Ashdale Rd. Stoke 1B 40
Ashendene Gro. Stoke 6J 39
Ashenhurst Rd. Als 7G 11
Ashenhurst Way. Leek 5G 17
Ashenough Rd. Tal P 5A 20
Ashfield Ct. New 3D 32
Ashfields Grange. New
. . . . .4E 32 (2B 6)
Ashfields New Rd.
New 4D 32 (2B 6)
(in two parts)
Ashfield Sq. Stoke 3F 35
Ashford St. Stoke 5A 34
Ash Grn. Clo. Stoke 7K 39
Ash Gro. Ash B 2A 36
Ash Gro. B'stn 6C 46
Ash Gro. B Bri 6D 42
Ash Gro. Cong 4C 8
Ash Gro. L'tn 4D 40
Ash Gro. New 3J 31
Ash Gro. Rode H 3G 11
Ashlands Av. Stoke 5H 33
Ashlands Cres. Stoke
. . . . .6H 33 (5H 7)
Ashlands Gro. Stoke . . .6H 33 (6H 7)
Ashlands Rd. Stoke . . .6H 33 (6H 7)
Ashlar Clo. Stoke 3K 21
Ashley Gro. New 1F 33
Ashman St. Stoke 2B 28
Ashmead Clo. Als 7F 11
Ashmead M. Als 7F 11
Ashmore's La. Als 7E 10
Ashmore Wlk. Stoke 3H 5
Ashover Gro. Stoke 3H 21
Ashridge Av. New 4E 38
Ashridge Gro. Stoke 1J 41
Ashton Clo. Cong 6K 9
Ashton Ct. New 4F 39
Ashton Ct. Werr 2B 36
Ash Tree Hill. C'dle 4F 45
Ashurst Gro. Stoke 7C 42
Ash Vw. Kid 1E 20
Ash Way. New 2C 38
Ash Way. Stoke 2A 36
Ashwell Rd. Stoke 5G 33 (4H 7)
Ashwood. Stoke 1G 41
Ashwood Gro. B Bri 1H 49
Ashwood Ter. Stoke 1H 41
(off Ashwood)
Ashworth St. Stoke 7C 34
Askern Clo. Stoke 5K 41
Aspen Clo. Har 7H 13
Asquith Clo. Bid 2C 14
Astbury. 7D 8
Astbury Clo. Kid 7F 13
Astbury La. Ends. Cong 7G 9
Astbury Marsh. 6D 8
Astbury Mere Country Pk. 5D 8
Astbury St. Cong 5E 8
Aster Clo. Stoke 7C 36
Aston Rd. New 3K 25
Astro Gro. Stoke 2F 41
Athelstan St. Stoke 1G 27
Athena Rd. Stoke 7E 28
Atherstone Rd. Stoke 7K 39
Athlone St. Stoke 2C 28
Atholl Rd. Stoke 5J 41
Atkin Clo. Cong 4C 8
Atlam Clo. Stoke 2F 35
Atlantic Gro. Stoke 6A 40
Atlas St. Stoke 1D 40
Attlee Rd. C'dle 4G 45
Attwood Ri. Kid 1D 20
Attwood St. Kid 1D 20
Aubrey St. Stoke 4E 20
Auckland St. Stoke 5K 27
Auden Pl. Stoke 3J 41
Audley. 2E 24
Audley Pl. New 7E 32
Audley Rd.
Als & Tal P 7F 11
Audley Rd. B'ly 7A 18
Audley Rd. Big E 5H 19
Audley Rd. New 2K 25
Audley St. New 2B 32
Audley St. Stoke 1G 27
Audley Theatre. 2E 24
Austen Clo. C'dle 4F 45
Austin Ho. Stoke 1F 35
Austin St. Stoke 3C 34
Austwick Gro. Stoke 1H 39
Aveling Grn. Stoke 4E 28
Aveling Rd. Stoke 4E 28
Avenue Rd. Stoke 4A 34
Avenue, The. Als 6D 10
Avenue, The. B Bri 7H 43
Avenue, The. End 4K 23
Avenue, The. Kid 2C 20
Avenue, The. New 3G 33 (1H 7)
Avenue, The. Stoc B 7K 23
Avion Clo. Stoke 7D 42
Avoca St. Stoke 7C 28 (1H 5)
Avon Clo. Kid 1E 20
Avon Clo. New 2E 38
Avon Ct. Als 5D 10
Avondale St. Stoke 4G 27
Avon Dri. Cong 6H 9
Avon Gro. C'dle 5H 45
Avonside Av. Stoke 7J 21
Avonwick Gro. Stoke 6F 29
Axbridge Wlk. Stoke 3B 28
(off Kinver St.)
Axon Cres. Stoke 3C 42
Aylesbury Rd. Stoke 3G 35
Aynsley Av. New 3E 38
Aynsley Clo. C'dle 5G 45
Aynsley Hall. Stoke 6B 34
Aynsley Rd. Stoke 4A 34
Aynsley's Dri. B Bri 7F 43
Ayreshire Gro. Stoke 5J 41
Ayr Rd. C'dle 1H 45

A-Z Stoke 51

Ayrshire Way—Berry La.

Ayrshire Way. Cong ... 6J 9
Ayshford St. Stoke ... 3G 41

B

Bk. Brook St. Brn L ... 5K 13
Bk. Bunt's La. Stoc B ... 7H 23
Bk. Cross La. Cong ... 7J 9
Bk. Ford Grn. Rd. Stoke ... 2C 28
Bk. Garden St. New ... 5F 33 (4E 7)
Bk. Heathcote St. Kid ... 1D 20
Back La. Brn E ... 4G 23 (Bank End)
Back La. Brn E ... 2G 23 (Hill Top)
Back La. Cong ... 2A 8
Back La. Leek ... 3E 16
Bk. Park St. Cong ... 5G 9
Bk. River St. Cong ... 4F 9
Baddeley Edge. ... 2H 29
Baddeley Green. ... 1F 29
Baddeley Grn. La. Stoke ... 2G 29
Baddeley Hall Rd. Stoke ... 2H 29
Baddeley Rd. Stoke ... 3G 29
Baddeley St. C'dle ... 4H 45
Baddeley St. Stoke ... 3J 27
Baden Rd. Stoke ... 3B 28
Baden St. New ... 3E 32 (1C 6)
Badger Gro. Stoke ... 7D 42
Badgers Brow. Stoke ... 2D 34
Badgers Ri. Leek ... 3F 17
Badgers Sett. Leek ... 3F 17
Badnall Clo. Leek ... 3E 16
Badnall St. Leek ... 3E 16
Baggott Pl. New ... 5C 32
Bagnall. ... 2K 29
Bagnall Rd. L Oaks ... 3J 29
Bagnall Rd. Stoke ... 3G 29
Bagnall St. Stoke ... 2B 34 (4F 5)
Bagot Gro. Stoke ... 4E 28
Bailey Ct. Als ... 7F 11
Bailey Cres. Cong ... 3J 9
Bailey Rd. Stoke ... 2D 40
Bailey's Bank. Bid ... 1J 15
Bailey's Hill. ... 1F 15
Bailey St. New ... 4D 32 (2B 6)
Bailey St. Stoke ... 4J 33
Bainbridge Rd. Stoke ... 7K 39
Bains Gro. New ... 4C 26
Baker Cres. Stoke ... 1G 29
Baker Cres. N. Stoke ... 1H 29
Baker Cres. S. Stoke ... 1G 29
Baker St. Stoke ... 7D 34
Bakers Vs., The. Cong ... 5F 9
Bakewell Clo. New ... 4J 31
Bakewell St. Stoke ... 1J 39
Bala Gro. C'dle ... 2J 45
Balcombe Clo. New ... 6E 32 (6C 6)
Balfour Gro. Bid ... 2D 14
Balfour St. Stoke ... 2C 34 (4H 5)
Ball Edge. ... 5H 23
Ball Green. ... 5D 22
Ball Haye Green. Leek ... 2G 17
Ball Haye Grn. Leek ... 3G 17
Ball Haye Rd. Leek ... 3G 17
Ball Hayes Rd. Stoke ... 6B 22
Ball Haye St. Leek ... 3G 17
Ball Haye Ter. Leek ... 3G 17
Ballington Gdns. Leek ... 4G 17 (in two parts)
Ballington Vw. Leek ... 5G 17
Ballinson Rd. Stoke ... 5D 40
Balliol St. Stoke ... 6K 33
Ball La. Leek ... 3F 17
Ball La. Stoke ... 6F 23
Balloon St. Stoke ... 4G 33 (3H 7)
Ball's Yd. New ... 5E 32 (3D 6)
Balmoral Clo. Stoke ... 4K 39
Balmoral Dri. C'dle ... 5E 44
Baltic Clo. Stoke ... 7A 40
Bamber Pl. New ... 6C 26
Bamber St. Stoke ... 5A 34
Bambury St. Stoke ... 7G 35
Bamford Gro. Stoke ... 7A 28
Banbury Gro. Bid ... 3B 14
Banbury St. Tal ... 2A 20
Bancroft La. B Bri ... 1G 49
Bank Ct. Kid ... 1D 20 (off Attwood St.)
Bank End. ... 3G 23
Bank End. Brn E ... 4G 23
Bankfield Gro. S Hay ... 2F 31 (in two parts)
Bankfield Rd. Stoke ... 6A 42
Bank Hall Rd. Stoke ... 2A 28
Bankhouse Dri. Cong ... 3J 9
Bank Ho. Dri. New ... 3H 33
Bankhouse Rd. For ... 6J 43
Bankhouse Rd. Stoke ... 6J 39
Banks Clo. Cong ... 4E 8
Bankside. New ... 5F 33 (4E 7)
Bankside Ct. Als ... 5F 11
Banksman Rd. Stoke ... 6J 35
Bank St. C'dle ... 3G 45
Bank St. Cong ... 5G 9
Bank St. Rook ... 6F 13
Bank St. Stoke ... 7G 21
Bank, The. ... 3E 12
Bank, The. Sch G ... 3E 12
Bank Top. ... 7A 22
Bank Top Av. Stoke ... 1K 27
Banky Brook Clo. Stoke ... 1B 28
Banky Fields. Cong ... 6E 8
Banky Fields Cres. Cong ... 6E 8
Baptist St. Stoke ... 4J 27
Barber Dri. Sch G ... 3B 12
Barber Pl. Stoke ... 5J 21
Barber Rd. Stoke ... 5J 21
Barber's Sq. New ... 1G 33
Barber St. Stoke ... 3J 27
Barbridge Rd. New ... 2A 26
Barbrook Av. Stoke ... 2K 41
Barclay St. Stoke ... 1H 41
Bardsey Wlk. Stoke ... 3F 41
Barford Rd. New ... 3C 38
Barford St. Stoke ... 3G 41
Bargrave Dri. New ... 4E 26
Bargrave St. Stoke ... 4J 35
Barhill Rd. Mad ... 3A 30
Barker Ho. Stoke ... 6E 40
Barker St. New ... 6C 26
Barker St. Stoke ... 3J 41
Barks Dri. Stoke ... 7C 22
Barlaston. ... 6D 46
Barlaston Common. ... 3K 47
Barlaston Old Rd. Stoke ... 1A 46
Barlaston Rd. Stoke ... 7E 40
BARLASTON STATION. RAIL ... 6C 46
Barley Cft. Als ... 1F 19
Barleycroft. C'dle ... 5H 45
Barleycroft Ter. Sch G ... 3C 12
Barleyfields. A'ly ... 2E 24
Barleyfields. Stoke ... 1B 28
Barleyford Dri. Stoke ... 7J 35
Barlow St. Stoke ... 3H 41
Barlstone Av. B Bri ... 1G 49
Barmouth Clo. Knyp ... 4D 14
Barmouth Gro. B Frd ... 1B 22
Barnbridge Clo. Sch G ... 3B 12
Barn Ct. New ... 3F 39
Barncroft Rd. Stoke ... 5A 22
Barnes Way. Stoke ... 5H 41
Barnett Gro. Cong ... 4C 8
Barnett Gro. Stoke ... 6J 21
Barnfield. Stoke ... 7J 33
Barnfield Rd. Stoke ... 5K 27
Barnfields. ... 5E 16
Barnfields Clo. Leek ... 5E 16
Barnfields Ind. Est. Leek ... 5E 16 (Barnfields Rd.)
Barnfields Ind. Est. Leek ... 6E 16 (Sunnyhills Rd.)
Barnfields Rd. Leek ... 5E 16
Barngate St. Leek ... 3E 16
Barnlea Gro. Stoke ... 2B 48
Barn Rd. Cong ... 3E 8
Barnsdale Clo. Stoke ... 2A 46
Barnwell Gro. Stoke ... 5K 39
Baron St. Stoke ... 1F 41
Barracks Rd. New ... 5F 33 (4E 7)
Barracks Sq. New ... 5F 33 (4E 7)
Barracks Way. Leek ... 3E 16
Barrage Rd. Bid M ... 4G 15
Barratt Rd. Als ... 7G 11
Barrett Cres. Stoke ... 6K 27
Barrett Dri. Stoke ... 6K 27
Barrie Gdns. Tal ... 3K 19
Barrington Ct. New ... 2G 33
Barry Av. Stoke ... 2F 35
Bartholomew Rd. Stoke ... 6A 42
Barthomley Rd. A'ly ... 7A 18
Barthomley Rd. Stoke ... 6C 28
Bartlem St. Stoke ... 1J 41
Barton Cres. Stoke ... 3H 27
Barton Rd. Cong ... 5H 9
Barwood Av. Chu L ... 5H 11
Basford. ... 4H 33 (3G 7)
Basford Pk. Rd. New ... 1G 33 (1H 7)
Basford Vs. New ... 1G 7
Basildon Gro. Stoke ... 4H 41
Baskerville Rd. Stoke ... 7C 28 (1H 5)
Baskeyfield Pl. Stoke ... 6A 22
Basnett's Wood. End ... 5K 23
Bassett Clo. C'dle ... 3G 45
Bassilow Rd. Stoke ... 6E 34
Bateman Av. Brn L ... 5A 14
Bath Rd. New ... 3G 31
Baths Pas. Stoke ... 2G 41 (off Strand, The)
Baths Rd. Stoke ... 2G 41
Bath St. Leek ... 3G 17
Bath St. Stoke ... 6K 33
Bath St. W Coy ... 1C 42
Bath Ter. Stoke ... 7K 33
Bathurst St. Stoke ... 2H 41
Bath Vale. ... 4K 9
Batkin Clo. Stoke ... 6A 22
Batten Clo. Stoke ... 7D 42
Battison Cres. Stoke ... 4H 41
Baulk La. Ful ... 7F 49
Bayham Wlk. Stoke ... 1F 35
Baytree Clo. Stoke ... 6E 28
Beaconsfield. New ... 5F 27
Beaconsfield Dri. Stoke ... 5D 40
Beadnell Gro. Stoke ... 5H 41
Beard Gro. Stoke ... 5G 29
Beasley. ... 5C 26
Beasley Av. New ... 6C 26
Beasley Pl. New ... 5C 26
Beatrice Clo. Stoke ... 4K 39
Beatrice Wlk. B Frd ... 1A 22
Beattie Av. New ... 2E 32
Beatty Dri. Cong ... 3J 9
Beatty Rd. Leek ... 3H 17
Beaufort Av. Werr ... 2B 36
Beaufort Rd. Stoke ... 4H 41
Beaulieu Clo. Werr ... 2C 36
Beaumaris Clo. Stoke ... 5G 33 (4H 7)
Beaumaris Ct. New ... 5D 32 (5A 6)
Beaumont Clo. Bid ... 2J 15
Beaumont Ct. New ... 3C 38 (off Bridle Path, The)
Beaumont Rd. Stoke ... 1H 27
Beaver Clo. Stoke ... 2H 39
Beaver Dri. C'dle ... 3E 44 (in two parts)
Beckenham Clo. Stoke ... 6D 42
Beckett Av. Stoke ... 5C 42
Beckfield Clo. Bid M ... 1G 15
Beckford St. Stoke ... 7C 28 (1H 5)
Beck Rd. Mad ... 6A 30
Beckton St. Stoke ... 1H 27
Bedale Pl. Stoke ... 5D 40
Bedcroft. B'stn ... 5E 46
Beddow Way. Stoke ... 5J 21
Bedford Cres. New ... 2F 39
Bedford Gro. Als ... 5C 10
Bedford Rd. Kid ... 7D 12
Bedford Rd. Stoke ... 3A 34 (6C 4)
Bedford St. Stoke ... 3K 33 (6B 4) (in two parts)
Beech Av. Rode H ... 2G 11
Beech Clo. Bid M ... 1G 15
Beech Clo. C'dle ... 4J 45
Beech Clo. Cong ... 3C 8
Beech Clo. Leek ... 7D 16
Beech Ct. B Bri ... 7E 42
Beechcroft. B'stn ... 5E 46
Beech Cft. Mad ... 1B 30
Beech Dri. Kid ... 3B 20
Beeches Row. Stoke ... 6G 21
Beeches, The. New ... 5F 27
Beechfield Rd. Stoke ... 1A 46
Beechfields. B'stn ... 5E 46
Beech Gro. Leek ... 3D 16
Beech Gro. New ... 1F 33
Beech Gro. Stoke ... 1B 40
Beechmont Gro. Stoke ... 6E 28
Beech Rd. Stoke ... 5E 40
Beech St. Stoke ... 3H 41
Beechwood Clo. B Bri ... 1G 49
Beechwood Clo. New ... 5F 39
Beechwood Dri. Als ... 6C 10
Beeston Dri. Als ... 7D 10
Beeston St. Stoke ... 1H 41
Beeston Vw. Kid ... 4D 20
Beggars La. Leek ... 5D 16
Belfast Clo. Stoke ... 2A 28
Belfield Av. New ... 1F 33
Belford Pl. Stoke ... 4J 33
Belgrave Av. Als ... 5E 10
Belgrave Av. Cong ... 4E 8
Belgrave Av. Stoke ... 4G 41
Belgrave Cres. Stoke ... 5H 41
Belgrave Rd. New ... 5F 33 (5E 7)
Belgrave Rd. Stoke ... 5H 41
Bell Av. Stoke ... 4J 41
Bellefield Vw. New ... 2F 33 (off High St.)
Bellerton La. Stoke ... 2D 28
Belle Vue. Leek ... 3E 16
Belle Vue Rd. Leek ... 3E 16
Bell Ho. Stoke ... 7E 40
Bellingham Gro. Stoke ... 6C 28
Bell La. B'stn ... 3D 46
Bellringer Clo. Bid ... 3B 14
Bellringer Rd. Stoke ... 7C 40
Bell's Hollow. New ... 2B 26
Bellwood Clo. Stoke ... 2B 48
Belmont Rd. Stoke ... 2K 33 (4A 4)
Belsay Clo. Stoke ... 2H 41
Belvedere Rd. Stoke ... 5K 39
Belvedere Ter. Rode H ... 3G 11
Belvoir Av. Stoke ... 2B 46
Bemersley Green. ... 2B 22
Bemersley Rd. B Frd & Brn E ... 7B 14
Benedict Pl. Stoke ... 7F 29
Benfleet Pl. Stoke ... 3F 41
Bengal Gro. Stoke ... 6B 40
Bengry Rd. Stoke ... 4K 41
Benjamins Way. Big E ... 2G 25
Bennett Pl. New ... 5E 26
Bennett Precinct. Stoke ... 3G 41 (off Strand, The)
Bennett St. Stoke ... 5H 27
Bennion St. Stoke ... 3H 41
Benson St. Stoke ... 6J 21
Bentilee. ... 4J 35
Bent La. A'bry ... 6B 8
Bentley Av. New ... 1E 32
Bentley Rd. Stoke ... 6B 22
Berdmore St. Stoke ... 1F 41
Beresford Cres. New ... 7D 32
Beresford Dale. Mad ... 1A 30
Beresford St. Stoke ... 4A 34
Beresford Trad. Est. Stoke ... 6G 21
Bergamot Dri. Stoke ... 1B 48
Berkeley Av. Als ... 5E 10
Berkeley Ct. New ... 4F 33 (3F 7)
Berkeley St. Stoke ... 2C 34 (5G 5)
Berkshire Dri. Cong ... 3F 9
Berkshire Gro. New ... 1F 39
Bernard Gro. Stoke ... 3A 48
Bernard St. Stoke ... 2C 34 (5G 5)
Berne Av. New ... 7B 32
Berryfield Gro. Stoke ... 2A 42
Berry Hill. ... 3F 35
Berry Hill Greenway. Stoke ... 3G 35
Berryhill-Normacot Greenway. Stoke ... 7J 35
Berry Hill Rd. Stoke ... 4C 34 (in two parts)
Berryhill Village. Stoke ... 4F 35
Berry La. Stoke ... 3H 41

52 A-Z Stoke

Berry St.—Bridgett Clo.

Berry St. Stoke 6A 34
Berwick Rd. Stoke 4D 28
Berwick Wlk. New 6C 32
Best St. Stoke 1E 40
Beswick Clo. C'dle 5G 45
Beswick Rd. Stoke 6J 21
Betchton Ct. Cong 4H 9
Betchton La. Chu L 2D 10
Bethell Rd. Stoke 5C 28
Bethesda Rd. Stoke 3C 34
Bethesda St. Stoke 2B 34 (4E 5)
Betley Pl. New 7F 33
Bettany Rd. Stoke 5K 27
Bevan Av. Tal P 5A 20
Bevandean Clo. Stoke 2B 46
Bevan Pl. Mad 1B 30
Beveridge Clo. Stoke 4C 42
Beverley Cres. For 6H 43
Beverley Dri. Stoke 3G 35
Beville St. Stoke 7D 34
Bevin La. Stoke 2F 35
Bewcastle Gro. Stoke 7B 42
Bew St. Stoke 6D 22
Bexhill Gro. Stoke 6E 28
Bexley St. Stoke 7A 28 (1D 4)
Bibby St. Rode H 3F 11
Bida La. Cong 7K 9
Biddulph. 2B 14
Biddulph Grange Gardens. 1K 15 (National Trust)
Biddulph Moor. 1G 15
Biddulph Rd. Cong 6J 9
Biddulph Rd. Har 4H 13
Biddulph Rd. Stoke 5K 21
Biddulph St. Cong 7K 9
Biddulph Valley Leisure Cen. 1C 14
Bignall End. 1G 25
Bignall End Rd. Big E 1H 25
Bignall Hill. 2H 25
Bignall Hill. Big E 2H 25
Bigsbury Wlk. Stoke 5K 27 (off Swainsley Clo.)
Billinge St. Stoke 4H 27
Bilton St. Stoke 7K 33
Birchall. 6G 17
Birchall Av. Stoke 6F 21
Birchall Clo. Leek 7G 17
Birchall La. Leek 7G 17
Birchall Pk. Av. Leek 6G 17
Bircham Wlk. New 4E 38
Birch Av. Als 1F 19
Birch Av. Knyp 4K 13
Birch Ct. Cong 4B 8
Birch Dale. Mad 2B 30
Birchdown Av. Stoke 1A 28
Birchenfields La. Dil 1C 44
Birchenwood Countryside Pk. 1F 21
Birchenwood Rd. Stoke 3H 21
Birches Farm M. Mad 7A 30
Birches Head. 7D 28
Birches Head Rd. Stoke 7C 28
Birches, The. C'dle 3G 45 (off Royal Wlk.)
Birches, The. C'dle 4G 45 (Lid La.)
Birches Way. Kid 1E 20
Birchfield Av. Rode H 3G 11
Birchfield Rd. Stoke 7H 29
Birchgate. Stoke 1H 35
Birchgate Gro. Stoke 1H 35
Birch Grn. Gro. Stoke 5D 28
Birch Gro. For 7H 43
Birch Gro. Stoke 3B 48
Birch Ho. Rd. New 4A 26
Birchlands Rd. Stoke 6E 28
Birchover Way. Stoke 3K 21
Birch Rd. Big E 3G 25
Birch Rd. Cong 4B 8
Birch St. Stoke 7D 28
Birch Ter. Stoke 2B 34 (4F 5)
Birch Tree La. Sch G 3E 12
Birch Wlk. Stoke 5F 41
Bird Cage Wlk. Stoke 2B 34 (4E 5)
Bird Rd. Stoke 4C 42
Birkdale Dri. Kid 7F 13
Birkholme Dri. Stoke 2B 48
Birks St. Stoke 1A 40
Birrell St. Stoke 1E 40
Biscay Gro. Stoke 6B 40
Bishop Ct. Stoke 7G 29
Bishop Rd. Stoke 6K 21
Bishop's Clo. Tal 3A 20
Bishop St. Stoke 1F 41
Bitterne Pl. Stoke 5J 35
Bittern La. C'dle 3H 45
Black Bank. 1H 31
Blackbank Rd. New 1H 31
Blackbird Way. Bid 2D 14
Blackbird Way. Pac 2J 21
Blackbrook Av. New 4A 26
Black Firs La. Som 2A 8
Blackfriars Rd. New 5E 32 (5C 6)
Blackheath Clo. Stoke 3J 41
Black Horse La. Stoke 1A 34 (3D 4)
Blacklake Dri. Stoke 3B 48
Blackshaw Clo. Cong 6K 9
Blackthorn Pl. New 4B 26
Blackwell's Row. Stoke 6A 28
Blackwood Hill. 5K 15
Blackwood Pl. Stoke 2K 41
Bladon Av. New 3E 38
Bladon Clo. Stoke 3K 21
Bladon Cres. Als 5D 10
Blakelow Rd. Stoke 7G 29
Blakeney Av. New 3E 38
Blake St. Cong 5E 8
Blake St. Stoke 4J 27
Blanchard Clo. Stoke 7D 42
Blantyre St. Stoke 4H 41
Blantyre Wlk. Stoke 4H 41
Blatchford Clo. Stoke 4C 42
Bleak Pl. Stoke 5K 27
Bleakridge Av. New 4E 26
Bleak St. New 2G 33
Bleeding Wolf La. Sch G 5B 12
Blencarn Gro. Stoc B 7H 23
Blenheim Ct. Als 5E 10
Blenheim St. Stoke 1C 40
Bleriot Clo. Stoke 7D 42
Blithe Vw. B Bri 1G 49
Blithfield Clo. Werr 3B 36
Bluebell Clo. Bid 3C 14
Bluebell Dri. New 2D 38
Bluebell Way. Als 7C 10
Bluestone Av. Stoke 2A 28
Blunt St. New 1F 33
Blurton. 4E 40
Blurton Priory. Stoke 6E 40
Blurton Rd. B'stn 5F 47
Blurton Rd. Stoke 2D 40
Blythe Av. Cong 5C 8
Blythe Av. Stoke 2B 48
Blythe Bridge. 7G 43
Blythe Bri. Rd. Cav 4F 43
BLYTHE BRIDGE STATION. RAIL 7G 43
Blythe Clo. B Bri 7E 42
Blythe Lodge. B Bri 7F 43 (off Grindley La.)
Blythe Marsh. 7H 43
Blythe Mt. Pk. B Bri 7H 43
Blythe Rd. For 7H 43
Blythe Vw. Sav G 5H 49
Boardmans Bank. Brn E 2F 23
Boathorse Rd. Kid 3C 20
Boathorse Rd. Stoke 5D 20
Bodmin Wlk. Smal 3C 28
Bogs La. B Bri 1G 49
Bolberry Clo. Stoke 5K 41
Bold St. Stoke 7D 28 (1H 5)
Bolina Gro. Stoke 7G 35
Bollin Clo. Als 7A 10
Bollin Dri. Cong 6H 9
Bollin Gro. Bid 1D 14
Bolney Gro. Stoke 7E 28
Bolsover Clo. Stoke 3K 21
Bolton Pl. Stoke 6A 42
Boma Rd. Stoke 6J 39
Bondfield Way. Stoke 4C 42
Bond St. Stoke 7G 21
Bonnard Clo. Stoke 1D 48
Bonner Clo. Stoke 1H 39
Boon Av. Stoke 7K 33
Boon Hill. 3G 25
Boon Hill Rd. Big E 3G 25
Boothen. 1A 40
Boothen Grn. Stoke 1A 40
Boothen Old Rd. Stoke 1A 40
Boothen Pk. Stoke 7A 34
Boothen Rd. Stoke 7A 34
Boothenwood Ter. Stoke 1K 39
Boothroyd St. Stoke 2B 34 (4F 5)
Booth St. A'ly 3E 24
Booth St. Cong 5E 8
Booth St. New 6C 26
Booth St. Stoke 7A 34
Bordeaux Rd. Stoke 6B 42
Bordeaux Wlk. New 3C 38
Borough Rd. Cong 4H 9
Borough Rd. New 4F 33 (2F 7)
Borrowdale Rd. Stoke 1D 28
Boscombe Gro. Stoke 2B 46
Bosinney Clo. Stoke 1G 41
Bosley Gro. Stoke 4F 21
Bosley Vw. Cong 6K 9
Boston Clo. Stoke 7F 21
Boswell St. Stoke 3J 33
Botany Bay Rd. Stoke 7D 28
Botesworth Gdns. Stoke 3G 27
Botteslow St. Stoke 2C 34 (5G 5)
Boughey Rd. Big E 2G 25
Boughey Rd. Stoke 5B 34
Boughey St. Stoke 7K 33
Boulevard, The. Stoke 1H 27 (off High St.)
Boulevard, The. Stoke 1H 27 (Scotia Rd.)
Boulton St. New 6F 27
Boulton St. Stoke 7C 28
Boundary. 4B 44
Boundary Clo. Leek 6G 17
Boundary Ct. Stoke 1F 5
Boundary La. Cong 7J 9
Boundary St. New 4G 33 (3G 7)
Boundary St. Stoke 7A 28 (1D 4)
Boundary Vw. C'dle 4E 44
Bourne Cotts. Stoke 4H 41
Bourne Pl. Leek 3D 16
Bourne Rd. Kid 1C 20
Bournes Bank. Stoke 4J 27
Bournes Bank S. Stoke 4J 27
Bourne St. Mow C 3G 13
Bourne St. Stoke 2D 40
Bouverie Pde. Stoke 5E 28
Bowden Clo. Cong 4B 8
Bowden St. Stoke 3A 28
Bower End La. Mad 2A 30
Bower St. Stoke 3B 34 (6F 5)
Bowfell Gro. Stoke 6G 35
Bowhill La. A'ly 6A 24
Bowland Av. New 2B 32
Bowlers Clo. Stoke 6K 27
Bowman Gro. Stoke 4A 22
Bowman Ho. Stoke 6A 42
Bowmead Clo. Stoke 1B 46
Bowmere Clo. Bid 1B 14
Bowness Ct. Cong 6C 8
Bowness St. Stoke 7A 28
Bowsey Wood Rd. Mad 1B 30
Bowstead St. Stoke 6A 34
Bow St. Stoke 7B 28 (1F 5)
Bowyer Av. Stoke 6D 22
Box La. Cong 4B 8
Box La. Stoke 4A 42
Boxwood Pl. New 4A 26
Boyles Hall Rd. Big E 2F 25
Brabazon Clo. Stoke 7D 42
Brackenberry. New 2E 32
Bracken Clo. Rode H 2G 11
Bracken Clo. Stoke 2A 48
Bracken Clo. T'sor 6A 46
Bracken Dale. Leek 5C 16
Brackenfield Av. Stoke 4H 35
Brackens, The. New 4E 38
Bracken St. Stoke 2D 40
Brackley Av. Stoke 3A 28
Bradbury Clo. Stoke 1D 28
Bradbury Gdns. Cong 7H 9
Braddocks Hay. 2D 14
Bradeley. 1B 28
Bradeley Village. Stoke 1A 28
Bradford Ter. Stoke 6D 28
Bradwell. 5D 26
Bradwell Ct. Cong 5H 9
Bradwell Grange. New 6E 26
Bradwell Gro. Cong 5H 9
BRADWELL HOSPITAL. 5D 26
Bradwell La. New 4C 26
Bradwell Lodge. New 6F 27
Bradwell St. Stoke 4G 27
Braemar Clo. Stoke 2J 35
Braemore Rd. Stoke 6G 29
Braithwell Dri. Stoke 2F 29
Brakespeare St. Stoke 4F 21
Brake, The. Sch G 3E 12
Brake Village. Sch G 3E 12
Bramble Lea. Mad 2B 30
Brambles Ct. Bid 3C 14
Brambles, The. New 4F 39
Bramfield Dri. New 3F 33 (1E 7)
Bramley Clo. C'dle 4H 45
Bramley Pl. Stoke 3H 39
Brammall Dri. B Bri 7F 43
Brammer St. Stoke 1B 28
Brampton Clo. End 1K 23
Brampton Ct. New 3F 33 (1E 7)
Brampton Gdns. New 2F 33
Brampton Ind. Est. New 3E 32 (1D 6)
Brampton Rd. New 3F 33 (1E 7)
Brampton Sidings. New 3E 32 (1D 6)
Brampton Sidings Ind. Est. New 3E 32 (1D 6)
Brampton, The. 3F 33 (1E 7)
Brampton Va. Gdns. New 3F 33
Brampton Wlk. Stoke 5H 41
Bramshaws Acre. C'dle 4H 45
Brandon Gro. Stoke 6J 39
Branson Av. Stoke 3K 41
Bransty Gro. Stoke 2B 46
Brant Av. New 1D 32
Brassington Way. Stoke 4H 35
Brattice Pl. Stoke 6J 35
Brattswood Dri. Chu L 5H 11
Braystones Clo. Stoke 3H 21
Breach Rd. Brn E 4H 23
Bream Way. Stoke 2A 28
Brecon Way. Stoke 3H 35
Breedon Clo. New 2C 32
Breeze Av. Stoke 7H 21
Brendale Clo. Stoke 5K 39
Brentnor Clo. Stoke 3A 42
Brentwood Dri. Werr 1C 36
Brentwood Gro. Stoc B 1H 29
Brentwood Gro. Werr 1C 36
Brereton Pl. Stoke 3H 27
Bretherton Pl. Stoke 5K 21
Brewery St. Stoke 1B 34 (2E 5)
Brewester Rd. Stoke 2E 34
Brianson Av. Stoke 5B 28
Briarbank Clo. Stoke 5J 39
Briars, The. New 3E 32
Briarswood. Kid 2E 20
Briarwood Pl. Stoke 5C 42
Brickfield Pl. Stoke 1H 41
Brick Ho. St. Stoke 4J 27
Brick Kiln La. P West 5B 26
Brick Kiln La. Stoke 3H 33
Bridal Path, The. Mad 1A 30
Bridestone Cen. Cong 4F 9
Bridestowe Clo. Stoke 7B 42
Bridge Clo. Big E 2G 25
Bridge Ct. Stoke 3H 39
Bridge Cft. Stoke 5A 22
Bridge Ind. Est. Stoke 5A 28
Bridgend. 2E 16
Bridge Rd. Stoke 3H 39
Bridge Row. Cong 3H 9
Bridge St. B Frd 1A 22
Bridge St. Cong 5F 9
Bridge St. New 4E 32 (3C 6)
Bridge St. Sil 4K 31
Bridgett Clo. Stoke 1H 39

A-Z Stoke 53

Bridgewater Clo. *Cong* 6K **9**
Bridgewater St. *Stoke* 4G **27**
Bridgewood St. *Stoke* 3H **41**
Bridgnorth Gro. *New* 2B **26**
Bridgwood Rd. *B Bri & For* . . .7H **43**
Bridle Path. *Dres* 5H **41**
(off Peel St.)
Bridle Path. *Stoke* 2B **36**
Bridle Path, The. *New* 3C **38**
Brierley Rd. *Cong* 6K **9**
Brierley St. *Stoke* 3B **28**
Brierly Brook. 1G **25**
Brieryhurst Clo. *Stoke* 7H **29**
Brieryhurst Rd. *Kid* 7E **12**
Brightgreen St. *Stoke* 7J **35**
Brighton St. *Stoke* 6K **33**
Brighton, The. *New* 3J **31**
Brights Av. *Kid* 1E **20**
Bright St. *Stoke* 5B **42**
Brindiwell Gro. *Stoke* 1B **46**
Brindley Clo. *Tal* 3B **20**
Brindley Clo. *New* 4G **27**
Brindley Ford. 1A **22**
Brindley La. *L Oaks* 1H **29**
Brindley Mill. 2E **16**
Brindley Pl. *Stoke* 5B **22**
Brindley St. *New* 4E **32** (2C **6**)
Brindleys Way. *Big E* 2G **25**
Brindley Way. *Cong* 6K **9**
Brindon Clo. *Stoke* 3C **42**
Brinscall Grn. *Stoke* 4K **21**
(off Charnock Pl.)
Brinsley Av. *Stoke* 7K **39**
Brisley Hill. *Stoke* 7J **33**
Bristol St. *New* 7G **27**
Britannia Pk. Ind. Est.
Stoke 5A **28**
Britannia St. *Leek* 4E **16**
Brittain Av. *New* 5B **26**
Brittle Pl. *Stoke* 2C **28**
Britton St. *Stoke* 4J **33**
Brixham Clo. *Stoke* 4E **34**
Broadfield Rd. *Stoke* 4E **20**
Broadhurst La. *Cong* 4E **8**
Broadhurst St. *Stoke* 3A **28**
Broad La. *Brn E* 2H **23**
Broadlawns Dri. *Stoke* 7G **35**
Broad Meadow. 6B **26**
Broadmeadow Ct. *Ches* 6B **26**
Broadmine St. *Stoke* 7D **34**
Broadoak Way. *Stoke* 5D **40**
Broad St. *Leek* 4F **17**
Broad St. *New* 4E **32** (2C **6**)
(in two parts)
Broad St. *Stoke* 3A **34** (6D **4**)
Broadway. *Stoke* 4A **42**
Broadway Ct. *Stoke* 5A **42**
Broadway Pl. *Stoke* 4A **42**
Brockbank Pl. *Stoke* 6A **22**
Brocklehurst Way. *Stoke* 5D **28**
Brockley Sq. *Stoke* 1B **34** (3E **5**)
Brocksford St. *Stoke* 1F **41**
Brock Way. *New* 3A **32**
Brocton Wlk. *Stoke* 5D **40**
Brogan St. *Stoke* 7E **34**
Bromford Pl. *Stoke* 3A **34** (6C **4**)
Bromley Ct. *Stoke* 7A **28** (1C **4**)
Bromley Farm. 5H **9**
Bromley Hough. *Stoke* 1J **39**
Bromley Rd. *Cong* 5G **9**
Bromley St. *Stoke* 7K **27** (1B **4**)
Brompton Dri. *Stoke* 1G **29**
Bromsberrow Way. *Stoke* 7B **42**
Bromsgrove Pl. *Stoke* 3F **41**
Bronant Wlk. *Stoke* 5K **27**
(off Leonora St.)
Bronte Gro. *Stoke* 2F **29**
Brook Clo. *B Bri* 7H **43**
Brook Clo. *End* 1K **23**
Brookes Ct. *Stoke* 7D **34**
Brookfield Av. *End* 4K **23**
Brookfield Ct. *Stoke* 1E **5**
Brookfield Dri. *Als* 5D **10**
Brookfield Rd. *Stoke* 1H **29**
Brookfield Rd. *T Vale* 1H **39**
Brook Gdns. *Bid* 1C **14**
Brookgate. *For* 6J **43**
Brookhouse Dri. *B'stn* 5B **46**

Brookhouse La. *Cong* 4J **9**
(in two parts)
Brookhouse La. *Stoke* 2J **35**
Brookhouse Rd. *Als* 7E **10**
Brookhouse Rd. *C'dle* 3D **44**
Brookhouse Rd. *New* 3C **26**
Brookhouse Rd. *Stoke* 4B **42**
Brookhouses. 4E **44**
Brookhouses Ind. Est. *C'dle* . . .4E **44**
Brookhouse Way. *C'dle* 4E **44**
Brookland Av. *Stoke* 5F **41**
Brooklands Cotts. *Stoke* 3H **21**
Brooklands Rd. *Cong* 5B **8**
Brooklands Rd. *Stoke* 6J **21**
Brook La. *End* 1K **23**
Brook La. *New* 6E **32** (6D **6**)
Brookmead Gro. *Stoke* 7G **35**
Brook Pl. *New* 1F **39**
Brook Pl. *Stoke* 4J **33**
Brook Rd. *Stoke* 7K **39**
Brookside. *Stoke* 4G **27**
Brookside Clo. *New* . . .6D **32** (6A **6**)
Brookside Ct. *C'dle* 3E **44**
Brookside Dri. *End* 1K **23**
Brookside Dri. *Stoke* 4D **40**
Brookside Ind. Est. *Stoke* 4G **27**
Brookside Rd. *Cong* 4F **9**
Brook St. *Brn L* 5K **13**
Brook St. *Cong* 4G **9**
Brook St. *Leek* 4F **17**
Brook St. *Sil* 3K **31**
Brook St. *Stoke* 6A **34**
Brookview Dri. *Stoke* 3A **42**
Brook Vs. *Als* 7F **11**
Brookwood Clo. *New* 3D **38**
Brookwood Dri. *Stoke* 3B **42**
Broome Hill. *New* 5F **39**
Broomfield Pl. N.
Stoke 2K **33** (4B **4**)
Broomfield Pl. S.
Stoke 2K **33** (5B **4**)
Broomfield Rd. *Stoke* 6C **22**
Broomfields. *Bid M* 1G **15**
Broomhill St. *Stoke* 7F **21**
Broom St. *Stoke* 7C **28** (1F **5**)
Brough Clo. *Leek* 3F **17**
Brough La. *Stoke* 7A **40**
Brough Pk. Leisure Cen. 3G **17**
Broughton Cres. *B'stn* 5D **46**
Broughton Rd. *New* . . .3G **33** (1H **7**)
Broughton Rd. *Stoke* 2E **34**
Brown Av. *Chu L* 6H **11**
Brown Edge. 4G **23**
Brownfield Rd. *Stoke* 4B **42**
Brownhill Rd. *Brn E* 4G **23**
Brownhills Bus. Pk. *Stoke* 2G **27**
Brownhills Rd. *Stoke* 3G **27**
Browning Clo. *C'dle* 4F **45**
Browning Gro. *Tal* 3K **19**
Browning Rd. *Stoke* 4E **40**
Brown Lees. 5A **14**
Brown Lees Ind. Est. *Brn L* . . .6A **14**
Brown Lees Rd. *Brn L* 5A **14**
Brown Lees Rd. *Har* 6J **13**
Brownley Rd. *Stoke* 3C **28**
Brownlow. 7A **8**
Brownsea Pl. *Stoke* 2D **40**
Brown St. *Cong* 4G **9**
Brown St. *Stoke* 4K **27**
Brundall Oval. *Stoke* 3J **35**
Brunel Wlk. *Stoke* 2H **41**
Brunswick Ind. Est. *Stoke* 4G **27**
Brunswick Pl. *Stoke* . . .2B **34** (5F **5**)
Brunswick St. *Cong* 4H **9**
Brunswick St. *Leek* 3G **17**
Brunswick St. *New* 4F **33** (3E **7**)
Brunswick St. *Stoke* . . .1B **34** (3E **5**)
Brunt St. *Stoke* 5G **27**
Brutus Rd. *New* 7A **26**
Bryan St. *Stoke* 1B **34** (1E **5**)
Bryant Rd. *Stoke* 7G **29**
Brymbo Rd. *New* 7C **26**
Buccleuch Rd. *Stoke* 4J **41**
Buckingham Cres. *Stoke* 5K **39**
Buckland Gro. *Stoke* 2B **46**
Buckley Rd. *Stoke* 5B **22**
Buckley's Row. *New* . . .5E **32** (4C **6**)

Buckmaster Av. *New* 7F **33**
Bucknall. 7F **29**
BUCKNALL HOSPITAL. 7G **29**
Bucknall New Rd.
Stoke 1C **34** (3G **5**)
Bucknall Old Rd.
Stoke 1C **34** (3G **5**)
Bucknall Rd. *Stoke* 1D **34**
Bude Clo. *Als* 7C **10**
Buglawton. 2K **9**
Buller St. *Stoke* 3C **34** (6H **5**)
Bull La. *B Frd* 1K **21**
Bullocks Ho. Rd. *Har* 7H **13**
Bulstrode St. *Stoke* 4H **27**
Bunny Hill. *New* 1F **39**
Bunts La. *Cong* 6G **9**
Bunt's La. *Stoc B* 7H **23**
Burford Av. *New* 3A **26**
Burford Way. *Stoke* 4F **35**
Burgess St. *Stoke* 5H **27**
Burgundy Gro. *Stoke* 6B **42**
Burland Rd. *New* 2K **25**
Burleigh Gro. *New* 2G **33**
Burlidge Rd. *Stoke* 5K **21**
Burlington Av. *New* 2G **33**
Burmarsh Wlk. *Stoke* 5J **27**
Burnaby Rd. *Stoke* 5F **21**
Burnett Pl. *Stoke* 7C **22**
Burnham St. *Stoke* 1F **41**
Burnhays Rd. *Stoke* 2J **27**
Burnley St. *Stoke* 6C **28**
Burns Clo. *Kid* 3D **20**
Burns Clo. *Rode H* 2F **11**
Burnside Clo. *Stoke* 7B **42**
Burns Rd. *Cong* 5J **9**
Burns Row. *Stoke* 4C **42**
Burnwood Ct. *Stoke* 2C **28**
Burnwood Gro. *Kid* 1E **20**
Burnwood Pl. *Stoke* 6A **22**
Burrington Dri. *Stoke* 2A **46**
Burslam St. *Cong* 5G **9**
Burslem. 4K **27**
Burslem Enterprise Cen.
Stoke 4K **27**
Burslem Greenway. *Stoke* 3J **27**
Burslem Walkway. *Stoke* 4K **27**
Bursley Rd. *Stoke* 5K **27**
Bursley Way. *New* 4D **26**
Burton Cres. *Stoke* 5D **28**
Burton Pl. *Stoke* 1B **34** (3F **5**)
Burton St. *Leek* 4E **16**
Burt St. *Stoke* 3C **42**
Bute St. *Stoke* 2F **41**
Butler St. *Stoke* 7A **34**
Butterfield Pl. *Stoke* 1H **27**
Buttermere Clo. *Stoke* 4H **27**
Buttermere Ct. *Cong* 5C **8**
Butters Green. 2H **25**
Butterton. 4B **38**
Butterton La. *But* 3A **38**
Butterton La. *Rad G* 2A **18**
Butt Lane. 2K **19**
Butts Grn. *Stoke* 6H **29**
Butts, The. *Als* 6E **10**
Buxton Av. *New* 3H **31**
Buxton Old Rd. *Cong* 3H **9**
Buxton Rd. *Cong* 3H **9**
Buxton Rd. *Leek* 3G **17**
Buxton St. *Stoke* 5C **28**
Byatt's Gro. *Stoke* 4F **41**
Bycars La. *Stoke* 3J **27**
Bycars Rd. *Stoke* 3J **27**
Bylands Pl. *New* 2D **38**
Byrom St. *Leek* 3E **16**
Byron Clo. *C'dle* 4E **44**
Byron Clo. *Rode H* 2F **11**
Byron Ct. *Kid* 3C **20**
Byron St. *Stoke* 4G **33** (3H **7**)
Bywater Gro. *Stoke* 7J **35**

C

Cadeby Gro. *Stoke* 2G **29**
Cadman Cres. *Stoke* 1D **28**
Cairn Clo. *Stoke* 2J **35**
Caistor Clo. *Stoke* 3F **29**

Caldbeck Pl. *Stoke* 1C **34** (3H **5**)
Caldew Gro. *Stoke* 2B **46**
Caldy Rd. *Als* 6D **10**
Caledonia Rd. *Stoke* 4A **34**
California Bus. Pk. *Stoke* 1A **40**
California St. *Stoke* 3F **41**
Callender Pl. *Stoke* 4K **27**
Callow Hill La. *C'dle* 3A **44**
Calrofold Dri. *New* 3A **26**
Calvary Cres. *Stoke* 5J **35**
Calverley St. *Stoke* 4J **41**
Calver St. *Stoke* 1G **27**
Calvert Gro. *New* 5E **26**
Camberwell Gro. *Stoke* 1B **46**
Camborne Clo. *Cong* 7G **9**
Camborne Cres. *New* 1C **38**
Cambrian Way. *Stoke* 1H **35**
Cambridge Clo. *Bid* 1B **14**
Cambridge Ct. *New* 1G **39**
Cambridge Dri. *New* 1G **39**
Cambridge St. *Stoke* . . .2A **34** (5D **4**)
Camden St. *Stoke* 2D **40**
Camellia Clo. *Stoke* 4H **33**
Camelot Clo. *Stoke* 3B **46**
Camillus Rd. *New* 3B **32**
Camoys Ct. *Stoke* 5K **27**
Camoys Rd. *Stoke* 5K **27**
Campbell Av. *Leek* 5E **16**
Campbell Clo. *Cong* 3J **9**
Campbell Pl. *Stoke* 6A **34**
Campbell Rd. *Stoke* 2A **40**
Campbell Ter. *Stoke* 6D **28**
Campion Av. *New* 2G **33**
Camp Rd. *Stoke* 3B **28**
Canal La. *Stoke* 3G **27**
Canal M., The. *Stoke* 1B **46**
Canal Rd. *Cong* 5G **9**
Canal Side. *B'stn* 6C **46**
Canal Side. *Stoke* 6E **22**
Canal St. *Cong* 5G **9**
Canal St. *Stoke* 4G **27**
Canary Rd. *Stoke* 6J **35**
Canberra Cres. *Stoke* 7D **42**
Canning St. *Stoke* 1E **40**
Cannon Pl. *Stoke* 3A **34** (5D **4**)
Cannon St. *Stoke* 2B **34** (5E **5**)
Canterbury Dri. *Stoke* 7A **22**
Canvey Gro. *Stoke* 7C **42**
Capesthorne Clo. *Als* 7D **10**
Capesthorne Clo. *Werr* 2C **36**
Capewell St. *Stoke* 2H **41**
Capitol Wlk. *Cong* 5F **9**
(off High St.)
Capper Clo. *Kid* 1D **20**
Cappers La. *B'ton* 1D **10**
Capper St. *Stoke* 1H **27**
Capricorn Way. *Stoke* 5J **21**
Caraway Pl. *Stoke* 1B **48**
Carberry Way. *Stoke* 2A **42**
Cardiff Gro. *Stoke* 2B **34** (5E **5**)
Cardigan Gro. *Stoke* 1B **46**
Cardington Clo. *New* 2D **38**
Card St. *Stoke* 5J **27**
Cardway, The. *New* 5E **26**
Cardwell St. *Stoke* 7D **28**
Carina Gdns. *Stoke* 3C **28**
Carisbrooke Way. *Stoke* 2B **46**
Carling Gro. *Stoke* 1F **41**
Carlisle St. *Stoke* 5G **41**
Carlos Pl. *New* 3E **26**
Carlton Av. *Brn E* 5G **23**
Carlton Av. *New* 3E **38**
Carlton Av. *Stoke* 6K **21**
Carlton Clo. *Brn E* 5G **23**
Carlton Clo. *C'dle* 5G **45**
Carlton Ho. Est. *Stoke* 5A **34**
Carlton Rd. *Stoke* 5B **34**
Carlton Ter. *Leek* 3H **17**
Carlyle Clo. *Rode H* 2F **11**
Carlyon Pl. *Stoke* 4C **28**
Carmounthead. 3H **29**
Carmount Rd. *Stoke* 5G **29**
Carmountside. 5G **29**
Carmountside Crematorium.
Stoke 4G **29**
Carnation Clo. *Stoke* 7C **36**

Carnforth Gro. *Stoke* 3H 21
Caroline Clo. *Werr* 1C 36
Caroline Cres. *Brn E* 5G 23
Caroline St. *Stoke* 2H 41
Carpenter Rd. *Stoke* 2F 41
Carriage Dri. *Bid* 1D 14
Carrick Pl. *Stoke* 5K 39
Carr La. *A'ly* 3B 24
Carroll Dri. *Stoke* 2J 41
Carron St. *Stoke* 1G 41
Carr St. *Pac* 2J 21
Carryer Pl. *New* 5C 32
Carson Rd. *Stoke* 1J 27
Cartlich St. *Stoke* 6G 21
Cartlidge St. *Stoke* 4G 33 (3G 7)
Cartmel Pl. *Stoke* 1A 28
Cartwright Ind. Est., The.
. . . . . . *Stoke* 4G 41
Cartwright St. *Stoke* 4G 41
Casewell Rd. *Stoke* 5B 28
Caspian Gro. *Stoke* 7A 40
Castel Clo. *New* 3B 38
Castledine Gro. *Stoke* 2J 41
Castlefield St. *Stoke* 3K 33
Castle Gro. *Stoke* 7G 29
Castle Hill Rd. *New* 4D 32 (3B 6)
Castle Keep Ct. *New* 5D 32 (4B 6)
Castle Keep Gdns.
. . . . *New* 4D 32 (3B 6)
Castle Keep M. *New* 5D 32 (3B 6)
Castle La. *Mad* 3B 30
Castle Mt. *New* 6B 26
Castle Ridge. *New* 5C 32 (5A 6)
Castle St. *Mow C* 3G 13
Castle St. *Ches* 5B 26
Castle St. *New* 4F 33 (3F 7)
Castleton Rd. *Stoke* 7K 41
Castletown Grange.
. . . . *New* 3D 32
Castle Vw. *Bid* 4B 14
Castleview Gro. *Stoke* 4J 21
Castleview Rd. *Kid* 7E 12
Castle Wlk. *New* 3D 6
Catalina Pl. *Stoke* 1D 48
Caterham Pl. *Stoke* 1C 48
Catharine Rd. *Stoke* 5A 22
Catherine St. *New* 1G 33
Caton Cres. *Stoke* 2E 28
Cauldon Av. *New* 5D 26
Cauldon Clo. *Leek* 5G 17
Cauldon Pl. *Stoke* 4A 34
Cauldon Rd. *Stoke* 4A 34
Caulton St. *Stoke* 3J 27
Causeley Gdns. *Stoke* 2G 35
Causeley Rd. *Stoke* 2G 35
Cavendish Cres. *Als* 5D 10
Cavendish Gro. *New* 3E 38
Cavendish St. *Stoke* . . .2K 33 (4B 4)
Caverswall. 4F 43
Caverswall Common. 1E 42
Caverswall Comn. *Cav* 7D 36
Caverswall La. *Stoke* 6D 42
Caverswall Old Rd. *For* 6G 43
Caverswall Rd. *B Bri* 7G 43
Caverswall Rd. *Dil* 3H 43
Caverswall Rd.
. . . . *Stoke & Cav* 2C 42
Caverswall Road Station. . . .5G 43
Cavour St. *Stoke* 3J 33
Cawdry Bldgs. *Leek* 3G 17
. . . . (off Fountain St.)
Cayley Pl. *Stoke* 1D 48
Cecil Av. *Stoke* 7A 28 (1D 4)
Cecilly St. *C'dle* 2H 45
Cecilly Ter. *C'dle* 2H 45
. . . . (off King Edward St.)
Cecil Rd. *Gil N* 2H 15
Cedar Av. *Stoke* 7D 10
Cedar Av. *B Bri* 1H 49
Cedar Av. *Tal* 2A 20
Cedar Clo. *C'dle* 4J 45
Cedar Clo. *Als* 6F 11
Cedar Ct. *Cong* 7H 9
Cedar Cres. *Big E* 3G 25
Cedar Cres. *End* 5K 23
Cedar Gro. *Bid M* 1F 15
Cedar Gro. *Stoke* 3D 40

Cedar Rd. *New* 3A 26
. . . . (in two parts)
Cedars, The. *Als* 7E 10
Cedartree Gro. *Stoke* 3C 28
Celandine Clo. *Stoke* 3G 29
Celebration Ct. *Stoke* 1B 28
Cellarhead. 1G 37
Cellarhead Rd. *Werr* 1E 36
Celtic Av. *Pac* 3J 21
Cemetery Av. *Stoke* 4G 41
Cemetery Rd. *Knut* 2B 32
Cemetery Rd. *Sil* 5A 32
Cemetery Rd. *Stoke* 3K 33
Cemetery Vw. *New* 2B 32
Cemetery Vw. *Stoke* 4G 41
Cemlyn Av. *Stoke* 3D 40
Centenary Pl. *Cong* 4G 9
Central Av. *Rad G* 2A 18
Central Av. *Stoke* 1F 35
Central Dri. *Stoke* 3D 40
Central St. *Mow C* 4E 12
Centre Ct. *Als* 6F 11
Centre 500. *Wol* 6H 27
Century Retail Pk.
. . . . *Stoke* 1A 34 (3C 4)
Century Rd. *High B* 2C 26
Century St. *Stoke* 7K 27 (1B 4)
. . . . (in two parts)
Ceramica. 4J 27
Chadwell Way. *Stoke* 4J 35
Chadwick St. *Stoke* 3H 41
Chadwyn Dri. *Stoke* 2G 29
Chaffinch Clo. *Cong* 6G 9
Chaffinch Dri. *Bid* 2D 14
Chain St. *Stoke* 2B 28
Chalfont Grn. *Stoke* 3G 35
Challenge Clo. *Stoke* 1B 28
. . . . (off Unwin St.)
Challinor Av. *Leek* 5F 17
Challinor St. *Stoke* 1H 27
Chamberlain Av. *Stoke* 7K 33
Chamberlain St. *Stoke* 3B 34
Chamberlain Way. *Bid* 2D 14
Chance Hall La. *Sch G* 2J 11
Chancery La. *Als* 7C 10
Chancery La. *Stoke* 3H 41
Chantree Row. *Mow C* 3G 13
Chantry Rd. *New* 7E 32
Chapel Bank. *Mow C* 4G 13
Chapel Clo. *Mow C* 4E 12
Chapel Cotts. *Stoke* 1G 23
Chapel Ct. *New* 3K 31
Chapel La. *A'ly* 2E 24
Chapel La. *Bid M* 2F 15
Chapel La. *Brn E* 2G 23
Chapel La. *Har* 6H 13
Chapel La. *Rode H* 3G 11
Chapel La. *Stoke* 4K 27
Chapel St. *Big E* 1F 25
Chapel St. *C'dle* 3G 45
Chapel St. *Cong* 5F 9
Chapel St. *For* 6H 43
Chapel St. *Knut* 2B 32
Chapel St. *Mow C* 4E 12
Chapel St. *New* 2F 33
Chapel St. *Sil* 3K 31
Chapel St. *Stoke* 1G 35
Chapel St. *Tal* 1A 20
Chaplin Rd. *Stoke* 6H 41
Chapter Wlk. *Stoke* 7F 29
Charles Cotton Dri. *Mad* 2A 30
Charles Sq. *Has G* 1A 10
Charles St. *Bid* 3B 14
Charles St. *C'dle* 3G 45
Charles St. *New* 2G 33
Charles St. *Stoke* 2C 34 (3F 5)
Charlestown Gro. *Stoke* 7B 42
Charlesworth Pl. *Cong* 3H 9
Charlotte St. *Stoke* 4F 21
Charlton St. *Stoke* 5A 34
Charminster Rd. *Stoke* 7B 42
Charmouth Clo. *Stoke* 6F 29
Charnock Pl. *Stoke* 4K 21
Charnwood. *Kid* 2E 20
Charnwood Clo. *Leek* 5D 16
Charnwood Rd. *Stoke* 5A 42
Charolais Cres. *Stoke* 6J 41

Charsley Pl. *Stoke* 5E 40
Charter Rd. *New* 2D 32
Chartley Clo. *B Bri* 1F 49
Chartwell Clo. *Werr* 2B 36
Chase La. *T'sor* 7A 46
Chase Wlk. *Stoke* 7A 42
Chasewater Gro. *C'dle* 2J 45
Chatfield Pl. *Stoke* 4J 41
Chatham St. *Stoke* 3A 34
Chatsworth Av. Pk. *Stoke* 5K 39
Chatsworth Dri. *Cong* 4B 8
Chatsworth Dri. *Stoke* 7D 22
Chatsworth Dri. *Werr* 3B 36
Chatsworth Pl. *New* 5C 26
Chatsworth Pl. *Stoke* 5A 42
Chatteris Clo. *Stoke* 1C 48
Chatterley. 1E 26
Chatterley Clo. *New* 4E 26
Chatterley Dri. *Kid* 4D 20
Chatterley Rd. *Stoke* 7E 20
Chatterley St. *Stoke* 3H 27
Chatterley Whitfield. 4B 22
Chatterton Pl. *Stoke* 3J 41
Chaucer Courts. *Stoke* 5G 41
Cheadle. 3G 45
CHEADLE HOSPITAL. 4G 45
Cheadle Rd.
. . . . *B Bri, For & C'dle* 7H 43
Cheadle Rd. *C'dle* 7C 44
Cheadle Shop. Cen. *C'dle* 3G 45
Cheapside. *New* 5E 32 (3D 6)
Cheapside. *Stoke* 1B 34 (3F 5)
Chebsey Clo. *Stoke* 1H 35
Checkley Dri. *Bid* 1C 14
Checkley Rd. *New* 3K 25
Checkly Gro. *Stoke* 7J 35
Cheddar Dri. *New* 3G 31
Cheddleton Rd. *Leek* 5F 17
Chelford Rd. *Som* 3A 8
Chell Grn. Av. *Stoke* 5K 21
Chell Grn. Ct. *Stoke* 5K 21
Chell Gro. *New* 5D 26
Chell Heath. 7A 22
Chell Heath Rd. *Stoke* 5A 22
Chells Hill. *B'ton* 2E 10
Chell St. *Stoke* 7C 28
Chelmorton Dri. *Stoke* 5K 41
Chelmsford Dri. *Stoke* 3H 35
Chelmsford Rd. *New* 7E 26
Chelsea Clo. *Bid* 1B 14
Chelson St. *Stoke* 3H 41
Cheltenham Av. *C'dle* 1H 45
Cheltenham Gro. *New* 3G 31
Cheltenham Rd. *Stoke* 7E 28
Chelwood St. *Stoke* . . .7A 28 (1D 4)
Chemical La. *Stoke* 2E 26
Chemical La. Ind. Est.
. . . . *Stoke* 3F 27
Chepstow Clo. *Bid* 1B 14
Chepstow Pl. *Stoke* 7H 35
Cheriton Grn. *Stoke* 4J 35
Cherry Clo. *Ful* 7F 49
Cherry Clo. *New* 3A 26
Cherry Gro. *Stoke* 3D 40
Cherry Hill. *Mad* 2B 30
Cherry Hill Av. *Stoke* 4B 42
Cherry Hill La. *New* 3B 32
. . . . (in two parts)
Cherry La. *C'dle* 1K 45
Cherry La. *Chu L & Rode H* . .4E 10
Cherry Orchard. *New*
. . . . .4E 32 (2D 6)
Cherry Tree Av. *Chu L* 5H 11
Cherry Tree La. *Stoke* 7K 39
Cherry Tree La. *Bid M* 1F 15
Cherry Tree Rd. *Big E* 3G 25
Cherry Tree Rd. *New* 3B 26
Cherrywood Gro. *Stoke* 1A 48
Chertsey Pl. *Stoke* 4C 28
Chervil Clo. *Stoke* 1B 48
Chesham Gro. *Stoke* 5D 16
Chessington Cres. *Stoke* 7B 40
Chester Clo. *Tal* 4B 20
Chester Cres. *New* 1D 38
Chester Rd. *A'ly* 2E 24
Chester Rd. *Tal* 4A 20
Chesterton. 5B 26

Chesterton Speedway Stadium.
. . . . .7A 26
Chesterwood Rd. *Stoke* 1A 28
Chestnut Av. *Rode H* 3G 11
Chestnut Cres. *B Bri* 1H 49
Chestnut Dri. *Als* 1F 19
Chestnut Dri. *Cong* 3B 8
Chestnut Gro. *New* 3B 26
Chestnut Rd. *Brn E* 4H 23
Cheswardine Rd. *New* 4E 26
Chetwynd Av. *Ash B* 2B 36
Chetwynd Dri. *Stoke* 6D 22
Chetwynd Rd. *New* 6E 26
Chetwynd St. *New* 7G 27
Cheviot Clo. *New* 2B 32
Cheviot Dri. *Stoke* 1B 28
Chichester Wlk. *Stoke* 1H 5
Childerplay Rd. *Bid* 7B 14
Chilgrove Clo. *Stoke* 7E 28
Chiltern Pl. *New* 2B 32
Chilton St. *Stoke* 1D 40
Chilworth Gro. *Stoke* 5E 40
China St. *Stoke* 1E 40
Chivelstone Gro. *Stoke* 1B 46
Cholerton Clo. *Stoke* 1D 40
Chorley Av. *Stoke* 5K 21
Chorley St. *Leek* 4F 17
Chorlton Rd. *Stoke* 6C 28
Christchurch St. *Stoke* 7D 34
Christie Pl. *Stoke* 1A 42
Christine St. *Stoke* 2F 35
Chubb Way. *Stoke* 2H 39
Chumleigh Gro. *Stoke* 2K 27
Church Av. *Stoke* 2G 29
Church Bank. *A'ly* 2E 24
Church Bank. *K'le* 6G 31
Church Clo. *Bid* 4C 14
Church Clo. *Stoke* 2A 48
Church Dri. *B'stn* 5D 46
Churchfield Av. *Stoke* 5H 41
Church Fields. 6D 26
Church Fields. *K'le* 6G 31
Church Gdns. *Stoke* 2H 41
Churchill Av. *Stoke* 7J 39
Churchill Clo. *B Bri* 1F 49
Churchill Dri. *Cong* 4C 8
Churchill Ho. *Stoke* . . .3B 34 (6F 5)
Churchill Rd. *C'dle* 1H 45
Churchill Way. *Stoke* 7J 39
Church La. *Bid M* 1G 15
Church La. *Chu L* 6K 11
Church La. *End* 1K 23
Church La. *Knut* 4B 32
Church La. *Leek* 3F 17
Church La. *Mow C* 3H 13
Church La. *New* 1G 33
Church La. *Sch G* 2J 11
Church La. *Stoke* 4J 39
Church Lawton. 5H 11
Church Plantation. *K'le* 6H 31
Church Rd. *Als* 6C 10
Church Rd. *Bid* 3C 14
Church Rd. *Brn E* 2F 23
Church Rd. *Stoke* 5E 40
Church Sq. *Stoke* 4H 27
Church St. *A'ly* 2E 24
Church St. *Big E* 3H 25
Church St. *C'dle* 3G 45
Church St. *Ches* 5B 26
Church St. *Kid* 6E 12
Church St. *Leek* 3F 17
Church St. *Mow C* 4F 13
Church St. *New* 4E 32 (3C 6)
Church St. *Sil* 3J 31
Church St. *Stoke* 6A 34
Church St. *Tal* 1A 20
Church Ter. *Stoke* 6A 28
Church Vw. *New* 3B 32
Church Vw. *S Hay* 2F 31
Church Wlk. *New* 5B 26
Churnet Gro. *C'dle* 5H 45
Churnet Rd. *For* 7H 43
Churnet Vw. *Leek* 1H 17
Churnet Works Ind. Est.
. . . . *Leek* 2D 16
Churston Clo. *New* 4E 38

Churston Pl. *Stoke* 4C 28
Cinderhill Ind. Est. *Stoke* 2A 42
Cinder-Hill La. *Sch G* 4B 12
Cinderhill La. *Stoke* 3J 41
City Bank. *Gil H* 2H 15
CITY GENERAL HOSPITAL (STOKE)
. . . . .6G 33 (6G 7)
City La. *Long* 5A 16
City Rd. *Stoke* 6B 34
Clandon Av. *Stoke* 7H 21
Clanway La. *Stoke* 6G 21
Clanway St. *Stoke* 6G 21
Clare Av. *New* 6E 26
Claremont Clo. *New* 5F 27
Clarence Rd. *Stoke* 2G 41
Clarence St. *New* 5G 33 (4G 7)
(Mount Pleasant)
Clarence St. *New* 7E 26
(Watlands Vw.)
Clarence St. *Stoke* 6D 34
Clarendon St. *Stoke* 7B 34
Clare St. *Har* 6H 13
Clare St. *Mow C* 4F 13
Clare St. *Stoke* 4G 33 (2H 7)
Clarice Cliff Ct. *Stoke* 6B 34
Claridge Rd. *Stoke* 4H 33 (3H 7)
Clark Clo. *Rode H* 2F 11
Clarke St. *Stoke* 3A 34 (6C 4)
Claud St. *Stoke* 2C 40
Claydon Cres. *New* 4E 38
Clayfield Gro. *Stoke* 7H 35
Clayfield Gro. W. *Stoke* 7G 35
Clayhanger Clo. *New* 4D 26
Clayhanger St. *Stoke* 4J 27
Clay Hills. *Stoke* 1F 27
Clay Lake. *End* 4J 23
Clayton. 1F 39
Clayton Av. *Cong* 2H 9
Clayton By-Pass. *Cong* 4E 8
Clayton La. *New & Stoke* 2F 39
Clayton Rd. *New* 6E 32 (6D 6)
Clayton Sports Cen. 1G 39
Clayton St. *Stoke* 3G 41
Claytonwood Rd. *Stoke* 3H 39
Cleadon Pl. *Stoke* 6G 29
Clematis Av. *B Bri* 1G 49
Clement Pl. *Stoke* 1D 28
Clement Rd. *Stoke* 6K 21
Clerk Bank. *Leek* 3F 17
Clermont Av. *Stoke* 4K 39
Cleveland Rd. *New* 2B 32
Cleveland St. *Stoke* . . .3B 34 (6E 5)
Cleveland St. *Stoke* 4J 27
Clewlow Pl. *Stoke* 1J 41
Clewlows Bank. *Bag* 7K 23
Clews St. *Stoke* 5H 27
Clews Wlk. *New* 7F 27
Cley Gro. *New* 4E 38
Cliffe Pl. *Stoke* 1K 27
Clifford Av. *Stoke* 6E 22
Clifford St. *Stoke* 3C 34 (6G 5)
Cliff St. *Smal* 3B 28
Cliff Vale. 4J 33
Cliff Va. *Stoke* 4J 33
Clifton Clo. *Stoke* 1D 40
Clifton St. *New* 1G 33
Clifton St. *Stoke* 1D 40
Clinton Sq. *Stoke* . . .2B 34 (5D 4)
Clive Av. *Stoke* 1G 29
Cliveden Pl. *Stoke* 4H 41
Cliveden Rd. *Stoke* 7G 29
Clive Rd. *New* 6G 27
Clive St. *Stoke* 7H 21
Cloister Wlk. *Stoke* 7F 29
Close La. *Als* 6A 10
Close La. *Mow C* 3G 13
Close, The. *Als* 7B 10
Close, The. *End* 2K 23
Close, The. *Mad* 1B 30
Close, The. *W Coy* 1C 42
Cloud Vw. *Cong* 5J 9
Clough Hall. 3C 20
Clough Hall Dri. *Kid & Tal* 4B 20
Clough Hall Rd. *Kid* 3C 20
Clough La. *Werr* 2B 36
Clough St. *Stoke* 2K 33 (5B 4)
Cloughwood Way. *Stoke* 3G 27

Clovelly Wlk. *Stoke* 5H 27
Cloverdale Pl. *Stoke* 3A 42
Cloverdale Rd. *New* 2E 32
Clover Rd. *New* 6G 27
Clowes Av. *Als* 7G 11
Clowes Rd. *Stoke* 2F 35
Club St. *Stoke* 7A 34
Clumber Av. *New* 7F 33
Clumber Gro. *New* 1F 39
Cluny Pl. *Stoke* 7F 29
Clyde Av. *Bid* 1D 14
Clyde Pl. *New* 2D 38
Clyde Rd. *Stoke* 5C 40
Clyde St. *Stoke* 2A 34 (5C 4)
Clyde Wlk. *Stoke* 2A 34 (5C 4)
Clynes Way. *Stoke* 3C 42
Coalpit Hill. 3J 19
Coalpit Hill. *Tal* 4A 20
Coalport Clo. *C'dle* 5F 45
Coalville Pl. *Stoke* 1C 42
Coates Pl. *Stoke* 3A 22
Cobden St. *Stoke* 6G 27
Cobden St. *Stoke* 5G 41
Cobham Pl. *Stoke* 6B 42
Cob Moor Rd. *Kid* 5D 12
Cobridge. 6A 28
Cobridge Ind. Est. *Stoke* 5A 28
Cobridge Rd. *Stoke* 1K 33 (3B 4)
Cocklessal La. *Ful* 7F 49
Cocknage. 2H 47
Cocknage Rd. *Stoke* 5G 41
Cockshuts. *Cong* 5F 9
Cocks La. *Stoc B* 1H 29
Cockster Brook La. *Stoke* 3E 40
Cockster Rd. *Stoke* 3E 40
Colclough Av. *New* 4D 26
Colclough La. *Stoke* 4G 21
Colclough Rd. *Stoke* 5B 42
Colehill Bank. *Cong* 5G 9
Colenso Way. *New* 4E 26
Coleridge Dri. *C'dle* 4F 45
Coleridge Rd. *Stoke* 4E 40
Cole St. *Bid* 3B 14
Colin Cres. *Stoke* 2C 42
Colindene Gro. *Stoke* 7J 33
Collard Av. *New* 2E 32
College Clo. *Mad* 1B 30
College Rd. *Als* 5C 10
College Rd. *Stoke* 3A 34 (6D 4)
Colley Rd. *Stoke* 5J 21
Collingbourne Clo. *Stoke* 1A 46
Collingwood Gro. *Stoke* 5H 33
Collin Rd. *Stoke* 2H 39
Collinson Rd. *Stoke* 4G 21
Collis Av. *Stoke* 4G 33 (3H 7)
Columbine Wlk. *Stoke* 1G 27
(off Ladywell Rd.)
Colville St. *Stoke* 7E 34
Colwyn Dri. *Knyp* 5C 14
Combe Dri. *Stoke* 2B 48
Combery Clo. *Stoke* 1B 48
Commerce St. *Stoke* 3H 41
Commercial Rd. *Stoke*
. . . . .2C 34 (5H 5)
Commercial St. *Stoke* 5K 27
Common La. *R'gh C* 3K 47
Commonside. 5C 44
Common, The. *Dil* 2K 43
Community Rd. *Stoke* 3C 28
Como Pl. *New* 7B 32
Compton. *Leek* 4F 17
Compton St. *Stoke* 2A 34 (5C 4)
Condlyffe Rd. *Leek* 5F 17
Conewood Pl. *Stoke* 5D 40
Coneygreave. 7D 44
Coneygreave Clo. *C'dle* 5G 45
Conford Clo. *Stoke* 3E 34
Congleton. 5F 9
Congleton Bus. Cen. *Cong* 4G 9
Congleton Bus. Pk. *Cong* 3D 8
Congleton Edge Rd. *Cong* 7K 9
Congleton Leisure Cen. 4G 9
Congleton Rd. *Bid* 1C 14
Congleton Rd.
Ker & Sch G 1B 12
Congleton Rd. *Mow C* 2H 13
Congleton Rd. *Tal* 3A 20

Congleton Rd. N.
Chu L & Sch G 7A 12
Congleton Rd. S. *Chu L* 7A 12
CONGLETON STATION. RAIL
. . . . .6J 9
CONGLETON WAR MEMORIAL
HOSPITAL. 6H 9
Congreve Rd. *Stoke* 4E 40
Conifer Gro. *Stoke* 4E 40
Conifers, The. *Als* 7C 10
Coniston Av. *Cong* 5B 8
Coniston Dri. *C'dle* 2J 45
Coniston Gro. *New* 2E 38
Coniston Pl. *Stoke* 7J 39
Connaught St. *Stoke* 2G 27
Conrad Clo. *Stoke* 3J 41
Consall Gro. *Stoke* 1B 46
Consall La. *Wet R* 1K 37
Consett Rd. *Stoke* 6E 40
Consort St. *Stoke* 6A 34
Constable Av. *New* 6B 26
Constable Clo. *Stoke* 7C 42
Constance Av. *Stoke* 6A 40
Convent Clo. *Stoke* 5K 33
Convent St. *Stoke* 5K 33
Conway Gro. *C'dle* 5H 45
Conway Rd. *Knyp* 4B 14
Conway St. *Stoke* 5B 34
Cookshill. 3E 42
Cookson Av. *Stoke* 5H 41
Coolidge St. *Stoke* 1G 27
Co-operative La. *Halm* 5E 24
Cooper Av. *New* 3H 33
Coopers Clo. *Leek* 4D 16
Cooper St. *Cong* 4G 9
Cooper St. *New* 6B 26
Cooper St. *Stoke* 3A 34 (6D 4)
Coopers Way. *Bid* 2A 14
Copeland Av. *New* 3E 38
Copeland Av. *T'sor* 6A 46
Copeland Clo. *C'dle* 5G 45
Copeland St. *Stoke* 5A 34
Copes Av. *Stoke* 7H 21
Cope St. *Stoke* 3F 29
Copperhill Rd. *Cong* 7K 9
Coppice Av. *New* 4H 31
Coppice Clo. *Bid* 3C 14
Coppice Gro. *Stoke* 3A 42
Coppice La. *C'dle* 6J 37
Coppice Rd. *Tal* 3K 19
Coppice, The. *Stoke* 5B 28
Coppice Vw. *New* 1D 32
Copp La. *Stoke* 2F 27
Copplestone Gro. *Stoke* 3K 41
Coppull Pl. *Stoke* 4K 21
Copthall Ho. *New* 3E 7
Copthorne Clo. *Cong* 5H 9
Coracle Gro. *Knyp* 4D 14
Coral Gro. *Stoke* 7A 40
Corbett Wlk. *Stoke* 1G 27
(off Ladywell Rd.)
Corby Pl. *Stoke* 3F 41
Corfe Grn. *Stoke* 1H 41
Corfield Pl. *Stoke* 6C 22
Corina Ct. *Stoke* 2J 41
Corina Way. *Stoke* 2J 41
Corinth Way. *Stoke* 1G 27
Cormie Clo. *Stoke* 6A 22
Cornelious St. *Stoke* 5B 42
Cornes St. *Stoke* 4C 34
Corneville Rd. *Stoke* 2G 35
Cornfield Rd. *Bid* 3C 14
Cornhill. .6D 22
Cornhill. *Leek* 5F 17
Cornhill Clo. *New* 3A 26
Cornhill Gdns. *Leek* 5F 17
Cornhill Rd. *Stoke* 6B 22
Cornhill St. *Leek* 4F 17
Cornwall Av. *New* 2F 39
Cornwall Clo. *Cong* 7J 9
Cornwallis St. *Stoke* 7A 34
Cornwall St. *Stoke* 2H 41
Cornwood Gro. *Stoke* 6K 41
Corona Pk. *New* 4B 26
Coronation Av. *Als* 7B 10
Coronation Av. *Knyp* 5A 14
Coronation Av. *Stoke* 3G 41

Coronation Cres. *Kid* 2B 20
Coronation Gdns. *Als* 6D 10
Coronation Rd. *Cong* 4H 9
Coronation Rd. *New* 5F 33 (4E 7)
Coronation Rd.
Stoke 5H 33 (5H 7)
Coronation St. *C'dle* 3G 45
Coronation St. *Stoke* 7H 21
Corporation St. *New* 4E 32 (3C 6)
Corporation St. *Stoke* 7K 33
Coseley St. *Stoke* 3B 28
Cotehill Rd. *Werr* 2C 36
Cotesheath St. *Stoke* 4C 34
Coton Ri. *B'stn* 6D 46
Cotswold Av. *New* 2B 32
Cotswold Cres. *Stoke* 3F 29
Cottage Clo. *Stoke* 5K 41
Cottage La. *Bid M* 2F 15
Cottages, The. 5B 36
Cotterill Dri. *New* 4E 26
Cotterill Rd. *Stoke* 5J 27
Cotton Rd. *Stoke* 5B 34
Cottons Row. *Stoke* 4G 33 (4H 7)
Cottonwood Gro. *Har* 7H 13
Cottonwood Gro. *Stoke* 2H 41
Country Pk. Vw. *Big E* 4H 25
Coupe Dri. *Stoke* 1B 42
Court La. *New* 1E 32
Courtney Pl. *Stoke* 6K 41
Court Number 1. *Stoke* 4K 41
Courtway Dri. *Stoke* 4C 28
Court Yd., The. *Cong* 4D 8
Coverdale Clo. *Stoke* 7B 42
Coverley Pl. *Stoke* 7J 33
Covert Gdns. *Tal* 3A 20
Covert, The. *K'le* 6J 31
Covert, The. *New* 4F 39
Cowall Moor. 6G 15
Cowallmoor La. *Lask E* 6G 15
Cowen St. *Stoke* 5D 22
Cowley Way. *Stoke* 6K 35
Cowlishaw Clo. *Brn L* 5K 13
Cowlishaw Rd. *Stoke* 2A 20
Cowper St. *Stoke* 7E 34
Coyney Gro. *Stoke* 3B 42
Crabtree Av. *Bid* 2B 14
Crabtree Clo. *Fen I* 5E 34
Crackley. .4B 26
Crackley Bank. *New* 2B 26
Crackley Gates. 2F 31
Crackley La. *S Hay* 2F 31
Craig Rd. *Cong* 3H 9
Craigside. *Bid* 2F 15
(in two parts)
Craig Wlk. *Als* 1G 19
Cranage Ct. *Cong* 4H 9
(off Brunswick St.)
Cranberry Dri. *New* 3A 26
Cranberry La. *Als* 6A 10
Cranberry Moss. 7B 10
Cranberry Moss La. *Als* 7B 10
Cranbourne Av. *Stoke* 2G 29
Cranbrook Clo. *Stoke* 7K 39
Crane St. *Stoke* 6A 28
Cranfield Dri. *Als* 7F 11
Cranfield St. *Stoke* 3G 35
Cranford M. *Als* 7B 10
Cranford Way. *Stoke* 2J 35
Cranleigh Av. *Stoke* 4C 28
Cranmer St. *Stoke* 6A 34
Cranswick Gro. *Stoke* 4J 35
Cranwell Pl. *Stoke* 6A 42
Cranworth Gro. *Stoke* 6K 41
Craven Clo. *Stoke* 6K 39
Crawford St. *Stoke* 1C 40
Crayford Av. *Cong* 2J 9
Crediton Av. *Stoke* 7B 22
Crescent Gro. *Stoke* 4H 33
Crescent Rd. *Cong* 5E 8
Crescent, The. *Cong* 5E 8
Crescent, The. *Leek* 3H 17
Crescent, The. *New* 7D 32
Crescent, The. *Sil* 3J 31
Crescent, The. *Stoke* 2H 39
(Springfields)
Crescent, The. *Stoke* 2C 42
(Weston Coyney)

Cresswell. 4K 49
Cresswell Av. *New* 3A 26
Cresswell La. *C'wll* 4K 49
Cresswell Old La. *C'wll* 4K 49
Cresswell Rd. *Stoke* 2D 34
Cresswellshawe Rd. *Als* 6E 10
Crestbrook Rd. *Stoke* 5G 29
Crestfield Rd. *Stoke* 6A 42
Crestway Rd. *Stoke* 2H 29
Crewe Rd. *Als* 1A 18
Crewe Rd. *Chu L* 6G 11
Crewe Rd. *Mad H* 5B 30
Crick Rd. *Stoke* 3D 34 (6H 5)
Critchlow Gro. *Stoke* 5F 41
Croft Av. *New* 6E 26
Croft Clo. *Cong* 5H 9
Croft Ct. *Stoke* 3B 28
Croft Cres. *Stoke* 7K 33
Crofter Clo. *Bid* 2A 14
Crofters Ct. *Red S* 1A 26
Croftfield St. *Stoke* 5J 35
Croft Rd. *C'dle* 3G 45
Croft Rd. *New* 3E 32 (1D 6)
Croft Rd. Ind. Est.
  New 3E 32 (1D 6)
Croft St. *Stoke* 5J 27
Croft, The. *C'dle* 1H 45
Croft, The. *New* 1J 39
Cromartie St. *Stoke* 4H 41
  (in two parts)
Cromer Cres. *Stoke* 1D 34
Cromer Rd. *Stoke* 1D 34
Cromer St. *New* 1G 33
Crompton Gro. *Stoke* 2B 46
Cromwell St. *Bid* 1B 14
Cromwell St. *Stoke* 6C 28
Cromwell Ter. *Leek* 4G 17
  (off Livingstone St.)
Crosby Rd. *Stoke* 3H 39
Crossdale Av. *Stoke* 2F 29
Cross Edge. *Brn E* 4G 23
Crossfield Av. *B Bri* 1G 49
Crossfield Av. *Knyp* 4B 14
Crossfields La. *Cong* 7H 9
Crossgate. 7E 48
Cross Heath. 2D 32
Cross Hill. *Stoke* 5J 27
Crossland Pl. E. *Stoke* 6B 42
Crossland Pl. W. *Stoke* 5B 42
Crosslands. *Cong* 6J 9
Cross La. *Big E* 7E 18
Cross La. *Cong* 7H 9
Crossledge. *Cong* 4D 8
Crossley Rd. *Stoke* 1K 27
Cross May St. *New* . . .5D 32 (5B 6)
Crossmead Gro. *Stoke* 6E 28
Cross St. *Als* 7D 10
Cross St. *Bid* 2B 14
Cross St. *C'dle* 3G 45
Cross St. *Ches* 4A 26
Cross St. *Cong* 4F 9
Cross St. *Leek* 4G 17
Cross St. *Long H* 4F 27
Cross St. *W Coy* 1C 42
Crossway Rd. *Chu L* 6H 11
Crossway Rd. *Stoke* 5B 28
Crossways. *Bid* 1D 14
Crossway, The. *New* 2F 33
Croston St. *Stoke* 3A 34
Crouch Av. *Stoke* 1K 27
Crowborough. 4F 15
Crowborough Rd.
  Bid M & Lask E 4E 14
Crowcrofts Rd. *Stoke* 7D 40
Crown Bank. *Stoke* 3F 5
Crown Bank. *Tal* 4A 20
Crown Bank Cres. *Tal P* 5A 20
Crowndale Pl. *Stoke* 3H 21
Crown Gdns. *Tal* 5A 20
Crown St. *New* 4K 31
Crown St. *Stoke* 2B 34 (4E 5)
Crowther St. *Stoke* 5B 34
Croxden Clo. *C'dle* 6G 45
Croxden Rd. *Stoke* 6G 29
Croyde Pl. *Stoke* 1C 48
Cruso St. *Leek* 4E 16
Crystal St. *Stoke* 6A 28

Cumberbatch Av. *Stoke* 4A 22
Cumberland Clo. *Kid* 4B 20
Cumberland Rd. *Cong* 4C 8
Cumberland St. *New* . . .4G 33 (3G 7)
Cumberland St. *Stoke* 6D 34
Cumbria Ho. *New* 1F 39
Cumming St. *Stoke* 4H 33
Curland Pl. *New* 7D 32
Curlew Rd. *Pac* 2H 21
Curtiss Pl. *Stoke* 1D 48
Curzon Av. *Als* 5E 10
Curzon Ri. *Leek* 4C 16
Curzon Rd. *Stoke* 2K 27
Curzon St. *New* 3G 33 (1H 7)
Cutts St. *Stoke* 3A 34 (6D 4)
Cygnet Clo. *Mad H* 5B 30
Cynthia Gro. *Stoke* 2K 27
Cypress Gro. *B Bri* 1H 49
Cypress Gro. *New* 4A 26

D

Dace Gro. *Stoke* 1A 28
Dahlia Clo. *Stoke* 7C 36
Dain Pl. *New* 6E 26
Dain St. *Stoke* 5H 27
Daintry Clo. *Stoke* 5F 17
Daintry St. *Leek* 4F 17
Daintry St. *Stoke* 2J 39
Dairy Clo. *Leek* 3H 17
Dairyfields Way. *Stoke* 5B 28
Dairyhouse La. *Dil* 3K 37
Dairylands Rd. *Chu L* 6G 11
Daisy Bank. *Als* 6B 10
Daisy Bank. *Leek* 3F 17
Daisybank Dri. *Cong* 2F 9
Daisy Pl. *Stoke* 2D 40
Dakota Gro. *Stoke* 7G 21
Dale Av. *Stoke* 5C 22
Dale Clo. *C'dle* 4H 45
Dalecot Grn. *Stoke* 5J 35
Dale Cres. *Cong* 5H 9
Dalegarth Gro. *Stoke* 6K 41
Dale Gro. *Cong* 5J 9
Dalehall Gdns. *Stoke* 4H 27
Dalehead Ct. *Stoke* 6A 42
Daleian Ct. *New* 4K 31
  (off Bridge St.)
Dale Pl. *Cong* 5H 9
Dales Clo. *Bid M* 2G 15
Dales Green. 5F 13
Dales Grn. Rd. *Mow C* 4F 13
Dale St. *Stoke* 4H 27
Dale, The. *Ful* 6F 49
Dale Vw. *Mow C* 5F 13
Dale Vw. *Stoke* 3C 42
Dale Vw. Ct. *Ful* 6F 49
Daleview Dri. *New* 4K 31
Dalewood Rd. *Lyme B* 7B 26
Dalton Gro. *Stoke* 4J 35
Daltry Way. *Mad* 6A 30
Daly Cres. *New* 4J 31
Dam La. *Bid M* 1F 15
Dampier St. *Leek* 4F 17
Dandillion Av. *C'dle* 6G 45
Dane Bank Av. *Cong* 3G 9
Danebower Rd. *Stoke* 1B 46
Danebridge Gro. *Stoke* 7D 28
Dane Clo. *Als* 7B 10
Dane Dri. *Bid* 1D 14
Dane Gro. *C'dle* 5H 45
Danehill Gro. *Stoke* 5J 39
Dane-in-Shaw. 7K 9
Danemead Gro. *Stoke* 7B 42
Danes Cft. *Stoke* 7A 40
Danesgate. *Leek* 3G 17
Dane Side. *Cong* 4E 8
Daneside Bus. Pk. *Cong* 3G 9
Daneside Theatre. 4G 9
Dane St. *Cong* 4E 8
Dane Wlk. *Stoke* 1C 34 (3H 5)
Darius Clo. *New* 4E 26
Darley Gro. *C'dle* 5H 45
Darnley St. *Stoke* 5B 34

Darrall Gdns. *Stoke* 3H 39
Darsham Gdns. *New* 4F 39
Dart Av. *Stoke* 7K 21
Dart Clo. *Bid* 1C 14
Dartford Pl. *Stoke* 7B 22
Dart Gro. *C'dle* 5H 45
Dartmouth Av. *New* 7D 32
Dartmouth Pl. *Stoke* 6A 42
Dartmouth St. *Stoke* 3A 28
Dart Pl. *New* 2D 38
Dash Gro. *Stoke* 3B 28
Davenport Clo. *Leek* 5C 16
Davenport St. *Cong* 5E 8
Davenport St. *Stoke* 4G 27
Davenport Way. *New* 3C 38
Daven Rd. *Cong* 6H 9
Daventry Clo. *Stoke* 3E 34
David Rd. *Stoke* 5A 42
Davidson Av. *Cong* 2J 9
Davis Clo. *Als* 6F 11
Davison St. *Stoke* 5K 27
Davis St. *Stoke* 3K 33 (6B 4)
Davy Clo. *Stoke* 2F 35
Dawlish Dri. *Stoke* 3G 35
Dawn Av. *Stoke* 7K 21
Dawn Vw. *Stoke* 3C 42
Day Green. 2A 10
Dayson Pl. *New* 5D 26
Deakin Gro. *New* 1F 39
Deakin Rd. *Stoke* 6A 22
Dean Hollow. *A'ly* 2E 24
Dean Pl. *Stoke* 3C 34
Deansberry Clo. *Stoke* 6K 39
Deanscroft Way. *Stoke* 2K 41
Deansgate. *New* 5D 32 (5A 6)
Dean's La. *New* 2K 25
Dean St. *Stoke* 1H 35
Deans Way. *Stoke* 1A 46
Deaville Rd. *Stoke* 2H 35
Debenham Cres. *Stoke* 3E 34
Decade Clo. *High B* 2C 26
Deebank Av. *Leek* 3J 17
Dee Clo. *Bid* 1D 14
Dee Clo. *Tal* 4B 20
Dee La. *New* 2E 38
Deepdale Clo. *Stoke* 2E 28
Defoe Dri. *Stoke* 2K 41
Delamere Ct. *Als* 6A 10
Delamere Gro. *New* 3F 33 (1D 6)
Delamere Gro. *Stoke* 7K 39
Delamere Rd. *Cong* 4B 8
Delaney Dri. *Stoke* 2A 42
Delius Gro. *Stoke* 7E 28
Dell, The. *New* 4K 31
Dellwood Gro. *Stoke* 7J 35
Delphouse Rd. *C'dle* 4B 44
Delph Side. *Big E* 2G 25
Delph Wlk. *Stoke* 7E 34
Delves Pl. *New* 1E 38
Denbigh Clo. *Knyp* 4B 14
Denbigh Clo. *New* 2G 39
Denbigh St. *Stoke* 7A 28 (1C 4)
Denby Av. *Stoke* 1H 41
Dency Gro. *Stoke* 1K 27
Denehurst Clo. *Stoke* 4B 42
Dene Side. *New* 5D 32 (5A 6)
Denewood Pl. *Stoke* 5C 42
Denford Pl. *Chu L* 4E 10
Denham Sq. *Stoke* 5D 40
Denmark Ho. *Stoke* 1E 40
Dennington Cres. *Stoke* 5D 40
Dennis Round Ct. *Als* 7D 10
Dennis St. *Stoke* 1E 40
Dennis Viollet Av. *Stoke* 3B 40
Denry Cres. *New* 5D 26
Denshaw Wlk. *Stoke* 2H 41
  (off Forrister St.)
Denstone Cres. *Stoke* 4E 40
Dentdale Clo. *Stoke* 7B 42
Denton Clo. *New* 3E 38
Denton Gro. *Stoke* 3K 41
Derby Pl. *New* 2F 39
Derby Rd. *Tal* 4A 20
Derby St. *Cong* 4F 9
Derby St. *Leek* 4F 17
Derby St. *Stoke* 2C 34 (5G 5)

Dereham Way. *Stoke* 4J 35
Derek Dri. *Stoke* 6D 28
Derry St. *Stoke* 2D 40
Derwent Clo. *Als* 6B 10
Derwent Cres. *Kid* 1F 21
Derwent Dri. *Bid* 1D 14
Derwent Dri. *C'dle* 5H 45
Derwent Dri. *Cong* 6H 9
Derwent Pl. *New* 2D 32
Derwent St. *Stoke* 7A 28
Devana Wlk. *Stoke* 4D 42
Devils La. *Long* 5A 16
Devon Clo. *New* 2F 39
Devon Gro. *Bid* 1B 14
Devon Pl. *Cong* 3G 9
Devonshire Sq. *Stoke* 4H 35
Devon Way. *Stoke* 5J 41
Dewsbury Rd. *Fen I* 6D 34
Diamond Av. *Kid* 1E 20
Diamond Clo. *B'stn* 7B 46
Diamond Clo. *Bid* 2B 14
Diamond Clo. *Stoke* 3B 48
Diamond Ridge. *B'stn* 6B 46
Diana Rd. *Stoke* 6E 28
Diarmid Rd. *Stoke* 5J 39
Dibden Ct. *Stoke* 6K 33
Dickenson Rd. E. *Stoke* 5B 28
Dickenson Rd. W. *Stoke* 5B 28
Dickens St. *Stoke* 1H 35
Dickinson Way. *Als* 7B 10
Dickson Ho. *Stoke* 4C 34
Diglake. 1H 25
Diglake Clo. *Tal P* 5K 19
Diglake St. *Big E* 1G 25
Dilhorne. 2K 43
Dilhorne Gro. *Stoke* 5H 41
Dilhorne La. *Cav* 3F 43
Dilhorne Rd. *C'dle* 3E 44
Dilhorne Rd. *Dil* 3J 37
Dilhorne Rd. *For & Dil* 6J 43
Dilke St. *Stoke* 7C 28 (1G 5)
Dill Gro. *Stoke* 1C 48
Dimensions Leisure Cen. 2J 27
Dimmelow St. *Stoke* 1C 42
Dimsdale. 7E 26
Dimsdale Pde. E. *New* 7E 26
Dimsdale Pde. W. *New* 6D 26
Dimsdale St. *Stoke* 5H 27
Dimsdale Vw. *New* 6C 26
Dimsdale Vw. E. *New* 6E 26
Dimsdale Vw. W. *New* 6E 26
Dingle, The. *Brn E* 4G 23
Dividy Rd. *Stoke* 2E 34
Dixon Rd. *Cong* 2J 9
Dobell Gro. *Stoke* 2J 41
Doctors Clo. *Bid* 2B 14
Doddington Pl. *New* 7E 32
Dodd's La. *A'bry* 7E 8
Doddswood Dri. *Cong* 3H 9
Dodson St. *Stoke* 5B 28
Dogcroft Rd. *Stoke* 6B 22
Dog La. *Leek* 3F 17
Dolespring Clo. *For* 6H 43
Dolly's La. *Stoke* 2K 27
Dominic St. *Stoke* 5K 33
Donald Bates Ho. *Stoke* 7J 33
Donald Rd. *Stoke* 6D 28
Doncaster La. *Stoke* 6J 33
Donkey La. *C'dle* 1H 45
Dorcas Dri. *Stoke* 2E 40
Dorchester Clo. *Kid* 7D 12
Dorchester Wlk. *Stoke* 3H 35
Doreen Av. *Cong* 7K 9
Dorian Way. *End* 2K 23
Doris Robinson Ct. *Stoke* 7A 42
Dorking Clo. *Stoke* 3E 34
Dorlan Clo. *Stoc B* 1H 29
Dorridge Gro. *New* 1H 33
Dorrington Clo. *Stoke* 2F 29
Dorrington Gro. *New* 6F 27
Dorset Clo. *Cong* 3G 9
Dorset Clo. *Stoke* 2H 35
Dorset Dri. *Bid* 2B 14
Dorset Pl. *Kid* 7D 12
Dorset Pl. *New* 2G 39
Douglas Av. *Bid* 3B 14
Douglas Av. *Stoke* 1J 39

Douglas Macmillan Hospice—Fairoak

DOUGLAS MACMILLAN HOSPICE. 7F 41
Douglas Pl. Stoke 3D 34 (6H 5)
Douglas Rd. New 2D 32 (1B 6)
Douglas St. Stoke 6A 28
Doulton Clo. C'dle 5G 45
Doulton Dri. New 5E 26
Doulton St. Stoke 4K 27
Dove Bank. 1D 20
Dovebank Gro. Stoke 1B 48
Dovecote Pl. Stoke 6K 41
Dovedale Clo. Cong 3J 9
Dovedale Clo. Stoke 4E 20
Dovedale Pl. New 4H 31
Dove Gro. Bid 1C 14
Dove Pl. New 2D 38
Doveridge St. Stoke 1C 40
Dove Rd. For 7H 43
Dover St. Stoke 7C 28 (1H 5)
Downey St. Stoke 2B 34 (5F 5)
Downfield Pl. Stoke 3E 28
Downham Rd. New 3B 32
Downing Av. New 2G 33
Downsview Gro. Stoke 3E 40
Dragon Sq. New 4B 26
Drake Clo. Stoke 4E 34
Drakeford Ct. Stoke 7D 22
Drakeford Gro. Stoke 7D 22
Draw-well La. Werr 1C 36
(in three parts)
Draycott Cross. 6C 44
Draycott Cross Rd. C'dle 6C 44
Draycott Dri. C'dle 5G 45
Draycott Dri. New 2A 26
Draycott Old Rd. For & Dray 7J 43
Drayton Grn. Stoke 3F 35
Drayton Rd. Stoke 2G 41
Drayton St. New 5D 32 (4B 6)
Drenfell Rd. Sch G 3C 12
Dresden. 5G 41
Dresden St. Stoke 2C 34 (4H 5)
Dreys, The. Stoke 7A 40
Driffield Clo. Stoke 4K 35
Drive, The. Als B & New 6G 25
Droitwich Clo. New 3G 31
Drubbery La. Stoke 5E 40
Drumber La. Sch G 2D 12
Drumburn Clo. Stoke 4J 21
Drummond St. Stoke 4F 21
Dryberg Wlk. Stoke 1F 35
Dryden Rd. Stoke 6K 27
Dryden Way. C'dle 4F 45
Duddell Rd. Stoke 2B 28
Dudley Pl. Stoke 6B 42
Dudson Cen., The. (Mus.) 1B 34 (2E 5)
Duesbury Grn. Stoke 3F 41
Duke Bank. 7E 22
Duke Bank Ter. Stoke 7E 22
Duke Pl. New 4K 31
Duke St. Bid 3C 14
Duke St. Cong 5F 9
Duke St. Leek 4F 17
Duke St. New 6F 33 (6F 7)
Duke St. Stoke 2D 40
(in two parts)
Dulverton Av. New 1D 38
Duncalf Gro. New 5E 26
Duncalf St. Stoke 4J 27
Duncan St. Stoke 7D 34
Dundas St. Stoke 7C 28 (1G 5)
Dundee Rd. Stoke 2K 33 (5A 4)
Dundee St. Stoke 4G 41
Dunham Clo. Als 7D 10
Dunkirk. 5H 19
Dunkirk. New 4D 32 (2B 6)
Dunkirk Ct. New 4D 32 (2B 6)
Dunning St. Stoke 7G 21
Dunnocksfold Rd. Als 6A 10
Dunnockswood. Als 6B 10
Dunnock Way. Bid 2D 14
Dunrobin St. Stoke 5H 41
Dunsany Gro. Stoke 6D 28
Dunsford Av. Stoke 2F 29
Dunster Rd. Stoke 1G 41
Dunwood Dri. Chu L 4E 10
Dunwood Dri. Stoke 1K 27
Durber Clo. A'ly 3E 24
Durber Clo. Stoke 2H 39
Durham Dri. Stoke 6H 41
Durham Gro. New 2G 39
Durston Pl. Stoke 3K 41
Dyke St. Stoke 1C 34 (2G 5)
Dylan Rd. Knyp 4D 14
Dylan Rd. Stoke 3J 41

E

Eagland Pl. Cong 3G 9
Eagle St. Stoke 1D 34 (3H 5)
Eamont Av. Stoke 7K 21
Eardley Cres. Cong 3G 9
Eardleyend Rd. A'ly & Big E 5E 18
Eardley St. Stoke 7J 33
Earlsbrook Dri. Stoke 7B 40
Earls Ct. New 4F 33 (2G 7)
Earl's Dri. New 7E 32
Earls Rd. Stoke 7A 40
Earl St. Leek 3G 17
Earl St. New 4G 33 (2G 7)
Earl St. Sil 4K 31
Earlswood Rd. Stoke 6F 29
Easdale Pl. New 1E 38
Easedale Clo. Stoke 2F 29
E. Bank Ride. For 6H 43
Eastbank Rd. Stoke 7A 28 (1C 4)
Eastbourne Clo. Leek 3E 16
Eastbourne Rd. Stoke 1C 34 (2H 5)
Eastbridge Av. Stoke 4C 28
Eastcott Clo. Cong 3B 8
East Ct. Als 5F 11
East Cres. New 2G 33
East Cres. Stoke 4D 28
Eastdean Av. Stoke 3F 35
East Dri. Bid 2C 14
Easters Gro. Stoke 3G 29
Eastfield Clo. Stoke 6D 40
East Gro. Stoke 5B 42
Easthead Wlk. Stoke 2A 34 (5C 4)
E. Precinct. Stoke 1C 34 (3G 5)
East St. Leek 3H 17
East St. Stoke 1C 42
East Ter. Stoke 5A 22
East Vw. Stoke 5J 27
Eastwick Cres. Stoke 6K 39
Eastwood Av. Stoke 7K 21
Eastwood Pl. Stoke 2B 34 (5F 5)
Eastwood Rd. Stoke 2C 34 (5G 5)
Eaton Bank. Cong 2G 9
Eaton Bank Ind. Est. Cong 3H 9
Eaton Rd. Als 6D 10
Eaton St. Stoke 1C 34 (2G 5)
Eaves La. C'dle 6G 45
Eaves La. Stoke 7H 29
Eaveswood Rd. Stoke 6H 29
Ebenezer Ho. New 2E 7
Ebury Gro. Stoke 5A 42
Ecclestone Pl. Stoke 5K 21
Edale Clo. New 4J 31
Edale Clo. Stoke 4E 20
Eddisbury Dri. New 2A 26
Eden Clo. Bid 1D 14
Eden Clo. Kid 1E 20
Eden Gro. C'dle 5H 45
Eden Gro. Stoke 5A 42
Edenhurst Av. Stoke 5C 42
Edensor Ct. New 5B 26
Edensor Rd. Stoke 4G 41
(in two parts)
Edensor St. New 5B 26
Edensor Ter. Stoke 4G 41
Edgar Pl. Stoke 7H 35
Edgbaston Dri. Stoke 6C 40
Edge Av. Stoke 5K 21
Edgefield La. Stoc B 5H 23
Edgefield Rd. Stoke 1H 41
Edgehill Rd. Leek 4D 16
Edge La. End 4J 23
Edgeley Rd. Bid 3C 14
Edge St. Stoke 2J 27
Edge Vw. Clo. Stoke 2H 29
Edge Vw. Ct. Bid 3B 14
Edgeview Rd. Cong 7K 9
Edge Vw. Rd. Stoke 1H 29
Edgeware St. Stoke 7A 28
Edinburgh Pl. Cong 5H 9
Edinburgh Rd. Cong 5H 9
Edison St. Stoke 7C 34
Edmonton Gro. Stoke 3E 28
Ednam Pl. Stoke 5B 42
Edwal Rd. Stoke 2B 42
Edward Av. New 7E 32
Edward Av. Stoke 7A 40
Edward Davies Rd. Stoke 2B 28
Edward St. Big E 1G 25
Edward St. New 1G 33
Edward St. Stoke 6D 34
Edwards Way. Als 6F 11
Egerton Rd. Stoke 5H 33 (4H 7)
Egerton St. Cong 5E 8
Egerton St. Stoke 4C 34
Elaine Av. Stoke 3A 28
Elburton Rd. Stoke 7F 35
Elder Pl. Stoke 6A 28
Elder Rd. Stoke 5A 28
Eldon St. Stoke 6C 28
Eleanor Cres. New 7D 32
Eleanor Pl. New 7D 32
Eleanor Vw. New 7E 32
Elenora St. Stoke 6A 34
Elers Gro. Stoke 5H 27
Elgar Cres. Stoke 7F 29
Elgin St. Stoke 4A 34
Elgood La. Stoke 4F 21
Elizabeth Ct. Stoke 5J 33
Elizabeth Ct. Tal P 6A 20
Elizabeth Dri. New 5B 26
Elizabeth St. Cong 5E 8
Elizabeth St. Stoke 1D 34 (3H 5)
Elkington Ri. Mad 6A 30
Elkstone Clo. Stoke 7H 21
Ellam's Pl. New 4B 32
Ellastone Gro. Stoke 7J 33
Elldawn Av. Stoke 2E 28
Ellerby Rd. Stoke 6D 40
Ellgreave St. Stoke 4H 27
Ellington Clo. Stoke 3F 35
Elliot Dri. Werr 1C 36
Elliot Rd. Stoke 7E 34
Elliott St. New 4G 33 (2G 7)
Ellison St. New 7G 27
Ellis St. Stoke 5B 28
Elmbrook Clo. Stoke 6A 42
Elm Clo. Kid 3E 20
Elm Clo. Leek 4D 16
Elmcroft Rd. Stoke 6G 29
Elmdon Pl. Stoke 7C 42
Elm Dri. C'dle 4J 45
Elm Gro. Als 6F 11
Elmhurst. New 2C 38
Elmhurst Clo. Stoke 3E 34
Elm Pl. Stoke 5E 40
Elm Rd. Cong 4D 8
Elmsmere Av. Stoke 5F 41
Elmsmere Rd. Stoke 6G 29
Elmstead Clo. Stoke 5J 39
Elms, The. New 5F 27
Elm St. New 3G 33
Elm St. Stoke 5K 27
Elms Way. Stoke 4B 42
Elm Tree Dri. Big E 3G 25
Elmwood Clo. B Bri 1H 49
Elmwood Clo. Chu L 6H 11
Elmwood Dri. B Bri 1H 49
Elphinstone Rd. Stoke 3J 39
Elsby Pl. Stoke 5K 21
Elsby Rd. Als 1G 19
Elsing St. Stoke 7C 34
Elstree Clo. Stoke 4A 42
Elstree Gro. Stoke 6F 29
Elswick Rd. Fen I 5D 34
Eltham Gdns. New 2G 33
Elton Ter. Stoke 4G 21
Elvington Clo. Cong 5G 9
Elworth Ct. Cong 4H 9
(off Herbert St.)
Ely Wlk. Stoke 2H 41
Embers Way. End 1K 23
Emberton St. Ches 5B 26
Emberton St. New 7F 27
Embleton Wlk. Stoke 5H 27
Emerson Rd. Stoke 6K 27
Emery Av. New 6C 32 (6A 6)
Emery Av. Stoke 4D 28
Emery St. Stoke 6A 28
Empire Pas. Stoke 7K 33
Empire St. Stoke 7K 33
Emsworth Rd. Stoke 6D 40
Encounter Pl. Stoke 7D 28
Enderley St. New 4E 32 (2C 6)
Endon. 3K 23
Endon Bank. 1K 23
Endon Dri. Brn L 5A 14
Endon Edge. 5J 23
Endon Rd. Stoke 7D 22
Englesea Av. Stoke 1B 42
Ennerdale Clo. Stoke 4H 27
Ennerdale Dri. Cong 5D 8
Enoch St. Stoke 5J 27
Enstone Clo. Stoke 6E 40
Enstone Ct. New 3E 38
Enterprise Cen. Stoke 3K 33
Ephraim St. Stoke 3C 34 (6G 5)
Epping Rd. Stoke 3H 39
Epsom Clo. C'dle 1H 45
Epworth St. Stoke 6K 33
Ernest Egerrton Clo. Stoke 6F 21
Ernest Pl. Stoke 6D 34
Eros Cres. Stoke 6D 28
Errill Clo. Stoke 7B 34
Erskine St. Stoke 5H 41
Eskdale Pl. New 1E 38
Eskdale Pl. Stoke 7J 39
Esk Way. New 2E 38
Esperanto Way. Smal 4B 28
Esporta Health & Fitness. 7K 27 (1B 4)
Essex Clo. Cong 2G 9
Essex Dri. Gil H 2J 15
Essex Dri. Kid 1C 20
Essex Pl. New 7D 32
Eton Av. New 2C 38
Etruria. 2K 33 (4A 4)
Etruria Industrial Mus. 3K 33 (6B 4)
Etruria Old Rd. Stoke 2J 33
Etruria Rd. Stoke & New 4G 33 (1G 7 & 4A 4)
Etruria Trad. Est. Stoke 2H 33
Etruria Va. Rd. Stoke 2K 33 (4A 4)
Etruria Way. Stoke 2H 33
Etruscan Ho. Stoke 3K 33 (6B 4)
Etruscan St. Stoke 3J 33 (6A 4)
Etruscan Wlk. B'stn 3E 46
Eva Gro. New 6G 39
Evans St. Stoke 3J 27
Evelyn St. Stoke 1D 40
Everest Rd. Kid 7E 12
Eversley Av. Leek 4F 17
Eversley Rd. Stoke 4K 41
Evesham Way. Stoke 3K 41
Excalibur Ind. Est. Als 7F 11
Exeter Grn. Stoke 3H 35
Exmouth Gro. Stoke 5K 27
Eyre St. Stoke 5H 27

F

Faceby Gro. Stoke 7D 42
Fairbank Av. Stoke 1J 39
Fairclough Pl. Stoke 1K 27
Fairfax St. Stoke 6C 28
Fairfield Av. Brn E 4G 23
Fairfield Av. New 1F 33
Fairfield Av. Stoke 6H 41
Fairfields. Big E 2G 25
Fairfields Rd. Bid M 1G 15
Fairhaven Gro. Stoke 6D 28
Fairlawn Clo. Stoke 6K 41
Fairlawns. New 3E 32
Fairlight Gro. Stoke 7B 42
Fairoak. New 2C 38

58 A-Z Stoke

Fair Oak Rd. *New* 3A **26**
Fairview Av. *Als* 6E **10**
Fair Vw. Rd. *Leek* 4H **17**
Fairway. *Stoke* 6H **39**
Fairway Rd. *Stoke* 1K **27**
Fairway, The. *Als* 6D **10**
Falcon Rd. *Stoke* 1B **48**
Falkirk Grange. *New* 6C **32**
Fallowfield. *Stoke* 6E **40**
Falmouth Rd. *Cong* 7G **9**
Fanny's Cft. *Als* 1F **19**
Faraday Pl. *Stoke* 6H **33**
Farams Rd. *Rode H* 3F **11**
Farcroft Av. *New* 6C **26**
Fareham Gro. *Stoke* 7K **41**
Far Grn. Ind. Est. *Stoke* 7C **28**
Farington Pl. *Stoke* 5K **21**
Farland Gro. *Stoke* 5K **21**
Farleigh Gro. *Stoke* 4H **35**
Farmadine. *Stoke* 7A **40**
Farman Clo. *Stoke* 7D **42**
Farmers Bank. *New* 4K **31**
Farmer St. *Stoke* 4H **41**
Farm Hollow. *Big E* 2H **25**
Farm Lea. *Stoke* 5D **22**
Farmside La. *Bid M* 1G **15**
Farmwood Clo. *Stoke* 5C **42**
Farnborough Dri. *Stoke* 7D **42**
Farndale St. *Stoke* 1G **27**
Farne Gro. *Stoke* 3F **41**
Farnham Dri. *Brn L* 5A **14**
Farnworth Clo. *Knyp* 4A **14**
Farnworth Rd. *Stoke* 2K **41**
Farrington Clo. *Stoke* 1D **28**
Faulkner Pl. *Stoke* 2A **42**
Fawcett Way. *Stoke* 1G **5**
Fawfield Dri. *Stoke* 5F **21**
Fawn Clo. *Stoke* 6B **42**
Fearns Av. *New* 3D **26**
Fearon Grn. *Stoke* 1D **28**
Featherstone Gro. *Stoke* 6K **33**
Federation Rd. *Stoke* 3H **27**
Fegg Hayes. 5A **22**
Fegg Hayes Rd. *Stoke* 5K **21**
Felcourt Gdns. *Stoke* 7D **28**
Fellbrook Ct. *Stoke* 1F **35**
Fellbrook La. *Stoke* 1F **35**
Fellgate Ct. *New* 4E **32** (3C **6**)
Fell St. *Stoke* 3B **28**
Felstead St. *Stoke* 1G **29**
Fenlow Av. *Stoke* 3E **34**
Fennel Gro. *Stoke* 1C **48**
Fenners Gro. *Stoke* 6C **40**
Fenpark Rd. *Stoke* 7E **34**
Fenton. 7D **34**
Fenton Clo. *Cong* 6J **9**
Fenton Ind. Est. *Fen I* 5D **34**
Fenton Ind. Est. *Stoke* 5D **34**
Fenton Low. 6D **34**
Fenton Manor Leisure Cen.
. . . . .6C **34**
Fenton Pk. *Stoke* 6F **35**
Fenton Rd. *Stoke* 4E **34**
Fermain Clo. *New* 3C **38**
Fern Cres. *Cong* 4J **9**
Ferncroft Clo. *Stoke* 7A **40**
Ferndown Dri. *New* 4F **39**
Ferndown Dri. S. *New* 5G **39**
Ferney Pl. *Stoke* 5F **21**
Fernhurst Gro. *Stoke* 6K **41**
Fernlea Cres. *End* 1K **23**
Fernleaf Clo. *Rode H* 2G **11**
Fernlea Gro. *Meir H* 3B **48**
Fernlea Gro. *W Coy* 1C **42**
Fern Pl. *Stoke* 4H **41**
Fernwood Cft. *Leek* 5D **16**
Fernwood Dri. *Leek* 5D **16**
Fernwood Grn. *Stoke* 7B **40**
Ferrand Clo. *Stoke* 4K **39**
Festing St. *Stoke* 7C **28** (1G **5**)
Festival Clo. *Stoke* 7K **27**

Festival Heights Retail Pk.
Stoke 7K **27** (1B **4**)
Festival Hall. *Cong* 5H **9**
Festival Park. 7K **27** (1B **4**)
Festival Way. *Stoke* . . .7J **27** (2A **4**)
Fiddlers Bank. *Brn E* 3G **23**
Field Av. *Stoke* 2G **29**
Field Clo. *Als* 6F **11**
Field Clo. *B Bri* 1F **49**
Fielden Clo. *Stoke* 2E **28**
Field End Clo. *Stoke* 7A **40**
Fielding St. *Stoke* 1A **40**
Field Pl. *Stoke* 1H **41**
Fields Rd. *Als* 6E **10**
Fields Rd. *Cong* 7G **9**
Field St. *Leek* 4F **17**
Field Vw. *Bid* 1C **14**
Field Vw. *Stoke* 2C **42**
Field Way. *Als* 6F **11**
Fieldway. *Ash B* 2A **36**
Fieldway. *B Bri* 7E **42**
Fieldway. *L'tn* 3D **40**
Fieldway. *Stoke* 7H **39**
Fife St. *Stoke* 2F **41**
Fifth Av. *Kid* 2B **20**
Filey Clo. *Stoke* 3J **35**
Finchdean Clo. *Stoke* 7B **42**
Finch Pl. *B Frd* 1A **22**
Finchsmith Pl. *Stoke* 4G **41**
Finch St. *B Frd* 2B **22**
Finney Green. 4E **30**
Finney Grn. *Stoke* 1F **35**
Finstock Av. *Stoke* 6D **40**
Firbank Pl. *Stoke* 2A **42**
Firbeck Clo. *Cong* 4B **8**
First Av. *Kid* 2B **20**
First Av. *New* 5F **27**
First Av. *Stoke* 1J **35**
Firs, The. 3F **33** (1F **7**)
(Mus. & Art Gallery)
Fir Tree Pl. *New* 4B **26**
Fir Tree Rd. *Stoke* 6K **41**
Firwood Rd. *Bid* 1E **14**
Fisher St. *B Frd* 1A **22**
Fishpond Way. *Stoke* 6F **29**
Fistral Clo. *Stoke* 2J **41**
Fitzgerald Clo. *Stoke* 2C **42**
Fitzherbert Rd. *Stoke* 4D **28**
Five Oaks Clo. *New* 3B **38**
Flackett St. *Stoke* 1H **41**
Flamborough Gro. *Stoke* 5H **27**
Flash La. *L Oaks* 2H **29**
Flash La. *Stoke* 3H **39**
Flatts Rd. *Stoke* 6D **22**
Flaxman Clo. *B'stn* 3D **46**
Flax St. *Stoke* 7A **34**
Fleckney Av. *Stoke* 3K **41**
Fleming Rd. *Stoke* 6A **34**
Fletcher Bank. *New* 4D **32** (2B **6**)
Fletcher Cres. *Stoke* 2G **29**
Fletcher Rd. *Stoke* 1K **39**
Fletcher St. *Stoke* 3A **34** (6D **4**)
Fleur Gro. *Stoke* 7G **35**
Flintsham Gro. *Stoke*
. . . . .7B **28** (1E **5**)
Flint St. *Stoke* 1C **42**
Florence. 6J **41**
Florence Rd. *Stoke* 5J **39**
Florence St. *New* 4E **32** (2D **6**)
Florida Clo. *Hot I* 4A **28**
Floyd St. *Stoke* 5A **34**
Flynn Rd. *Fen I* 5D **34**
Foden Av. *Als* 7G **11**
Foden St. *Stoke* 1K **39**
Fogg St. *New* 4E **32** (3D **6**)
Fogg St. E. *New* 4E **32** (3D **6**)
Fogg St. W. *New* 4E **32** (3D **6**)
Fold La. *Bid* 1J **15**
Foley Pl. *Stoke* 2F **41**
Foley Rd. *Stoke* 3F **41**
(in two parts)
Foley St. *Stoke* 2G **41**
Fol Hollow. *A'bry* 6D **8**
Fontaine Pl. *Stoke* 1K **39**
Fonthill Wlk. *Stoke* 1G **35**
Forber Rd. *Stoke* 2J **39**

Ford Av. *Stoke* 6A **22**
Ford Green. 2C **28**
Ford Green Hall. (Mus.) 2C **28**
Ford Green Nature Reserve.
. . . . .1C **28**
Ford Grn. Rd. *Stoke* 3B **28**
Ford Hayes La. *Stoke & Hul* . .5J **35**
Fords La. *Mow C* 4G **13**
Ford St. *Leek* 3G **17**
Ford St. *Sil* 3J **31**
Ford St. *Stoke* 4H **33** (2H **7**)
Forest Clo. *New* 2B **38**
Forest Ct. *Stoke* 1F **5**
Forest Edge. *Stoke* 6B **28**
Forest Rd. *Stoke* 7A **42**
Forestside Gro. *Stoke* 4J **39**
Forge La. *Cong* 4D **8**
Forge La. *Stoke* 1J **33**
Forge Way. *Knyp* 6A **14**
Forrester Clo. *Bid* 2B **14**
Forresters Bank. *L Oaks* 1H **29**
Forrister St. *Stoke* 2H **41**
Forsbrook. 7J **43**
Forster St. *Stoke* 1G **27**
Forsyte Rd. *Stoke* 7G **35**
Forum Rd. *New* 7A **26**
Fosbrook Pl. *Stoke* . . .5G **33** (5H **7**)
Foster Clo. *Stoke* 4E **40**
Foster Ct. *Stoke* 4E **40**
Foundry Bank. *Cong* 4G **9**
Foundry La. *Sch G* 3C **12**
Foundry La. *Stoke* 2F **35**
Foundry Sq. *Stoke* 2F **35**
Foundry St. *Stoke* 1B **34** (2E **5**)
Fountain Ct. *Bid* 1C **14**
Fountain La. *Stoke* 4J **27**
(off Westport Rd.)
Fountain Pl. *Stoke* 4J **27**
Fountains Av. *New* 2E **38**
Fountain Sq. *Stoke* . . .1B **34** (3F **5**)
Fountain St. *Cong* 5F **9**
Fountain St. *Leek* 3G **17**
Fountain St. *Stoke* 7D **34**
Fourth Av. *Kid* 2C **20**
Fourth Av. *Stoke* 1J **35**
Fowlchurch Rd. *Leek* 2G **17**
Fowler's La. *L Oaks* 2J **29**
Foxfield Clo. *Stoke* 1H **45**
Foxfield Railway Mus. 5G **43**
Foxfield Steam Railway. 5G **43**
Foxfield Way. *Stoke* 6E **40**
Fox Gdns. *Tal* 3A **20**
Foxglove Clo. *Stoke* 1C **42**
Foxglove La. *New* 5F **39**
Fox Gro. *New* 4F **39**
Foxlands Clo. *Stoke* 2J **35**
Foxley. 4E **18**
Foxley La. *Stoke* 3E **28**
Fox St. *Cong* 4G **9**
Frampton Gro. *Stoke* 5H **21**
Francis St. *Stoke* 6J **21**
Franklin Rd. *Stoke* 6J **33**
Franklyn St. *Stoke* 3C **34** (6H **5**)
Frank St. *Stoke* 7K **33**
Fraser St. *Stoke* 5A **28**
Freckleton Pl. *Stoke* 7D **42**
Frederick Av. *Stoke* 6K **33**
Frederick St. *Stoke* 7D **34**
Freebridge Clo. *Stoke* 2K **41**
Freedom Dri. *Har* 7H **13**
Freedom Wlk. *Stoke* 1B **28**
(off Bradeley Village)
Freehay. 6J **45**
Freehold St. *New* 5F **33** (5F **7**)
Free Trade St. *Stoke* . . .7C **28** (1G **5**)
Fremantle Rd. *Stoke* 2J **39**
Frenchmore Gro. *Stoke* 5K **41**
Freshwater Gro. *Stoke* 2E **34**
Friars Clo. *C'dle* 3G **45**
Friars Ct. *C'dle* 3G **45**
(off Prince George St.)
Friars Pl. *Stoke* 5G **29**
Friars Rd. *Stoke* 5G **29**
Friars St. *New* 5E **32** (4D **6**)
Friar St. *Stoke* 2H **41**
Friars Wlk. *New* 7E **32**
Friarswood Rd. *New* . . .5E **32** (5C **6**)

Friendly Av. *New* 4E **26**
Friesian Gdns. *New* 2K **25**
Frith St. *Leek* 3E **16**
Frobisher St. *Stoke* 6F **23**
Frodingham Rd. *Stoke* 4J **35**
Froghall. *New* 4E **32** (3C **6**)
Froghall Rd. *C'dle* 2G **45**
Frome Wlk. *Stoke* 6K **21**
Frozer Ho. *Stoke* 6A **42**
Fulford. 6F **49**
Fulford Dale. *Ful* 5C **48**
Fulford Rd. *Ful* 7E **48**
Fuller St. *Stoke* 7H **21**
Fullwood Wlk. *Stoke* 4H **35**
Fulman Pl. *Stoke* 7C **42**
Furlong Ind. Est. *Stoke* 5H **27**
Furlong La. *Stoke* 5H **27**
Furlong Pde. *Stoke* 4J **27**
Furlong Pas. *Stoke* 4J **27**
Furlong Rd. *Stoke* 7H **21**
Furmston Pl. *Leek* 2H **17**
Furnace La. *Mad* 1A **30**
Furnace Rd. *Stoke* 4J **41**
Furnival St. *Stoke* 6A **28**
Fynney St. *Leek* 4G **17**

G

Gables, The. *Als* 6D **10**
Gable St. *Stoke* 7A **34**
Gainsborough Rd. *New* 6B **26**
Gainsborough Rd. *Stoke* 6D **40**
Galbraith Clo. *Cong* 5E **8**
Galleys Bank. *Kid* 7E **12**
Gallimore Clo. *Stoke* 3H **27**
Galloway Rd. *Stoke* 5K **35**
Gallowstree La. *New* 6B **32**
Galsworthy Rd. *Stoke* 7G **35**
Galveston Gro. *Stoke* 1E **40**
Garbett St. *Stoke* 4F **21**
Gardeners Clo. *Brn L* 5A **14**
Gardenholm Clo. *Stoke* 6A **42**
Garden Pl. *Stoke* 5H **33** (5H **7**)
Garden Rd. *Leek* 3E **16**
Garden St. *Cong* 4E **8**
Garden St. *New* 5F **33** (4E **7**)
Garden St. *Stoke* 7J **33**
Gardiner Dri. *Stoke* 4F **41**
Garfield Av. *Stoke* 5J **39**
Garfield Ct. *Stoke* 5J **39**
Garfield Cres. *Stoke* 5J **39**
Garfield St. *Stoke* 3A **34** (6C **4**)
Garibaldi St. *Stoke* 2J **33** (5A **4**)
Garlick St. *Stoke* 3A **28**
Garner St. *Stoke* 2H **33**
(in two parts)
Garner's Wlk. *Mad* 1B **30**
Garnet St. *Stoke* 2K **33** (4B **4**)
Garnett Rd. E. *Stoke* 7E **26**
Garnett Rd. W. *New* 6E **26**
Garsdale Cres. *Stoke* 6E **40**
Garth St. *Stoke* 1C **34** (2G **5**)
Gaskell Rd. *Stoke* 2J **35**
Gas Works Ind. Est. *Kid* 1B **20**
Gate St. *Stoke* 1C **42**
Gateley Gro. *Stoke* 1C **48**
Gate Way. *New* 2A **26**
Gedney Gro. *New* 4E **38**
Geen St. *Stoke* 6A **34**
Gemini Gro. *Stoke* 5H **21**
Geneva Dri. *New* 7B **32**
Geneva Dri. *Stoke* 5E **28**
Geoffrey Av. *Stoke* 4E **16**
Geoffrey Gro. *Stoke* 2B **42**
George Av. *Stoke* 5C **42**
George Bates Clo. *Als* 7D **10**
George Ct. *Stoke* 3G **41**
George Eardley Clo.
Stoke 6F **21**
George Eastham Av.
Stoke 3C **40**
George St. *A'ly* 3E **24**

George St. *Ches* 5B **26**
George St. *New* 6F **27**
 (Boulton St.)
George St. *New* 4F **33** (3F **7**)
 (Brunswick St.)
George St. *Sil* 4J **31**
George St. *Stoke* 6D **34**
Georges Way. *Big E* 2G **25**
Gerrard St. *Stoke* 5K **33**
Giantswood La.
 Hul W & Cong 1C **8**
Gibbins St. *Stoke* 7C **28**
Gibson Dri. *New* 4A **26**
Gibson Pl. *Stoke* 4B **42**
Gibson St. *Stoke* 2H **27**
Gifford Pl. *Stoke* 7J **33**
Gilbern Dri. *Knyp* 5A **14**
Gilbert Clo. *Kid* 1D **20**
Gilbert St. *Stoke* 4F **21**
Gilchrist Ct. *Stoke* 6A **28**
 (off Grange St.)
Giles Clo. *C'dle* 3G **45**
Giles Wlk. *Stoke* 7D **28**
Gill Bank Rd. *Kid* 3E **20**
Gill Bank Rd. *Stoke* 4E **20**
Gilliat Wlk. *Stoke* 5H **35**
Gillow Heath. **2H 15**
Gill Wlk. *Stoke* 5D **4**
Gillyflower Clo. *Stoke* 2D **28**
Gilman Av. *Stoke* 2G **29**
Gilman Pl. *Stoke* 1C **34** (3G **5**)
Gilman St. *Stoke* 2C **34** (4G **5**)
Gimson St. *Stoke* 7D **34**
Girsby Clo. *Stoke* 2B **46**
Gitana St. *Stoke* 1B **34** (3E **5**)
Glades, The. *Stoke* 7J **27**
Glade, The. *New* 4D **38**
Gladstone Gro. *Bid* 2C **14**
Gladstone Pl. *Stoke* 1J **39**
Gladstone Pottery Mus. 3H **41**
Gladstone St. *Leek* 4F **17**
Gladstone St. *Stoke* . .3H **33** (1H **7**)
Gladwyn St. *Stoke* 1H **35**
Glaisher Dri. *Stoke* 7D **42**
Glandore Rd. *Stoke* 2A **42**
Glass St. *Stoke* 1B **34** (2F **5**)
Glastonbury Clo. *Stoc B* 1J **29**
Glebe Clo. *B Bri* 1H **49**
Glebe Ct. *C'dle* 4E **44**
Glebe Ct. *Stoke* 6B **34**
Glebedale Ct. *Stoke* 1D **40**
Glebedale Rd. *Stoke* 7D **34**
Glebe Rd. *King* 4E **44**
Glebe St. *Stoke* 6A **34**
Glebe St. *Tal* 1A **20**
Glebeville. *Leek* 5F **17**
Glencastle Way. *Stoke* 2B **46**
Glencoe St. *Stoke* 4G **41**
Glendale Ct. *New* 4F **39**
Glendale St. *Stoke* 5K **27**
Glendue Gro. *Stoke* 1B **46**
Gleneagles Cres. *Stoke* 6D **28**
Glenfield Way. *Stoke* 5K **35**
Glenroyd Av. *Stoke* 4F **35**
Glenroyd Wlk. *Stoke* 4H **35**
Glenwood Clo. *New* 4K **31**
Glenwood Clo. *Stoke* 2G **41**
Globe St. *Stoke* 4H **27**
Gloucester Grange. *New* 1F **39**
Gloucester Rd. *Kid* 1C **20**
Glover St. *Stoke* 7C **28**
Glyn Pl. *Stoke* 1J **27**
Goddard St. *Stoke* 2H **41**
Godfrey Rd. *Stoke* 2G **35**
Godleybarn La. *Dil* 1A **44**
Godleybrook. **1A 44**
Godley La. *Dil* 2A **44**
Golborn Av. *Stoke* 3B **48**
Golborn Clo. *Stoke* 3B **48**
Goldcrest Way. *Bid* 2D **14**
Goldenhill. **4F 21**
Goldenhill Rd. *Stoke* 2G **41**
Goldfinch Clo. *Cong* 6G **9**
Goldfinch Dri. *Als* 7C **10**
Goldsmith Pl. *Stoke* 2J **41**
Gold St. *Stoke* 3G **41**
Golf Links Clo. *Stoke* 4F **21**

Goms Mill Rd. *Stoke* 5F **41**
 (Drubbery La.)
Goms Mill Rd. *Stoke* 4G **41**
 (Ladysmith St.)
Goodfellow St. *Stoke* 7G **21**
 (in two parts)
Goodson St. *Stoke* 1B **34** (3F **5**)
Goodwick Clo. *Stoke* 2B **46**
Goodwin Av. *New* 3E **32**
Goodwin Rd. *Stoke* 4C **42**
Goodwood Av. *C'dle* 2J **45**
Goodwood Pl. *Stoke* 7K **39**
Goosemoor Gro. *Stoke* 7C **42**
Goose St. *New* 5E **32** (5D **6**)
Goostrey Ct. *Cong* 4H **9**
 (off Brunswick St.)
Gordale Clo. *Cong* 2J **9**
Gordon Clo. *Leek* 5D **16**
Gordon Av. *C'dle* 3E **44**
Gordon Av. *Stoke* 5B **28**
Gordon Banks Dri. *Stoke* 3C **40**
Gordon Ct. *New* 2B **32**
Gordon Cres. *Stoke* 7C **42**
Gordon Rd. *Stoke* 5F **21**
Gordon St. *New* 2B **32**
Gordon St. *Stoke* 3A **28**
Gorse St. *Stoke* 2D **40**
Gorsey Bank. *Stoke* 5D **22**
Gorsty Bank. **2K 31**
Gort Rd. *New* 1C **32**
Gosforth Gro. *Stoke* 7D **42**
Gosling Way. *Cong* 4C **8**
Govan Rd. *Fen I* 7D **34**
Gowan Av. *Stoke* 7K **21**
Gower St. *New* 4F **33** (2F **7**)
Gower St. *Stoke* 3H **41**
Gowy Clo. *Als* 7A **10**
Grace Rd. *Stoke* 7B **40**
Grace St. *Leek* 3D **16**
Graffam Gro. *C'dle* 2J **45**
Grafton Av. *Stoke* 3A **28**
Grafton Rd. *Stoke* 2H **41**
Grafton St. *Stoke* 7C **28** (1G **5**)
Graham St. *New* 2F **35**
Granby Wlk. *Stoke* 7J **33**
Grancaster Clo. *Stoke* 1C **48**
Grange Ct. *Bid* 2J **15**
Grangefields. *Bid* 1K **15**
Grange Gdns. *Leek* 5E **16**
Grange La. *New* 1G **33**
 (in two parts)
Grange Pk. Dri. *Bid* 1K **15**
Grange Rd. *Bid* 1K **15**
Grange Rd. *Stoke* 1A **48**
Grange St. *Stoke* 6A **28**
Grange, The. *Stoke* 4B **42**
Grangewood Av. *Stoke* 1A **48**
Grangewood Rd. *Stoke* 6B **42**
Granstone Clo. *Stoke* 4K **21**
Grantham Pl. *Stoke* 6F **29**
Grantley Clo. *Stoke* 5F **41**
Grant St. *Stoke* 6B **34**
Granville Av. *New* 3F **33** (1F **7**)
Granville Rd. *Stoke* 5C **28**
Granville Rd. *Stoke* 1G **35**
Grasmere Av. *Cong* 5B **8**
Grasmere Av. *New* 2E **38**
Grasmere Ter. *Stoke* 1K **27**
Grass Rd. *Dray* 7B **44**
Grass Rd. *Stoke* 6F **23**
Grassygreen La. *A'ly* 3E **24**
Gratton La. *End* 1K **23**
Gratton Rd. *Stoke* 7J **35**
Gravelly Bank. *Stoke* 7A **42**
Grayling Gro. *Stoke* 1A **28**
Grayling Willows. *Mad* 3E **30**
Gray's Clo. *Sch G* 3E **12**
Grayshott Rd. *Stoke* 6H **21**
Greasley Rd. *Stoke* 6G **29**
Greatbatch Av. *Stoke* 6J **33**
Great Chell. **5K 21**
Great Eaves. **7H 29**
Gt. Fenton Bus. Pk. *Stoke* 2C **40**
Greatoak Rd. *Big E* 7G **19**
Greenacres Av. *B Bri* 6D **42**
Greenacres Rd. *Cong* 5B **8**
Greenbank Rd. *New* 2F **33**

Greenbank Rd. *Stoke* 1J **27**
Greenbirches Ind. Est.
 Stoke 7G **21**
Greenbrook Ct. *New* 2E **32**
Green Clo. *B'stn* 6C **46**
Green Clo. *B Bri* 7E **42**
Greendale Dri. *New* 3A **26**
Greendock St. *Stoke* 3G **41**
Green Dri. *Als* 6E **10**
Greenfield. *Bid* 4C **14**
Greenfield Av. *Brn E* 4H **23**
Greenfield Clo. *Brn E* 4H **23**
Greenfield Ct. *Cong* 4D **8**
Greenfield Cres. *C'dle* 2H **45**
Greenfield Farm Trad. Est.
 Cong 3D **8**
Greenfield Pl. *Brn E* 4H **23**
Greenfield Rd. *Cong* 4D **8**
Greenfield Rd. *End* 3K **23**
Greenfield Rd. *Stoke* 6H **21**
Greenfields Dri. *Als* 7F **11**
Greengate Rd. *Chu L* 5G **11**
Greengates St. *Stoke* 7H **21**
Greenhead St. *Stoke* 4J **27**
Greenhill Rd. *Stoke* 5D **22**
Greenlea Clo. *Stoke* 2B **46**
Greenmeadow Gro. *End* 5K **23**
Greenmeadows Rd. *Mad* 1B **30**
Greenmoor Av. *Stoke* 3K **21**
Greenock Clo. *New* 5C **32**
Green Pk. *Ful* 6F **49**
Green Rd. *Stoke* 3H **39**
Greenside. *New* 4D **32** (2B **6**)
Greenside Av. *Stoc B* 1H **29**
Greenside Clo. *Kid* 4D **20**
Green's La. *Stoke* 2K **35**
Green, The. *Brn E* 4G **23**
Green, The. *Cav* 3E **42**
Green, The. *C'dle* 4E **44**
Green, The. *Chu L* 5H **11**
Green, The. *Cong* 5E **8**
Green, The. *New* 3F **39**
Green, The. *Stoc B* 1G **29**
Green, The. *Stoke* 5H **33** (5H **7**)
Greenway. *Als* 5C **10**
Greenway. *Cong* 4D **8**
Greenway. *L'tn* 3D **40**
Greenway. *Tren* 7H **39**
Greenway Av. *Stoke* 2A **28**
Greenway Bank. *B Frd* 1B **22**
Greenway Bank. *L Oaks* 2H **29**
Greenway Bank Country Pk.
 .6E **14**
Greenway Clo. *Rode H* 2G **11**
Greenway Hall Rd. *L Oaks* 2J **29**
Greenway Hall Rd. *Stoc B* 1H **29**
Greenway Pl. *Stoke* 5G **29**
Greenway Rd. *Bid* 2K **15**
Greenways. *Big E* 2G **25**
Greenways Dri. *C'dle* 2G **45**
Greenway, The. *New* 2F **33**
Greenwood Av. *Cong* 4H **9**
Greenwood Av. *Stoke* 4H **39**
Greenwood Rd. *For* 6H **43**
Greeting St. *Stoke* 5K **27**
Gregory St. *Stoke* 3G **41**
Gregson Clo. *Stoke* 3F **41**
Grenadier Clo. *Stoke* 3B **46**
Grendon Grn. *Stoke* 3H **35**
Gresley Way. *Big E* 2G **25**
Gresty St. *Stoke* 6K **33**
Greville St. *Stoke* 7C **28** (1G **5**)
Greyfriars Rd. *Stoke* 7F **29**
Greyhound Ct. *Mad* 2B **30**
Greyhound Way. *Stoke*
 . . . . .7K **27** (1B **4**)
Greysan Av. *Pac* 3J **21**
Greystones. *New* 5F **27**
 (off First Av.)
Greyswood Rd. *Stoke* 3H **39**
Grice Rd. *Stoke* 5H **33**
Griffin St. *Stoke* 2G **41**
Grig Pl. *Als* 5D **10**
Grindley Hill Ct. *Stoke* 6G **33**

Grindley La. *B Bri* 7F **43**
Grindley La. *Stoke* 2B **48**
Grindley Pl. *Stoke* 7J **33**
Grisedale Clo. *Stoke* 7B **42**
Gristhorpe Way. *Stoke* 4J **35**
Gritter St. *Stoke* 2G **27**
Grosvenor Av. *Als* 5E **10**
Grosvenor Av. *Stoke* 2J **39**
Grosvenor Clo. *Als* 5E **10**
Grosvenor Clo. *Stoke* 1K **23**
Grosvenor Gdns. *New*
 . . . . .5F **33** (5E **7**)
Grosvenor Pl. *New* 7F **27**
Grosvenor Pl. *Stoke* 7G **21**
Grosvenor Rd. *Cong* 4C **8**
Grosvenor Rd. *New* 5F **33** (5E **7**)
Grosvenor Rd. *Stoke* 5A **42**
Grosvenor St. *Leek* 4G **17**
Grosvenor St. *Stoke* 3G **41**
Grove Av. *Chu L* 6H **11**
Grove Av. *Kid* 2B **20**
Grove Av. *Stoke* 2D **40**
Grovebank Rd. *Stoke* 3H **39**
Grove Ct. *Als* 6F **11**
Grove Pk. Av. *Chu L* 6H **11**
Grove Pl. *Stoke* 3A **34** (6C **4**)
Grove Rd. *Stoke* 2C **40**
Grove Rd. Ind. Est. *Stoke* 2C **40**
Grove St. *Leek* 3E **16**
Grove St. *New* 2B **32**
Grove St. *Stoke* 6K **27**
Grove Ter. *Leek* 3E **16**
 (off Westwood Gro.)
Grove, The. *B Bri* 1F **49**
Grove, The. *Chu L* 6H **11**
Grove, The. *New* 7E **32**
Grove, The. *Stoke* 2A **38**
Guernsey Clo. *Cong* 6J **9**
Guernsey Dri. *New* 2B **38**
Guernsey Wlk. *Stoke* 3F **41**
 (off Anglesey Dri.)
Guildford St. *Stoke* 5B **34**
Gun Battery La. *Bid M* 2F **15**
Gunderson Clo. *B Bri* 6J **43**
Gunn St. *Bid* 2B **14**
Guy St. *Stoke* 1G **35**
Gwenys Cres. *Stoke* 2D **40**
Gwyn Av. *Knyp* 5C **14**

H

Hackett Clo. *Stoke* 2J **41**
Hackwood Clo. *B'stn* 3E **46**
Hadden Clo. *Werr* 3C **36**
Haddon Gro. *New* 6C **26**
Haddon Pl. *Stoke* 7H **29**
Hadfield Grn. *Stoke* 2C **28**
Hadleigh Clo. *New* 4E **38**
Hadleigh Rd. *Stoke* 6G **29**
Hadrian Way. *New* 7A **26**
Haig Rd. *Leek* 2H **17**
Haig St. *Stoke* 4J **41**
Hailsham Clo. *Stoke* 6J **21**
Hales Hall Rd. *C'dle* 2J **45**
Halesworth Cres. *New* 4F **39**
Halfway Pl. *New* 4B **32**
Halifax Clo. *Stoke* 7D **42**
Haliford Av. *Stoke* 5C **28**
Hallahan Gro. *Stoke* 5K **33**
Hallam St. *Stoke* 7C **34**
Hallam St. *New* 2H **17**
Halldearn Av. *Cav* 3E **42**
Hall Dri. *Als* 7D **10**
Hall Dri. *Stoke* 2C **42**
Hall Green. **5B 12**
Hall Hill Dri. *Stoke* 5J **35**
Hall Orchard. *C'dle* 3G **45**
Halls Rd. *Bid* 1B **14**
Halls Rd. *Mow C* 3F **13**
Hall St. *A'ly* 2E **24**
Hall St. *New* 4E **32** (2C **6**)
Hall St. *Stoke* 4H **27**
Hallwater. *End* 1K **23**

Halmer End. 6F 25
Halton Grn. Stoke 6D 40
Hambleton Pl. Knyp 5A 14
Hamble Way. Stoke 4J 35
Hambro Pl. Stoke 4A 22
Hamil Dri. Leek 3E 16
Hamil Rd. Stoke 3K 27
Hamilton Ct. New 4F 39
Hamilton Ind. Cen. Stoke 1D 40
Hamilton Ri. Stoke 2G 29
Hamilton Rd. Stoke 4J 41
Hamilton St. Stoke 1B 40
Hamlett Pl. Stoke 1D 28
Hammersley Hayes Rd.
    C'dle 1H 45
Hammersley St. Stoke 6D 28
Hammerton Av. Stoke 3E 34
Hammond Av. Brn E 4G 23
Hammond Ho. Stoke 3C 34
Hammond Rd. P West 4B 26
Hammoon Gro. Stoke 3G 35
Hamner Grn. Stoke 5J 35
Hampshire Clo. Cong 3F 9
Hampshire Clo. End 2K 23
Hampshire Cres. Stoke 6H 41
Hampstead Gro. Stoke 7B 40
Hampton Ct. Leek 4E 16
Hampton St. Join I . . .3C 34 (6G 5)
Hams Clo. Bid 3B 14
Hanbridge Av. New 6D 26
Hanchurch. 7E 38
Hanchurch La. Han 7E 38
Hancock Rd. Cong 3H 9
Hancock St. Stoke 6B 34
Handel Gro. Stoke 6F 29
Handley Banks. Cav 3F 43
Handley Dri. B Frd 1A 22
Handley St. Pac 1K 21
Handsacre Rd. Stoke 1J 41
Hand St. Stoke 2H 27
Hanford. 5J 39
Hanley. 1B 34 (3F 5)
Hanley Bus. Pk. Stoke
    . . . . .3B 34 (6D 4)
Hanley Mall. Stoke 2F 5
Hanley Rd. Stoke 3B 28
Hanover Ct. New 2E 7
Hanover St. New 4F 33 (2E 7)
    (in three parts)
Hanover St. Stoke 1B 34 (1E 5)
Harber St. Stoke 3H 41
Harborne Cotts. C'dle 2H 45
Harborne Cres. C'dle 2H 45
Harborne Rd. C'dle 2G 45
Harcourt Av. Stoke 5A 42
Harcourt St. Stoke 3A 34
Hardewick Clo. Werr 2C 36
Hardinge St. Stoke 7C 34
Harding Rd. Stoke . . .3B 34 (6F 5)
Hardings Bank. 3J 9
Hardings Row. Mow C 3G 13
Hardings Wood. 1A 20
Hardingswood Rd. 1B 20
Hardingswood Ind. Est.
    Kid 1B 20
Hardingswood Rd. Kid . . .1B 20
Harding Ter. Stoke 7K 33
Hardman St. Stoke 3F 29
Hardwick Clo. Stoke 3B 46
Hardy Clo. C'dle 4F 45
Hardy St. Stoke 7G 21
Harebell Gro. Pac 2J 21
Harecastle Av. Tal 2B 20
Harecastle Vs. Kid 1B 20
Haregate. 1H 17
Haregate Rd. Leek 2H 17
Haregate Ter. Leek 2H 17
Hareshaw Gro. Stoke 3K 21
Harewood Clo. C'dle 2G 45
Harewood Est. C'dle 1E 44
Harewood Rd. Stoke 2G 27
Harewood St. Stoke 2G 27
Hargreave Clo. Stoke 7D 42
Harington Dri. Stoke 1K 41
Harlech Av. Stoke 5K 41
Harlech Dri. Knyp 4B 14
Harlequin Dri. Stoke 2B 28

Harley St. Stoke . . .2C 34 (5G 5)
    (in two parts)
Harold St. Stoke 3B 28
Harper Av. New 1D 32
Harper Gro. Cong 3G 9
Harpers St. Stoke 5H 27
Harpfield Rd. Stoke 7H 33
Harplow La. C'dle 5D 44
Harptree Wlk. Stoke 4J 39
Harpur Cres. Als 5C 10
Harrier Clo. Stoke 1B 48
Harriseahead. 5G 13
Harriseahead La. Har 6F 13
Harrison Clo. Halm 6E 24
Harrison Ct. New 6F 33 (6F 7)
    (off Occupation St.)
Harrison Rd. Stoke 1D 28
Harrison St. New 5F 33 (5F 7)
Harris St. Stoke 5K 33
Harrogate Gro. New 3G 31
Harrop St. Stoke 6C 28
Harrowby Dri. New 2C 38
Harrowby Rd. Stoke 6B 42
Hart Ct. New 4E 32 (2C 6)
Hartill St. Stoke 5B 34
Hartington Clo. Leek 5F 17
Hartington St. Leek 4F 17
Hartington St. New 7E 26
Hartland Av. Stoke 7B 22
Hartley Gdns. Cong 7K 9
Hartshill. 5H 33 (3H 7)
Hartshill Rd. Stoke . . .4G 33 (3G 7)
Hartwell. 5G 47
Hartwell Ct. New 2C 38
Hartwell La.
    Stone & R'gh C 5F 47
Hartwell Rd. Stoke 6B 42
Harvey Rd. Cong 2J 9
Harvey St. Stoke 4B 42
Haslemere Av. Stoke 3G 29
Haslington Clo. New 3A 26
Hassall Grn. 1A 10
Hassall Rd. Has G & Als 2A 10
Hassall St. Stoke 2C 34 (4G 5)
Hassam Av. New 3D 32
Hassam Pde. New 7E 26
Hassell St. New 5E 32 (4D 6)
Hatfield Rd. Stoke 6D 40
Hathersage Clo. Stoke 1H 41
Hatherton Clo. New 2A 26
Hatrell St. New 5F 33 (5D 6)
Hatter St. Cong 4G 9
Havannah. 2J 9
Havannah La. Cong 3J 9
Havannah La. Hav 1H 9
Havelet Dri. New 3C 38
Havelock Gro. Bid 3B 14
Havelock Pl. Stoke . . .3A 34 (6C 4)
Haven Av. Stoke 4C 28
Haven Cres. Werr 1C 36
Haven Gro. New 5F 27
Havergal Wlk. Stoke 1H 41
Hawes St. Stoke 7G 21
Hawfinch Rd. C'dle 3H 45
Hawk Clo. Stoke 7B 42
Hawkins St. Stoke 7B 34
Hawksdale Clo. Stoke 7B 42
Hawksmoor Clo. Stoke 7A 42
Hawkstone Clo. New . . .5F 33 (5F 7)
Hawksworth Av. Leek 5E 16
Hawksworth Clo. Leek 5E 16
Haworth Av. Stoke 2H 9
Hawthorne Av. Big E 3G 25
Hawthorne Av. Stoke 1H 39
Hawthorne Clo. Cong 3C 8
Hawthorne Ct. Als 6E 10
Hawthorne Ter. Leek 3G 17
Hawthorn Gdns. Tal 3A 20
Hawthorn Gro. Bid 3D 14
Hawthorn Pl. Stoke 6A 42
Hawthorn Rd. New 3B 26
Hawthorns, The. K'le 5G 31
Hawthorn St. Stoke 6K 27
Hawthorn Vs. Als 7H 11
Haydock Clo. C'dle 1H 45
Haydock Ct. Sil 4K 31

Haydon Ct. Stoke 3H 33
Haydon St. Stoke 3H 33
Hayes. 6D 24
Hayes Clo. Leek 3G 17
Hayes St. Stoke 2B 28
Hayeswood La. Halm 6F 25
Hayfield Cres. Stoke 6D 34
Hayfield Rd. New 4J 31
Hayhead Clo. Kid 1E 20
Hayling Pl. Stoke 3E 40
Haymarket. Stoke 1G 27
Hayner Gro. Stoke 2C 42
HAYWOOD AND STANFIELD
    HOSPITAL 1K 27
Haywood Rd. Stoke 2J 27
Haywood St. Leek 4G 17
Haywood St. Stoke 4A 34
Hazel Clo. Kid 7E 12
Hazel Clo. Stoke 1J 39
Hazeldene Rd. Stoke 7B 40
Hazel Gro. Als 7H 11
Hazel Gro. Bid M 1G 15
Hazel Gro. Leek 5D 16
Hazel Gro. Stoke 4A 42
Hazelhurst Rd. Stoke 5J 21
Hazelhurst St. Stoke . .3C 34 (6H 5)
Hazel Rd. New 4A 26
Hazelwood Clo. Stoke 6B 28
Hazelwood Rd. End 5K 23
Hazlitt Way. Stoke 1K 41
Headingley Gro. Stoke 6C 40
Heakley Av. Stoke 7E 22
Healey Av. Knyp 5A 14
Heanor Pl. Stoke 3F 41
Heath Av. New 2F 33
Heath Av. Rode H 2F 11
Heath Av. Werr 1F 37
Heathcote Ct. Stoke 1J 41
Heathcote Ri. Stoke 2C 42
Heathcote Rd. Halm 5F 25
Heathcote Rd. Stoke 3F 41
    (in two parts)
Heathcote St. Kid 2D 20
Heathcote St. New 4B 26
Heathcote St. Stoke 7H 35
Heath Ct. Chu L 4G 11
Heathdene Clo. Stoke 2G 41
Heath End Rd. Als 4C 10
Heather Clo. Werr 1B 36
Heather Cres. Stoke 3B 48
Heather Glade. Mad 1A 30
Heatherleigh Gro. Stoke 6E 28
Heatherside. Mow C 5F 13
Heather Vw. Stoke 5D 22
Heathfield Clo. Cong 4B 8
Heathfield Ct. Stoke 4F 21
Heathfield Dri. New 3A 26
Heathfield Gro. Stoke 1A 48
Heathfield Rd. Stoke 6B 22
Heath Gro. Stoke 2B 48
Heath La. Stoke 1E 34
Heath Pl. New 2F 33
Heath St. New 4E 32 (2D 6)
Heath St. Stoke 4F 21
Heath View. Als 5F 11
Heathwood Dri. Als 5C 10
Heaton Ter. New 6E 26
Heaton Ter. Werr 1K 23
Heaton Vs. Brn E 4G 23
Heber St. Stoke 2D 42
Hedley Pl. New 5C 32 (4A 6)
Heighley. 7A 24
Heighley Castle Way. Mad
    . . . . .4A 30 & 1B 30
Heighley La. Bet 7A 24
Heights, The. Leek 7C 16
Hellyar-Brook Rd. Als 6C 10
Helston Av. Stoke 3K 41
Hem Heath. 1B 46

Hem Heath Wood Nature Reserve.
    .1B 46
Heming Pl. Stoke 2F 35
Hemingway Rd. Stoke 2J 41
Hemlock Rd. Stoke 2J 41
Hempstalls Ct. New . . .3E 32 (1D 6)
Hempstalls Gro. New 2E 32
Hempstalls La. New . . .3E 32 (2D 6)
Hemsby Way. New 4E 38
Hencroft. Leek 3F 17
Henderson Gro. Stoke 3C 42
Henley Av. Knyp 4K 13
Henrietta St. Cong 4E 8
Henry St. Stoke 7G 21
Henshall Hall Dri. Cong 6K 9
Henshall Pl. Stoke 5G 21
Henshall Rd. P West 4B 26
Herbert St. Cong 4H 9
Herbert St. Stoke 7C 34
Herd St. Stoke 3J 27
Hereford Av. New 2F 39
Hereford Gro. Stoke 3J 35
Herm Clo. New 2B 38
Hermes Clo. Stoke 7D 42
Heron Clo. Mad 6A 30
Heron Cross. 2D 40
Heron St. Stoke 1D 40
Hertford Clo. Cong 3G 9
Hertford Gro. New 2G 39
Hertford St. Stoke 2D 40
Hesketh Av. Stoke 6C 22
Heskin Way. Stoke 5K 21
Hester Clo. Stoke 7H 35
Hethersett Wlk. Stoke 3J 35
Hewitt Cres. Werr 2C 36
Hewitt St. Stoke 5J 21
Heyburn Cres. Stoke 4H 27
Heyfield Cotts. T'sor 7A 46
Heysham Clo. Stoke 2C 42
Heywood St. Cong 5C 8
Hickman St. New 4E 32 (3C 6)
Hick St. New 4D 6
Hidden Hills. Mad 5A 30
Hide St. Stoke 6A 34
Higginson Clo. Cong 6K 9
High Bank Pl. Stoke 3A 28
High Carr. 2C 26
High Carr Bus. Pk. New 2C 26
Highcroft Av. Cong 5H 9
Highcroft Wlk. Stoke 2A 28
Higher Ash Rd. Tal 2A 20
Higherland. New 5D 32 (5B 6)
Higherland Ct. Kid 1D 20
    (off Attwood St.)
Higher Woodcroft. Leek 5E 16
Highfield Av. C'dle 2G 45
Highfield Av. Kid 1E 20
Highfield Av. New 1G 39
Highfield Av. Stoke 5A 42
Highfield Clo. B Bri 7E 42
Highfield Ct. New 7F 33
Highfield Cres. C'dle 2G 45
Highfield Dri. Stoke 2D 40
Highfield Grange. New 1H 33
Highfield Pl. Bid 2C 14
Highfield Ri. Stoke 6J 39
Highfield Rd. Cong 6G 9
Highfield Rd. E. Bid 3C 14
Highfield Rd. W. Bid 3C 14
Highgate Clo. Stoke 1D 28
Highgrove Rd. Stoke 3J 39
Highland Clo. Bid M 2G 15
Highland Clo. B Bri 1F 49
Highland Dri. Stoke 5J 41
High La. Als B 7G 25
High La. Brn E 5F 23
High La. Stoke 5K 21
High Lowe Av. Cong 3J 9
High St. Bid 2B 14
High St. Big E 3H 25
High St. Cav 3F 43
High St. C'dle 3G 45
High St. Ches 5B 26
High St. Cong 5F 9
High St. Dil 2K 43

High St. *Halm* 5D **24**
High St. *Har* 6H **13**
High St. *Kid* 7F **13**
High St. *Knut* 2B **32**
High St. *Leek* 3F **17**
High St. *Mow C* 3G **13**
High St. *New* 2G **33**
(May Bank)
High St. *New* 4E **32** (3C **6**)
(Newcastle-under-Lyme,
in three parts)
High St. *N'cpl* 1H **21**
High St. *Sand* 4F **21**
High St. *Sil* 3H **31**
High St. *Tal P* 5A **20**
High St. *Tun* 6G **21**
High St. *Wol* 6F **27**
Highton St. *Stoke* 3H **29**
Hightown. **6K 9**
Highup Rd. *Leek* 1C **16**
High View. *Mow C* 5E **12**
High Vw. *Stoke* 2B **48**
High Vw. Rd. *End* 1K **23**
Highview Rd. *Ful* 7F **49**
High Vw. Rd. *Leek* 4J **17**
Highway La. *K'le* 7E **30**
Higson Av. *Stoke* 5K **33**
Hilderstone Rd.
  Stoke & Spot A 3A **48**
Hilgreen Rd. *Stoke* 1J **41**
Hillary Av. *Cong* 5J **9**
Hillary Rd. *Kid* 7E **12**
Hillary St. *Stoke* 6A **28**
Hillberry Clo. *Stoke* 3F **35**
Hillchurch St. *Stoke* 1B **34** (2F **5**)
Hillcott Wlk. *Stoke* 3J **41**
Hill Cres. *Als B* 6G **25**
Hillcrest. *Leek* 3E **16**
Hillcrest Ho. *Stoke* 1C **34** (3G **5**)
Hillcrest St. *Stoke* 1C **34** (3G **5**)
Hillesden Ri. *Cong* 5H **9**
Hillfield Av. *Stoke* 2H **39**
Hillfields. *Cong* 3F **9**
Hill Fields Clo. *Cong* 3F **9**
Hillman St. *Stoke* 3H **29**
Hillport Av. *New* 5E **26**
Hillport Ho. *New* 5F **27**
(off Claremont Clo.)
Hillside. *New* 5D **32** (5A **6**)
Hillside Av. *End* 1K **23**
Hillside Av. *For* 6H **43**
Hillside Av. *Kid* 4D **20**
Hillside Av. *Stoke* 5A **42**
Hillside Clo. *Bid M* 1G **15**
Hillside Clo. *Ful* 7F **49**
Hillside Clo. *Mow C* 3G **13**
Hillside Clo. *Stoke* 1H **29**
Hillside Dri. *Leek* 5D **16**
Hillside Rd. *Stoke* 1H **29**
Hillside Rd. *Werr* 1C **36**
Hillside Wlk. *Stoke* 5G **33** (5H **7**)
Hill St. *New* 3D **32** (1B **6**)
Hill St. *Stoke* 6K **33**
Hillswood Av. *Leek* 3D **16**
Hillswood Clo. *End* 4K **23**
Hillswood Dri. *End* 3K **23**
Hill Ter. *A'ly* 2E **24**
Hill Top. 2G **23**
Hilltop Av. *New* 3H **33**
Hilltop Clo. *Brn E* 2G **23**
Hill Top Cres. *Stoke* 2B **48**
Hillview. *Leek* 4H **17**
Hill Vw. *Stoke* 2G **29**
Hill Village Rd. *Werr* 1D **36**
Hillwood Rd. *Mad H* 5B **30**
Hilton Ho. *Stoke* 6H **33**
Hilton Rd. *Stoke* 6G **33** (6H **7**)
Hincho Pl. *Stoke* 7D **22**
Hinckley Ct. *Cong* 4C **8**
Hinckley Gro. *Stoke* 2A **46**
Hinde St. *Stoke* 3B **34** (6E **5**)
Hines St. *Stoke* 1D **40**
Hinton Clo. *Stoke* 6E **40**
Hitchman St. *Stoke* 7D **34**
Hobart St. *Stoke* 5K **27**
Hobby Clo. *Stoke* 7B **42**
Hobson St. *Stoke* 4K **27**

Hodgefield. 1G **23**
Hodgkinson St. *New* 6C **26**
Hodnet Gro. *Stoke* 7A **28**
Hogarth Pl. *New* 6B **26**
Holbeach Av. *Stoke* 3F **35**
Holborn. *New* 4E **32** (3C **6**)
Holborn, The. *Mad* 3B **30**
Holbrook Wlk. *Stoke* 4H **35**
Holdcroft Dwellings. *Stoke* 1J **27**
(off Queens Av.)
Holdcroft Rd. *Stoke* 7G **29**
Holden Av. *New* 2G **33**
Holden Av. N. *Stoke* 4C **28**
Holden Av. S. *Stoke* 4C **28**
Holder St. *Stoke* 7A **28**
Holding Cres. *Halm* 5E **24**
Holditch Ind. Est. *New* 7C **26**
Holditch Rd. *New* 7C **26**
Holecroft St. *Stoke* 4K **27**
Holehouse La. *Brn E & End* 1H **23**
Holehouse La. *Sch G* 3K **11**
Holehouse Rd. *Stoke* 6G **29**
Holford St. *Cong* 4F **9**
Holland St. *Stoke* 1G **27**
Hollies Dri. *Stoke* 4J **27**
Hollies, The. *New* 3F **33** (1E **7**)
Hollings St. *Stoke* 1F **41**
Hollington Dri. *Stoke* 3K **21**
Hollins. **3A 20**
Hollins Cres. *Tal* 2B **20**
Hollins Grange. *Tal* 3A **20**
Hollinshead Av. *New* 1D **32**
Hollinshead Clo. *Sch G* 3C **12**
Hollinwood Clo. *Kid* 3B **20**
Hollinwood Rd. *Kid* 3B **20**
Hollowood Pl. *Stoke* 6D **22**
Hollowood Wlk. *Stoke* 6C **22**
Hollow, The. *Cav* 4F **43**
Hollow, The. *Mow C* 5E **12**
Holly Bank. *Stoke* 7H **39**
Holly Bank Cres. *Stoke* 1K **39**
Hollybush. **3D 40**
Hollybush Cres. *Stoke* 2D **40**
Hollybush Rd. *Stoke* 3D **40**
Holly Cross. *K'le* 7H **31**
Holly Dri. *Stoke* 2B **36**
Holly La. *Als* 7F **11**
Holly La. *Har* 5H **13**
Holly M. *K'le* 6G **31**
Holly Pl. *Stoke* 2D **40**
Holly Rd. *New* 3A **26**
(Birch Ho. Rd.)
Holly Rd. *New* 3A **26**
(Cedar Rd.)
Holly Tree Dri. *Gil H* 2H **15**
Holly Wall. **6F 21**
Hollywall La. *Stoke* 7E **20**
(in two parts)
Hollywood La. *New* 4D **30**
Holmes Chapel Rd. *Cong* 3A **8**
Holmesfield Wlk. *Stoke* 3J **41**
Holmesville Av. *Cong* 5D **8**
Holmes Way. *Stoke* 3A **22**
Holm Oak Dri. *Mad* 1B **30**
Holst Dri. *Stoke* 6F **29**
Holwell Cres. *Stoke* 2C **42**
Holywell Clo. *Knyp* 4D **14**
Homer Pl. *Stoke* 6A **22**
Homer St. *Stoke* 1D **34** (3H **5**)
Homeshire Ho. *Als* 7E **10**
Homestead, The. *Stoke* 5J **35**
Homestead, The. *Stoke* 1H **29**
Honeysuckle Av. *B Bri* 1G **49**
Honeywall. *Stoke* 6K **33**
Honeywall Ho. *Stoke* 6K **33**
Honeywall La. *Mad H* 5C **30**
Honeywood. *New* 2C **42**
Honiton Wlk. *Stoke* 3J **41**
Hood & Broomfield Fine
  Art Gallery. 4G **33** (2G **7**)
Hoon Av. *New* 1E **32**
Hoover St. *Stoke* 1G **27**
Hopedale Clo. *New* 3E **38**
Hopedale Clo. *Stoke* 6G **35**
Hope St. *Big E* 2E **25**
Hope St. *Stoke* 1B **34** (2E **5**)

Hopkins Clo. *Cong* 4D **8**
Hopton Way. *Stoke* 3K **21**
Hopwood Pl. *Stoke* 2G **35**
Horace Lawton Ct. *Cong* 4F **9**
Horatius Rd. *New* 6A **26**
Hordley St. *Stoke* 2C **34** (4G **5**)
Hornby Dri. *Cong* 4C **8**
Hornby Row. *Stoke* 6K **33**
Horsecroft Cres. *Leek* 1H **17**
Horsecroft Gro. *Leek* 2H **17**
Horsley Gro. *Stoke* 6D **40**
Horton Dri. *Stoke* 2B **42**
Horton St. *Leek* 3G **17**
Horton St. *New* 4G **33** (2G **7**)
Horwood. *K'le* 7K **31**
Horwood Gdns. *Stoke* 3B **28**
Horwood Hall. *K'le* 6K **31**
Hose St. *Stoke* 1G **27**
Hoskins Rd. *Stoke* 6H **21**
Hot La. *Bid M* 1G **15**
Hot La. *Hot I & Stoke* 5A **28**
Hot La. Ind. Est. *Stoke* 4A **28**
Hougher Wall Rd. *A'ly* 3E **24**
Hough Hill. *Brn E* 2G **23**
Houghton St. *Stoke* 3B **34** (6F **5**)
Houghwood. **1K 29**
Houghwood La. *Stoc B* 7J **23**
Houldsworth Dri. *Stoke* 4A **22**
Housefield Rd. *Stoke* 5J **35**
Houseman Dri. *Stoke* 1A **42**
Houston Av. *End* 3K **23**
Hoveringham Dri. *Stoke* 4E **34**
Howard Clo. *Leek* 5D **16**
Howard Clo. *Werr* 1C **36**
Howard Cres. *Stoke* 3D **34**
Howard Gro. *New* 7D **32**
Howard Pl. *New* 7D **32**
Howard Pl. *Stoke* 3A **34**
Howard St. *Stoke* 4H **41**
Howard Wlk. *Stoke* 4H **41**
Howe Gro. *New* 3B **32**
Howey Hill. *Cong* 6F **9**
Howey La. *Cong* 5F **9**
Howson St. *Stoke* 2C **34** (5G **5**)
Hudson Wlk. *Stoke* 4H **41**
(off Caroline St.)
Hugh Bourne Pl. *B Frd* 1A **22**
Hughes Av. *New* 3E **32**
Hughes St. *Stoke* 5K **27**
Hughson Gro. *Stoke* 1D **28**
Hugo St. *Leek* 4F **17**
Hulland Clo. *New* 4J **31**
Hullock's Pool Rd. *Big E* 6E **18**
Hulme. **5B 36**
Hulme Clo. *New* 4J **31**
Hulme La. *Werr & Hul* 3B **36**
Hulme Rd. *Stoke* 1A **42**
Hulme St. *Stoke* 5H **33**
Hulme Walfield. **1D 8**
Hulse St. *Stoke* 7G **35**
Hulton Clo. *Cong* 6K **9**
Hulton Gro. *Stoke* 6G **29**
Hulton St. *Stoke* 7C **28**
Humber Dri. *Bid* 2D **14**
Humbert St. *Stoke* 2J **33**
Humber Way. *New* 3E **38**
Hungerford La. *Mad* 7A **30**
Hunsford Clo. *Stoke* 2H **41**
(off Goddard St.)
Huntbach St. *Stoke* 1B **34** (3F **5**)
Hunters Clo. *Bid* 2B **14**
Hunters Dri. *Stoke* 7J **33**
Hunters Way. *Stoke* 1J **39**
Huntilee Rd. *Stoke* 1H **27**
Huntingdon Pl. *Stoke* 6E **28**
Huntley. **7F 45**
Huntley Av. *Stoke* 7K **33**
Huntley Clo. *C'dle* 6G **45**
Huntley La. *C'dle* 6E **44**
Huntsbank Dri. *New* 3A **26**
Hunt St. *Stoke* 1H **27**
Huron Gro. *Stoke* 6K **39**
Hurricane Dri. *Stoke* 7F **21**
Hurst Clo. *Tal P* 5A **20**
Hurst St. *Stoke* 3F **41**
Hutchinson Wlk. *Stoke* 3F **41**
Hutton Dri. *Cong* 5J **9**

Hutton Way. *Stoke* 3J **35**
Huxley Pl. *Stoke* 2J **41**
Hyacinth Ct. *New* 3F **33**
Hyacinth Rd. *Stoke* 4H **33**
Hyde Pk. Ind. Est. *Stoke* 7B **34**
Hyndley Clo. *Stoke* 2F **35**
Hyssop Pl. *Stoke* 2C **28**

I

Ian Rd. *N'cpl* 1G **21**
Ibsen Rd. *Stoke* 2B **42**
Ikins Dri. *Big E* 2G **25**
Ilam Clo. *New* 4J **31**
Ilford Side. *Stoke* 6D **40**
Ilkley Pl. *New* 3G **31**
Imandra Clo. *Stoke* 7K **39**
Imex Bus. Pk. *Stoke* 7C **40**
(Bellringer Rd.)
I-Mex Bus. Pk. *Stoke* 1E **40**
(Old Tramway)
Imogen Clo. *Stoke* 7G **35**
Imperial Ct. *Stoke* 3C **34** (6G **5**)
Ingelow Clo. *Stoke* 4F **41**
Ingestre Sq. *Stoke* 6D **40**
Ingleborough Pl. *Stoke* 3J **29**
Ingleby Rd. *Stoke* 6D **40**
Inglefield Av. *Stoke* 3A **28**
Ingleton Gro. *Stoke* 7B **42**
Inglewood Dri. *New* 6F **27**
Inglewood Gro. *New* 6F **27**
Inkerman Ter. *Leek* 2E **16**
Inglis St. *Stoke* 5B **34**
Intone Fitness Cen. 7E **10**
Iona Pl. *Stoke* 3E **40**
Ipswich Wlk. *Stoke* 3G **35**
Irene Av. *New* 3G **33**
Irene Av. *Stoke* 1J **27**
Iris Clo. *Stoke* 1D **42**
Ironbridge Dri. *New* 3C **32**
Ironmarket. *New* 4E **32** (3D **6**)
Irvine Rd. *Werr* 1D **36**
Isherwood Pl. *Stoke* 2J **41**
Isis Clo. *Cong* 6H **9**
Islay Wlk. *Stoke* 3F **41**
Ivy Clo. *B Bri* 1G **49**
Ivy Gdns. *Stoke* 5E **8**
Ivy Ho. *Stoke* 6J **39**
Ivyhouse Dri. *B'stn* 3D **46**
Ivy Ho. Rd. *Gil H* 2H **15**
Ivy Ho. Rd. *Stoke* 2D **34**
Ivy La. *Als* 1F **19**
Izaac Walton Way. *Mad* 3B **30**

J

Jack Ashley Ct. *Stoke* 7C **34**
Jackfield St. *Stoke* 3A **28**
Jack Haye La. *L Oaks* 3J **29**
Jack Hayes. **4K 29**
Jackson Rd. *Cong* 2G **9**
Jackson St. *Stoke* 4K **27**
Jacqueline St. *Stoke* 7F **21**
Jade Ct. *Stoke* 2J **41**
Jamage Ind. Est. *Tal P* 5K **19**
Jamage Rd. *Tal P* 5A **20**
(in two parts)
James Brindley Clo. *Stoke*
  ....3K **33** (6B **4**)
James Brindley Mus. 3E **16**
James Cres. *Werr* 1D **36**
James St. *Leek* 4E **16**
James St. *New* 1J **39**
James St. *Stoke* 1J **39**
James Way. *Knyp* 4K **13**
Jamieson Clo. *Als* 6F **11**
Janet Pl. *Stoke* 1D **34**
Janson St. *Stoke* 5J **39**
Jasmine Clo. *B Bri* 7G **43**
Jasmine Cres. *N'cpl* 1G **21**
Jasmin Way. *Pac* 1J **21**
Jason St. *New* 3D **32** (1B **6**)
Jasper Clo. *B'stn* 3E **46**
Jasper Clo. *New* 5E **26**

Jasper St. *Stoke* 2B **34** (5F **5**)
Java Cres. *Stoke* 7A **40**
Jaycean Av. *Stoke* 7H **21**
Jean Clo. *Stoke* 2K **27**
Jefferson St. *Stoke* 7G **21**
Jenkinson Clo. *New* 5C **32** (5A **6**)
Jenkins St. *Stoke* 4J **27**
Jerbourg Clo. *New* 2B **38**
Jeremy Clo. *Stoke* 7J **33**
Jersey Clo. *Cong* 5J **9**
Jersey Clo. *New* 2B **38**
Jersey Cres. *Stoke* 5H **41**
Jervison St. *Stoke* 7J **35**
Jervis St. *Stoke* 7C **28** (2H **5**)
　　　　　　　　　(in two parts)
Jesmond Gro. *Stoke* 6D **40**
Joanhurst Cres. *Stoke*
　　　　　. . . . . .3A **34** (6C **4**)
Jodrell Vw. *Kid* 3E **20**
John Bright St. *Stoke* . .7C **28** (1H **5**)
John Offley Rd. *Mad* 2A **30**
John O'Gaunt's Rd. *New*
　　　　　. . . . . .4D **32** (3B **6**)
John Rhodes Way. *Stoke* 6F **21**
Johnson Av. *New* 1D **32**
Johnson Clo. *Cong* 6J **9**
Johnson Pl. *Stoke* 5A **22**
Johnstone Av. *Werr* 1D **36**
John St. *Bid* 3B **14**
John St. *Ches* 4B **26**
John St. *Cong* 5E **8**
John St. *Knut* 3B **32**
John St. *Leek* 4F **17**
John St. *New* 4G **33** (3G **7**)
John St. *Stoke* 2B **34** (4F **5**)
Joiner's Square. **3D 34**
Joiner's Sq. Ind. Est. *Stoke* 6G **5**
Jolley St. *Stoke* 3B **28**
Jolliffe St. Leek 4F **17**
　　　　　　　　(off Cornhill St.)
Jolyon Clo. *Stoke* 7G **35**
Jonathan Rd. *Stoke* 3B **46**
Jordan St. *Stoke* 3A **34** (6C **4**)
Joseph Cres. *Als* 1G **19**
Joseph St. *Stoke* 4H **27**
Josiah Wedgwood St.
　　　Stoke 2K **33** (4B **4**)
Joyce Av. *Stoke* 2A **28**
Jubilee Av. *Stoke* 2K **33** (5B **4**)
Jubilee Clo. *Bid* 3C **14**
Jubilee Rd. *Cong* 5G **9**
Jubilee Rd. *New* 2G **33**
Jubilee Rd. *Stoke* 6J **39**
Jubilee Ter. Leek 3E **16**
Judgefield La. *Brn E* 1E **22**
Judith Gro. *Stoke* 1B **40**
Jug Bank. *Stoke* 6A **28**
June Rd. *Stoke* 7G **35**
Juniper Clo. *New* 3B **26**
Juniper Clo. *Stoke* 1B **48**
Jupiter St. *Stoke* 3B **28**
Justin Clo. *New* 6G **27**

K

Kara Pl. *Stoke* 6A **40**
Kaydor Clo. *Werr* 1C **36**
Kearsley Way. *Stoke* 6D **40**
Keary St. *Stoke* 7A **34**
Keates St. *Stoke* 4J **27**
Keats Dri. *Rode H* 2F **11**
Keats Gdns. *Kid* 3D **20**
Keble Way. *Stoke* 4E **40**
Kedleston Rd. *Stoke* 2K **27**
Keele. **6G 31**
Keele By-Pass. *K'le* 5F **31**
Keele Observatory. **6K 31**
Keele Rd. *K'le & New* . . .6H **31** (5A **6**)
Keele Rd. *Mad H* 5C **30**
Keele Science Pk. *Uni K* 5A **31**
Keele St. *Stoke* 7G **21**
Keele University Leisure Cen.
　　　　　. . . . . .6J **31**
Keeling Rd. *C'dle* 3H **45**
Keelings Dri. *Stoke* 2H **39**
Keelings Rd. *Stoke* 7C **28** (1H **5**)

Keeling St. *New* 6F **27**
Keene Clo. *Stoke* 1D **28**
Keepers Clo. *B Bri* 1H **49**
Kelly Grn. *Stoke* 5A **22**
Kelman Rd. *Stoke* 7F **35**
Kelmore Clo. *Stoke* 2G **41**
Kelsall St. *Cong* 4G **9**
Kelsall St. *Stoke* 3A **28**
Kelsall Way. *A'ly* 3E **24**
Kelvin Av. *Stoke* 6C **28**
Kelvin St. *New* 1G **33**
Kemball Av. *Stoke* 2B **40**
Kemnay Av. *Stoke* 3A **22**
Kempthorne Rd. *Stoke*
　　　　　. . . . . .3C **34** (6H **5**)
Kempton Gro. *C'dle* 1H **45**
Kendal Ct. *Cong* 5C **8**
Kendal Gro. *Stoke* 3J **35**
Kendal Pl. *New* 7E **32**
Kendrick St. *Stoke* 3H **41**
Kenelyn Cres. *Stoke* 2D **40**
Kenilworth Gro. *New* 2H **33**
Kenilworth Gro. *Stoke* 5A **42**
Kenilworth Wlk. *C'dle* 4E **44**
Kenley Av. *End* 1K **23**
Kennedy Rd. *Stoke* 7A **40**
Kennedy Wlk. *Werr* 1C **36**
Kennermont Rd. *Stoke* 7H **29**
Kennet Clo. *New* 3E **38**
Kennet Dri. *Cong* 6H **9**
Kennington Oval. *Stoke* 6B **40**
Kensington Ct. *Als* 6A **10**
Kensington Ct. *Stoke* 7H **21**
　　　　　　　　　(Trent Vale)
Kensington Ct. *Stoke* 7H **21**
　　　　　　　　　(Tunstall)
Kensington Rd. *Stoke* 2J **39**
Kensworth Clo. *New* 3D **38**
Kent Dri. *Cong* 3F **9**
Kent Dri. *End* 5K **23**
Kent Gro. *New* 4A **26**
Kentmere Clo. *Stoke* 1G **41**
Kentmere Pl. *New* 7E **32**
　　　　　　　　　(in two parts)
Kent Pl. *Stoke* 7D **34**
Kents Row. *Stoke* 5D **46**
Kenworthy St. *Stoke* 7H **21**
Kerry Hill. **5K 29**
Kersbrook Clo. *Stoke* 1B **46**
Kervis Gro. *Stoke* 1C **48**
Kesteven Wlk. *Werr* 2G **35**
Kestrel Av. *Stoke* 7D **42**
Kestrel Clo. *Cong* 6G **9**
Kestrel Clo. *Knyp* 4A **14**
Kestrel La. *C'dle* 3H **45**
Keswick Ct. *Cong* 5C **8**
Keswick Pl. *New* 7E **32**
Kettering Dri. *Stoke* 3E **34**
Ketton Clo. *Stoke* 3A **22**
Keynsham Wlk. *Stoke* 2C **28**
Keyworth Wlk. *Stoke* 3F **35**
Kibworth Gro. *Stoke* 7B **28**
Kidbrooke Pl. *Stoke* 6C **40**
Kidsgrove. **2C 20**
Kidsgrove Bank. *Kid* 3E **20**
Kidsgrove Rd. *Stoke* 3F **21**
KIDSGROVE STATION. RAIL
　　　　　. . . . .**2C 30**
Kilburn Pl. *Stoke* 3E **34**
Kildare St. *Stoke* 4J **27**
　　　　　　　　　(in two parts)
Kildown Clo. *Stoke* 3K **33** (6A **4**)
Kiln La. *Leek* 3D **16**
Kilsby Gro. *Stoke* 2G **29**
Kimberley Grange.
　　　New 3E **32** (1C **6**)
Kimberley Rd. *New* . . .3E **32** (1C **6**)
Kimberley Rd. *Stoke* . . .2K **33** (5A **4**)
Kimberley St. *Stoke* 4G **41**
Kinder Pl. *New* 4J **31**
King Charles Clo. *Stoke* 7B **42**
Kingcross St. *Stoke* 3H **41**
King Edward St. *C'dle* 2H **45**
Kingfisher Clo. *Cong* 6G **9**
Kingfisher Clo. *Mad* 6A **30**
Kingfisher Cres. *C'dle* 3J **45**

Kingfisher Cres. *Ful* 7F **49**
Kingfisher Gro. *Stoke* 1B **28**
King George St. *Stoke*
　　　　　. . . . . .7C **28** (1H **5**)
King's Av. *New* 7F **27**
Kingsbridge Av. *New* 1E **38**
Kingsbury Gro. *Stoke* 6E **28**
Kingsclere Gro. *Stoke* 5D **28**
King's Cft. *Stoke* 4G **33** (3H **7**)
Kingsdale Clo. *Stoke* 7B **42**
Kingsdown M. *New* 2F **39**
Kingsfield Cres. *Bid* 2C **14**
Kingsfield Oval. *Stoke* . .4G **33** (2G **7**)
Kingsfield Rd. *Bid* 2C **14**
Kingsfield Rd. *Stoke* . . .4G **33** (2H **7**)
Kingsford Pl. *Stoke* 6B **42**
Kingside Gro. *Stoke* 2B **46**
Kingsland Av. *Stoke* 2J **39**
Kingsley Clo. *Tal P* 5A **20**
Kingsley Rd. *Cong* 4J **9**
Kingsley Rd. *Tal P* 5A **20**
Kingsley St. *Werr & Dil* 1G **37**
Kingsmead Rd. *Stoke* 7A **42**
Kingsnorth Pl. *Stoke* 1C **48**
Kings Pl. *Stoke* 3G **33** (1H **7**)
Kings Rd. *Stoke* 5K **39**
Kings Ter. *Stoke* 4G **33** (2H **7**)
Kingston Av. *Stoke* 5D **28**
Kingston Pl. *Bid* 2K **15**
Kingston Pl. *Stoke* 1D **28**
King St. *C' H'th* 2D **32**
King St. *A'ly* 3E **24**
King St. *Bid* 2B **14**
King St. *Bug* 3H **9**
King St. *Ches* 5B **26**
King St. *Kid* 1D **20**
King St. *Leek* 4F **17**
King St. *New* 4F **33** (3E **7**)
King St. *Stoke* 7D **34**
King St. *Tal P* 6A **20**
　　　　　　　　　(in two parts)
Kingsway. *Stoke* 6A **34**
Kingsway E. *New* 7E **32**
Kingsway W. *New* 7D **32**
Kingswell Rd. *Stoke* . . .4G **33** (3H **7**)
Kingswinford Pl. *Stoke* 5C **28**
Kingswood. *Kid* 2E **20**
King William St. *Stoke* 1H **27**
Kinnersley Av. *Kid* 3C **20**
Kinnersley St. *Kid* 1D **20**
Kinsey Av. *Cong* 5G **9**
Kinsey St. *New* 4J **31**
Kinver St. *Stoke* 3B **28**
Kipling Way. *Stoke* 4J **35**
Kirby St. *Stoke* 6K **27**
Kirkbride Clo. *Stoke* 2J **41**
Kirkham St. *Stoke* 7K **33**
Kirkland La. *Stoke* 6K **33**
Kirkstall Pl. *New* 2E **38**
Kirkstone Ct. *Cong* 6C **8**
Kirk St. *Stoke* 2B **28**
Kirkup Wlk. *Stoke* 3F **41**
Kirkwall Gro. *Stoke* 5D **28**
Kite Gro. *Kid* 7G **13**
Kite Gro. *Stoke* 7B **42**
Knarsdale Clo. *Stoke* 1J **41**
Knaworth Ct. *Cong* 7K **9**
Knenhall. **7K 47**
Knenhall Clo. *Stoke* 6J **47**
Knenhall Bk. La. *Knen* 7K **47**
Knightley. *Mad* 7A **30**
Knightsbridge Way. *Stoke* 1G **27**
　　　　　　　　(off Madeira Pl.)
Knights Cft. *K'le* 6G **31**
Knight St. *Stoke* 7G **21**
Kniveden La. *Leek* 4H **17**
Knowl Bank. **6A 24**
Knowlbank Rd. *A'ly* 6A **24**
Knowle Av. *Bid* 3B **14**
Knowle St. *Stoke* 5K **33**
Knowle Style. **3B 14**
Knowle Wood Vw. *Stoke* 3E **40**
Knowsley La. *Chu L* 6B **12**
Knutsford Old Rd. *Chu L* 5G **11**
Knutsford Rd.
　　　Chu L & Rode H 5G **11**

Knutton. **2B 32**
Knutton La. *New* 3C **32** (2A **6**)
Knutton Recreation Cen. **3B 32**
Knutton Rd. *New* 7F **27**
Knype Clo. *New* 5D **26**
Knypersley. **4B 14**
Knypersley Gdns. *Knyp* 5C **14**
Knypersley Rd. *Stoke* 6D **22**
Knype Way. *Knyp* 4A **14**
Knype Way. *New* 5D **26**
Kyffin Rd. *Stoke* 6G **29**

L

Laburnum Clo. *B Bri* 1H **49**
Laburnum Clo. *Cong* 3B **8**
Laburnum Clo. *Kid* 3B **20**
Laburnum Gro. *Stoke* 3D **40**
Laburnum Pl. *New* 3A **26**
Laburnum Pl. *Stoke* 6A **42**
Lacy Ct. *Cong* 5H **9**
Ladderedge. *Leek* 7B **16**
Ladderedge Country Pk. **6E 16**
Lad La. *New* 4E **32** (3D **6**)
Ladybank Gro. *Stoke* 6D **40**
Lady Bennett Ct. *Stoke* 3F **41**
　　　　　　　　(off Grosvenor St)
Ladydale Clo. *Leek* 5G **17**
Ladymoor Gate. **6G 15**
Ladymoor La. *Brn E* 6G **15**
Ladysmith Rd. *Stoke*
　　　　　. . . . . .2K **33** (5A **4**)
Ladysmith St. *Stoke* 4G **41**
Ladywell Rd. *Stoke* 1G **27**
　　　　　　　　　(in two parts)
Lagonda Clo. *Knyp* 5A **14**
Lakeside. *Stoke* 7J **27**
Lake Vw. *Als* 1D **18**
Lake Vw. *Cong* 5D **8**
Lakewood Dri. *B'stn* 3D **46**
Lakewood Gro. *Stoke*
　　　　　. . . . . .1K **33** (3A **4**)
Lally Pl. *B Frd* 1A **22**
Lambert's La. *A'bry* 6D **8**
　　　　　　　　　(in three parts)
Lambert's La. *Cong* 7G **9**
Lambert St. *Stoke* 1H **27**
Lambourne Dri. *Stoke* 3H **29**
Lambourn Pl. *Stoke* 6C **40**
Lamb St. *Kid* 1D **20**
Lamb St. *Stoke* 1B **34** (3F **5**)
Lamerton Gro. *Stoke* 4A **42**
Lamotte Clo. *Stoke* 1G **41**
Lanark Walks. *New* 6C **32**
Lancaster Av. *Ful* 6F **49**
Lancaster Av. *Leek* 2G **17**
Lancaster Av. *New* 5G **33** (4G **7**)
Lancaster Bldgs. New
　　　　　. . . . . .4E **32** (3D **6**)
　　　　　　　　(off Ironmarket)
Lancaster Cres. *Stoke*
　　　　　. . . . . .5G **33** (5G **7**)
Lancaster Dri. *Stoke* 7E **22**
Lancaster Rd. *New* 5G **33** (4G **7**)
Lanchester Clo. *Knyp* 4A **14**
Lancia Clo. *Knyp* 5A **14**
Lander Pl. *Stoke* 5B **22**
Landon St. *Stoke* 3H **41**
Landrake Gro. *Stoke* 4J **21**
Landseer Pl. *New* 6B **26**
Lane Ends. **1J 21**
La. Farm Gro. *Stoke* 5D **28**
Lanehead Rd. *Stoke* 2J **33** (5A **4**)
Langdale Ct. *Cong* 6C **8**
Langdale Cres. *Stoke* 5C **28**
Langdale Rd. *Stoke* 1E **38**
Langford Rd. *Stoke* 2D **38**
Langford Rd. *Stoke* 2G **35**
Langford St. *Leek* 4E **16**
Langham Rd. *Stoke* 3F **29**
Langland Dri. *Stoke* 4E **40**
Langley Clo. *New* 2A **26**
Langley St. *Stoke* 4G **33** (2H **7**)
Langton Ct. *Werr* 1B **36**
Lansbury Gro. *Stoke* 3C **42**
Lansdell Av. *New* 6D **26**

Lansdowne Clo.—Lower Heath

Lansdowne Clo. *Leek* 4C 16
Lansdowne Cres. *Werr* 1C 36
Lansdowne Rd. *Stoke*
. . . . .5H 33 (4H 7)
Lansdowne St. *Stoke* 5G 41
Lapwing Clo. *Pac* 2H 21
Lapwing Rd. *Kid* 7G 13
Larch Clo. *Kid* 3D 20
Larch Ct. Stoke *5K 27*
(off Commercial St.)
Larch Gro. *Stoke* 4D 40
Larchmount Clo. *Stoke* 7A 40
Larch Pl. *New* 4B 26
Larchwood. *K'le* 7H 31
Lark Av. *Kid* 7G 13
Larkfield. *Kid* 2E 20
Larkin Av. *Stoke* 2J 41
Larksfield Rd. *Stoke* 3C 28
Larkspur Gro. *New* 3F 33 (1E 7)
Lascelles St. *Stoke* 1G 27
Lask Edge. 3J 15
Laski Cres. *Stoke* 4C 42
Latebrook. 5E 20
Latebrook Clo. *Stoke* 4F 21
Latham Gro. *Stoke* 4A 22
Latimer Way. *Stoke* 3H 35
Lauder Pl. N. *Stoke* 5K 35
Lauder Pl. S. *Stoke* 5K 35
Laurel Cres. *Werr* 2B 36
Laurel Dri. *Har* 7H 13
Laurel Gro. *Stoke* 4C 40
Lauren Clo. *Stoke* 7D 34
Lavender Av. *B Bri* 1G 49
Lavender Clo. *Stoke* 1D 42
Laverock Gro. *Mad* 2B 30
Lawley St. *Stoke* 3J 41
Lawn Farm Cres. *Stoke* 6J 35
Lawrence St. *Stoke* 3A 34 (6D 4)
Lawson Ter. *Knut* 2B 32
Lawson Ter. *New* 6E 26
Lawton Av. *Chu L* 7A 12
Lawton Coppice. *Chu L* 6B 12
Lawton Cres. *Bid* 2C 14
Lawton-gate. 5H 11
Lawtongate Est. *Chu L* 5H 11
Lawton Heath. 4G 11
Lawton Heath End. 4E 10
Lawton Heath Rd. *Chu L* 4F 11
Lawton Rd. *Als* 6E 10
Lawton St. *Bid* 2C 14
Lawton St. *Cong* 5G 9
Lawton St. *Rook* 6F 13
Lawton St. *Stoke* 2K 27
Laxey Rd. *New* 3D 32
Laxton Gro. *Stoke* 3B 46
Leacroft Rd. *Stoke* 6B 42
Leadbeater Av. *Stoke* 1J 39
Leadendale. 4A 48
Leadendale La. *R'gh C* 4K 47
Leadendale M. *Stoke* 6A 42
Leaford Wlk. *Stoke* 3E 34
Leaks All. *Stoke* 4G 41
Leamington Gdns. *New* 2H 33
Leamington Rd. *Cong* 4B 8
Lea Pl. *Stoke* 4C 42
Leaside Rd. *Stoke* 1H 39
Leason Rd. *Stoke* 4B 42
Leason St. *Stoke* 6A 34
Leaswood Clo. *New* 4F 39
Leaswood Pl. *New* 4F 39
Lea, The. *Stoke* 7A 40
Lea Way. *Als* 7E 10
Leawood Rd. *Stoke* 3H 39
Ledbury Cres. *Stoke* 7E 28
Ledstone Way. *Stoke* 2K 41
Leech Av. *New* 6C 26
Leech St. *New* 5F 33 (5F 7)
Leeds St. *Stoke* 1E 40
Lee Gro. *New* 2E 38
Leek. 3F 17
LEEK MOORLANDS HOSPITAL.
. . . . .4H 17
Leek New Rd.
Stoke & Stoc B (ST2,ST9)
. . . . .2F 29
Leek New Rd. *Stoke* (ST6,ST1)
. . . . .5A 28
Leek Rd. *Brn E* 4H 23
Leek Rd. *C'dle* 1E 44
Leek Rd. *Cong* 7H 9
Leek Rd. *Stoc B & End* 6J 23
Leek Rd. *Stoke* (ST1)
. . . . .3C 34 (6H 5)
Leek Rd. *Stoke* (ST2) 7F 29
Leek Rd. *Stoke* (ST4) 5B 34
Leek Rd. *W Coy & Werr* 7C 36
Leek Rd. *Wet R & C'dle* 1J 37
Leek Town F.C. (Harrison Pk.)
. . . . .3D 16
Leese St. *Stoke* 6A 34
Legge St. *New* 5F 33 (5F 7)
Leicester Av. *Als* 5D 10
Leicester Clo. *New* 1F 39
Leicester Pl. *Stoke* 3H 35
Leigh La. *Stoke* 3F 27
Leigh Rd. *Cong* 2K 9
Leigh St. *Stoke* 2K 27
Leighton Clo. *Stoc B* 7H 23
Lennox Rd. *Stoke* 4J 41
Lenthall Av. *Cong* 7H 9
Leonard Av. *Bad G* 1G 29
Leonard Dri. *Brn E* 5G 23
Leonard St. *Leek* 4G 17
Leonard St. *Stoke* 2A 28
Leonora St. *Stoke* 5J 27
Leopold St. *Stoke* 7D 34
Lessways Clo. *New* 4E 26
Lessways Wlk. *Stoke* 5J 27
Lester Clo. *Als* 6E 10
Leveson Rd. *Stoke* 5J 39
Leveson St. *Stoke* 4H 41
Levita Rd. *Stoke* 2J 39
Lewisham Dri. *Stoke* 4F 21
Lewis St. *Stoke* 5A 34
Lexham Pl. *Stoke* 4K 41
Leycett. 3D 30
Leycett La. *Mad H & Ley* 5C 30
Leycett Rd. *S Hay* 1E 30
Leyfield Rd. *Stoke* 1A 46
Ley Gdns. *Stoke* 4F 41
Leyland Grn. Stoke *4K 21*
(off Coppull Pl.)
Leys Dri. *New* 2B 38
Leys La. *Stoke* 2H 29
Liberty La. Stoke *1B 28*
(off Bradeley Village)
Libra Pl. *Stoke* 5J 21
Lichfield Clo. *New* 3A 32
Lichfield Rd. *Tal* 4A 20
Lichfield St. *Stoke* 2B 34 (4F 5)
Liddle St. *Stoke* 7K 33
Lidgate Gro. *Stoke* 4E 40
Lidgate Wlk. *New* 4F 39
Lid La. *C'dle* 3F 45
(in two parts)
Light Oaks. 3J 29
Light Oaks Av. *L Oaks* 3J 29
Lightwater Gro. *Stoke* 3E 28
Lightwood. 7K 41
Lightwood Rd. *New* 3A 26
Lightwood Rd.
Stoke & R'gh C 4H 41
Lilac Clo. *New* 3A 26
Lilac Clo. *Stoke* 1D 42
Lilac Ct. *Cong* 5G 9
Lilac Gro. *Stoke* 3D 40
Lilleshall Rd. *New* 1G 39
Lilleshall St. *Stoke* 4H 41
Lillydale Rd. *Stoke* 2G 35
Lily St. *New* 7F 27
Limbrick Rd. *A'ly* 3B 24
Lime Clo. *Stoke* 1D 42
Lime Gro. *Als* 7F 11
Lime Gro. *B'stn* 3E 46
Limeheath Pl. *Stoke* 6H 21
Lime Kiln La. *Chu L* 1B 20
Limes, The. *New* 5F 27
Lime St. *Cong* 5F 9
Lime St. *Stoke* 1A 40
Lime Tree Av. *Cong* 4D 8
Limewood Clo. *B Bri* 1H 49
Linacre Way. *Stoke* 1K 41
Lincoln Av. *New* 1F 39
Lincoln Gro. *New* 1F 39
Lincoln Rd. *Kid* 1C 20
Lincoln Rd. *Stoke* 5K 27
Lincoln St. *Stoke* 2C 34 (4H 5)
Lindale Clo. *Cong* 2J 9
Lindale Gro. *Stoke* 7C 42
Linda Rd. *Stoke* 6H 21
Linden Clo. *Cong* 7J 9
Linden Clo. *New* 2E 32
Linden Dri. *Gil H* 1B 14
Linden Gro. *Gil H* 2H 15
Linden Gro. *New* 2E 32
Linden Pl. *Stoke* 5E 40
Lindley Pl. *Stoke* 3B 48
Lindley St. *Stoke* 5A 28
Lindop Ct. *Stoke* 3G 5
Lindops La. *Mad* 6A 30
Lindop St. *Stoke* 1C 34 (3G 5)
Lindsay Hall. *K'le* 7J 31
Lindsay St. *Stoke* 2A 34 (5D 4)
Lindsay Way. *Als* 6B 10
Lindum Av. *Stoke* 7B 40
Line Houses. 5E 20
Linfield Rd. *Stoke* 1C 34 (3G 5)
Lingard St. *Stoke* 4K 27
Lingfield Av. *Brn E* 3F 23
Linhope Gro. *Stoke* 7C 42
Linkend Clo. *Stoke* 7E 28
Links Av. *New* 1E 32
Linksway. *Cong* 7G 9
Linksway Clo. *Cong* 7H 9
Linley Gro. *Als* 7G 11
Linley La. *Als* 6G 11
Linley Rd. *Als* 7G 11
Linley Rd. *Stoke* 5H 33 (4H 7)
Linley Rd. *Tal* 2J 19
Linley Trad. Est. *Tal* 2K 19
Linnburn Rd. *Stoke* 2J 41
Linnet Way. *Bid* 2D 14
Linwood Way. *Stoke* 6H 21
Lionel Gro. *Stoke* 6H 33
Lion Gro. *New* 4B 26
Lion St. *Cong* 5F 9
Lion St. *Stoke* 6K 33
Lisbon Pl. *New* 6B 32
Liskeard Clo. *Stoke* 4F 35
Litley Dri. *C'dle* 6G 45
Little Chell. 6J 21
Lit. Chell La. *Stoke* 6J 21
Lit. Cliffe Rd. *Stoke* 2D 40
Lit. Eaves La. *Stoke* 6H 29
Little-Field. *Stoke* 2H 39
Little La. *R'gh C* 3K 47
Little Madeley. 6B 30
Little-moss. 5B 12
Lit. Moss Clo. *Sch G* 5B 12
Lit. Moss La. *Sch G* 5B 12
Little Row. *Fen I* 5E 34
Little Row. Kid *1E 20*
(off Brights Av.)
Little St. *Cong* 5F 9
Littondale Clo. *Cong* 2H 9
Liverpool Rd. *Kid* 1C 20
Liverpool Rd. *New* 7D 26 (1C 6)
(in two parts)
Liverpool Rd. *Red S* 1A 26
Liverpool Rd. *Stoke* 6A 34
Liverpool Rd. E.
Chu L & Kid 7A 12
Liverpool Rd. W. *Chu L* 6G 11
Livingstone St. *Leek* 4G 17
Livingstone St. *Stoke* 2B 28
Lloyd St. *Stoke* 4H 41
Loachbrook Av. *Cong* 5C 8
Lockerbie Clo. *Leek* 4J 17
Locketts La. *Stoke* 4H 41
(Lightwood Rd.)
Locketts La. *Stoke* 4J 41
(Normacot Rd.)
Lockett St. *Stoke* 6C 28
Lockington Av. *Stoke* 3J 35
Lockley St. *Stoke* 7D 28
Lockwood St. *New* 4G 33 (3G 7)
Lockwood St. *Stoke* 1G 29
Lodge Barn Rd. *Knyp* 4E 14
Lodge Gro. *New* 6F 27
Lodge Rd. *Als* 6D 10
Lodge Rd. *Stoke* 6H 33 (6H 7)
Lodge Rd. *Tal P* 5A 20
Loftus St. *Stoke* 7A 28 (1D 4)
Loganbeck Gro. *Stoke* 1J 41
Lomas St. *Stoke* 3K 33
Lombardy Gro. *Stoke* 4B 42
Lomond Gro. *C'dle* 2H 45
Lomond Wlk. *Stoke* 7E 40
London Rd. *Ches & New* 4B 26
London Rd. *New* 5F 33 (5E 7)
London Rd. *Stoke* 3H 39
London St. *Leek* 4G 17
Longbridge Hayes Rd.
Stoke 4F 27
Longbrook Av. *Stoke* 4E 40
Longclough Rd. *New* 2A 26
Longdoles Av. *Stoke* 3K 41
Longdown Rd. *Cong* 4A 8
Longfield Rd. *Stoke* . . .5G 33 (5H 7)
Longford Wlk. *Stoke* 3F 35
Long La. *Ful* 7F 49
Long La. *Har* 6H 13
Longley Rd. *Stoke* 1H 41
Long Mdw. *New* 3F 39
Longnor Pl. *Stoke* 3F 35
Longport. 4G 27
Longport Rd. *Stoke* 5G 27
LONGPORT STATION. RAIL
. . . . .5G 27
Long Row. *Cav* 3E 42
Long Row. *Kid* 2D 20
Longsdon. 7A 16
Longsdon Clo. *New* 3K 25
Longsdon Gro. *Stoke* 2K 41
Longshaw Av. *New* 5E 26
Longshaw St. *Stoke* 4G 27
Longton. 3H 41
Longton Exchange. Stoke *3G 41*
(off Strand, The)
Longton Hall Rd. *Stoke* 4E 40
LONGTON COTTAGE HOSPITAL.
. . . . .5J 41
Longton Rd. *B'stn* 6D 46
Longton Rd. *Knen* 7J 47
Longton Rd. *Stoke* 7K 39
LONGTON STATION. RAIL . . .2G 41
Long Valley Rd. *Gil H* 2H 15
Longview Av. *Als* 6F 11
Longview Clo. *Stoke* 1J 41
Lonsdale St. *Stoke* 7A 34
Loomer Rd. *New* 7A 26
Loomer Rd. Ind. Est. *New* 7B 26
Lords Clo. *Stoke* 7C 40
Lordship La. *Stoke* 6B 34
Lordshire Pl. *Pac* 2J 21
Lord St. *Bid* 3C 14
Lord St. *Stoke* 3B 28
Lorien Clo. *Leek* 5D 16
Loring Rd. *New* 6E 26
Loring Ter. S. *New* 6F 27
Lorne St. *Stoke* 3K 27
Lorraine St. *Pac* 2J 21
Lotus Av. *Knyp* 4A 14
Loughborough Wlk. *Stoke* 2H 41
Louise Dri. *Stoke* 3E 40
Louise St. *Stoke* 3K 27
Louvain Av. *Stoke* 5C 28
Lovatt Av. *New* 1D 32
Lovatt St. *Stoke* 6A 34
Loveage Dri. *Stoke* 2G 35
Love La. *B'ton* 1D 10
Loveston Gro. *Stoke* 2J 41
Lowe Av. *Cong* 5G 9
Lowe Hill. 6J 17
Lowell Dri. *Stoke* 2K 41
Lwr. Ash Rd. *Kid* 3B 20
Lwr. Bedford St.
Stoke 3K 33 (6A 4)
Lwr. Bethesda St.
Stoke 2B 34 (5F 5)
Lwr. Bryan St. *Stoke* . . .7B 28 (1E 5)
Lower Cres. *Stoke* 5H 33 (5H 7)
Lwr. Cross St. *L'tn* 2H 41
Lwr. Foundry St.
Stoke 1B 34 (3E 5)
Lower Hadderidge. *Stoke* 4J 27
Lower Heath. 2G 9
Lower Heath. *Cong* 3G 9

64 A-Z Stoke

Lwr. Heath Av.—Mellard St.

Lwr. Heath Av. Cong 2G 9
Lwr. Heath Ter. Cong 3G 9
Lwr. High St. Mow C 3G 13
Lwr. Mayer St. Stoke . . .7C 28 (1G 5)
Lwr. Milehouse La. Knut 3C 32
Lwr. Oxford Rd. New . . .3H 33 (1H 7)
Lwr. Park St. Cong 4G 9
Lwr. Spring Rd. Stoke 4J 41
(in two parts)
Lower St. New 4E 32 (2C 6)
Lower St. Stoke 5K 27
Lowe's Pas. Stoke 4J 41
Lowe St. Stoke 6A 34
Lowfield Dri. New 7H 27
Lowhurst Dri. Stoke 4J 21
Lowlands Rd. Stoke 7D 20
Lowndes Clo. Stoke 7J 33
Low St. Rode H 2F 11
Lowther Pl. Leek 4H 17
Lowther St. Stoke 7A 28 (1C 4)
Lowthorpe Way. Stoke 4K 35
Loxley Pl. Stoke 7A 42
Lucas St. Stoke 5H 27
Lucerne Pl. New 6B 32
Ludbrook Rd. Stoke 1G 41
Ludford Clo. New 2A 26
Ludlow St. Stoke 1C 34 (3H 5)
Ludwall Rd. Stoke 5K 41
Lugano Clo. New 7C 32
Lukesland Av. Stoke 7H 33
Luke St. Stoke 5H 27
Lulworth Gro. Stoke 5J 21
Lumpy St. Cong 4E 8
Lundy Rd. Stoke 3E 40
Lune Clo. Cong 6H 9
Lunt Moss. 3A 12
Lydford Pl. Stoke 3A 42
Lydia Dri. Stoke 6E 28
Lyme Brook Pl. Stoke 3H 39
Lyme Ct. New 6F 7
Lymedale Pk. New 7B 26
Lymedale Small Firms Cen.
Lyme B 7C 26
Lyme Dri. Park 7G 33
Lyme Gro. New 2F 33
Lyme Rd. Stoke 5C 42
Lymes Rd. But . . . . . .7G 31 & 2A 38
Lymes, The. 3A 38
Lymevale Rd. Stoke 2H 39
Lyme Valley Rd. New . . .6E 32 (5D 6)
Lymewood Clo. New . . .5E 32 (5C 6)
Lymewood Gro. New . . .6E 32 (6C 6)
Lyminster Gro. Stoke 3G 29
Lynalls Clo. Cong 4B 8
Lynam St. Stoke 6K 33
Lynam Way. Mad 1B 30
Lyndhurst Dri. Brn L 4K 13
Lyndhurst St. Stoke 4H 27
Lyneside Rd. Knyp 4A 14
Lynmouth Clo. Bid 4B 14
Lynmouth Gro. Stoke 4J 21
Lynn Av. Tal 3K 19
Lynn St. Stoke 1C 42
Lynsey Clo. Halm 5F 25
Lynton Gro. Stoke 6A 42
Lynton Pl. Als 6E 10
Lynton Rd. New 1C 38
Lysander Rd. Stoke 7B 42
Lytton St. Stoke 6B 34

M

Macclesfield Rd. Cong 2G 9
Macclesfield Rd. Leek 1C 16
Macclesfield St. Stoke 3A 28
Macdonald Cres. Stoke 3B 42
Mace St. Stoke 2J 39
McGough St. Stoke 1G 27
Machin Cres. New 5D 26
Machin St. Stoke 7H 21
Macintyre St. Stoke 5K 27
McKellin Clo. Big E 2F 25
Mackenzie Cres. C'dle 5H 45
McKinley St. Stoke 1G 27
(in two parts)
Maclagan St. Stoke 7A 34
Maddock St. A'ly 3E 24
Maddock St. Stoke 5H 27
Madeira Pl. Stoke 1G 27
Madeley. 2B 30
Madeley Heath. 5C 30
Madeley St. New 4J 31
Madeley St. Stoke 7G 21
Madeley St. N. New 3J 31
Madison St. Stoke 7G 21
Mafeking St. Stoke 4G 41
Magdalen Rd. Stoke 6D 40
Magdalen Wlk. Stoke 7D 40
Magenta Dri. New 3B 32
Magnolia Dri. Stoke 2E 28
Magnus St. Stoke 5J 27
Magpie Cres. Kid 1E 20
Maidstone Gro. Stoke 3H 35
Main St. Stoke 1C 42
Maitland Gro. Stoke 1A 46
Majors Barn. 4F 45
Majors Barn. C'dle 4F 45
Malam St. Stoke 7B 28 (1E 5)
Malcolm Clo. Stoke 2G 29
Malcolm Ct. Stoke 7H 29
Malcolm Dri. Stoke 7H 29
Malhamdale Rd. Cong 2J 9
Malham Rd. New 2B 32
Malkin Way. Stoke 6H 27
Mallard Way. Stoke 1B 28
Mallorie Rd. Stoke 7C 22
Mallory Ct. Cong 4B 8
Mallory Way. C'dle 3J 45
Mallowdale Clo. Stoke 1B 46
Malpas Wlk. Stoke 4F 21
Malstone Av. Stoke 2H 29
Malthouse La. B'stn 5D 46
Malthouse La. Stoke 5C 36
Malthouse Rd. Stoke 2G 35
Malt La. Stoke 4J 41
Malton Gro. Stoke 6G 21
Malvern Av. New 3G 31
Malvern Clo. Cong 4B 8
Malvern Clo. Stoke 7K 39
Manchester Rd. Cong 1G 9
Mandela Way. Stoke 4J 41
Mandeville Clo. Stoke 1B 28
Manifold Clo. New 4J 31
Manifold Rd. For 6G 43
Manifold Wlk. Stoke 4H 35
Mannin Clo. Stoke 2B 42
Mann St. Stoke 4D 42
Manor Clo. Cong 6J 9
Manor Clo. Dray 1K 49
Manor Ct. St. Stoke 7J 33
Manor Rd. Mad 3B 30
Manor Rd. Mow C 3G 13
Manor St. Stoke 7D 34
Manse Clo. Stoke 2H 41
Mansfield Clo. New 4F 39
Mansfield Dri. Brn L 5K 13
Mansion Clo. C'dle 4H 45
Maple Av. Als 1F 19
Maple Av. New 3B 26
Maple Av. Tal 3A 20
Maple Clo. C'dle 4J 45
Maple Clo. Cong 3B 8
Maple Clo. Stoke 6F 23
Maple Cres. B Bri 1H 49
Maplehurst Clo. Hot I 4A 28
Maple Pl. Rode H 3G 11
Maple Pl. Stoke 4C 42
Maples Clo. Stoke 2K 41
Marcel Clo. Stoke 4K 39
March La. Werr 2H 37
March Rd. Stoke 2G 41
Marchwood Ct. Stoke 7H 33
Marcus Ind. Est. Stoke 2E 34
Mardale Clo. Cong 2J 9
Margaret Av. Stoke 6J 39
Margaret St. Stoke 1D 34 (3H 5)
Margery Av. Sch G 3B 12
Margill Clo. Stoke 2A 34 (5D 4)
Maries Way. Sil 4A 32
Marina Dri. New 1F 33
Marina Rd. Stoke 3J 39
Marina Way. Stoke 1J 33 (4A 4)
Market La. New 4E 32 (3D 6)
Market La. Stoke 1B 34 (3F 5)
Market Pas. Stoke 4J 27
Market Pl. C'dle 3G 45
Market Pl. Leek 3F 17
(off Church St.)
Market Pl. Stoke 4J 27
Market Sq. Cong 5F 9
Market Sq. Stoke 1B 34 (3F 5)
Market Sq. Arc. Stoke 3F 5
Market St. Cong 5F 9
Market St. Kid 2D 20
Market St. Leek 3G 17
Market St. Stoke 2H 41
Marlborough Cres. End 3K 23
Marlborough Rd. Stoke 2H 41
Marlborough St. Stoke 1C 40
Marldon Pl. Stoke 5F 21
Marlow Clo. Stoke 1J 41
Marlow Rd. Stoke 1J 41
Marney Wlk. Stoke 2A 28
Marriott St. Stoke 1F 41
Marsden St. Stoke 1C 34 (2G 5)
Marshall Av. Brn E 4G 23
Marshall Gro. Cong 6K 9
Marshall St. Stoke 3J 27
Marsh Av. New 7F 27
Marsh Av. N'cpl 1H 21
Marsh Av. Stoke 2A 28
Marsh Clo. Als 7B 10
Marsh Clo. Werr 1B 36
Marshfield La. Gil H 2H 15
Marsh Grn. Clo. Bid 2J 15
Marshgreen Rd. Bid 1J 15
Marsh Gro. Gil H 1H 15
Marshland Gro. Stoke 3K 21
Marsh La. Als 7B 10
Marsh Pde. New 5F 33 (4F 7)
Marsh St. N. Stoke 1B 34 (2E 5)
Marsh St. S. Stoke 1B 34 (3E 5)
Marsh Vw. Stoke 2B 48
Marsh Way. New 7F 27
Mars St. Stoke 3B 28
Marston Gro. Stoke 4C 28
Martindale Clo. Stoke 6A 42
Martin St. Stoke 5A 28
Marton Clo. Cong 2G 9
Marychurch Rd. Stoke 2G 35
Maryfield Wlk. Stoke 6H 33
Maryhill Clo. Kid 7D 12
Maryrose Clo. Stoke 2G 35
Masefield Clo. C'dle 1G 45
Masefield Rd. Stoke 4F 41
Maskery Pl. Cong 4F 9
Mason Dri. Bid 2A 14
Mason St. Stoke 1E 40
Masterson St. Stoke 7C 34
Mathews Wlk. Stoke 3G 5
Matlock Pl. New 3H 31
Matlock St. Stoke 3B 34
Matrix Health & Leisure Club.
. . . . .3G 27
Matthews Ct. Stoke 4H 5
Matthews Pl. Cong 5J 9
Maud St. Stoke 6D 34
Maunders Rd. Stoke 3F 29
Maureen Av. Stoke 5G 21
Maureen Gro. New 2F 33
Mawdesley St. Stoke 6A 28
Mawdsley Clo. Als 7A 10
Mawson Gro. Stoke 4C 34
Maxton Way. Stoke 4C 42
Maxwell Pl. Stoke 6H 33
Maxwell Rd. Cong 7J 9
May Av. New 2G 33
May Av. Stoke 1H 27
May Bank. 2G 33
May Bank. New 2G 33
Maybury Way. Stoke 3F 29
Mayer Av. New 3E 32
Mayer Bank. Stoke 4K 27
Mayers Ct. Leek 4E 16
Mayer St. Stoke 1C 34 (2F 5)
Mayfair Gdns. Stoke 1G 27
(off Wesley St.)
Mayfair Gro. End 3K 23
Mayfield Av. New 5D 32 (5A 6)
Mayfield Av. Stoke 7D 28
Mayfield Clo. Leek 4C 16
Mayfield Cres. Stoke 7D 28
Mayfield Dri. B Bri 6E 42
Mayfield Pl. New 1F 33
Mayfield Pl. E. Stoke 1H 39
Mayfield Pl. W. Stoke 1H 39
Mayfield Rd. Bid 4C 14
Maylea Cres. Stoke 5B 28
Mayneford Pl. Stoke 5J 39
Mayne St. Stoke 4J 39
May Pl. New 2F 33
May Pl. Stoke 1G 41
May St. New 4K 31
May St. Stoke 3A 28
Maythorne Rd. Stoke 5F 41
Mead Av. Sch G 3B 12
Meadow Av. Cong 6E 8
Meadow Av. New 1D 32
Meadow Av. Stoke 6H 41
Meadow Clo. B Bri 1F 49
Meadow Clo. For 6J 43
Meadow Clo. Leek 4H 17
Meadow Cotts. Cong 4F 9
(off Stonehouse Grn.)
Meadow Ct. B'stn 5B 46
Meadow Ct. N'cpl 1H 21
Meadow Cft. Als 1F 19
Meadowcroft Av. Stoke 6D 42
Meadow Dri. C'dle 3G 45
Meadow Dri. Stoke 6F 41
Meadow La. Ful 7F 49
Meadow La. New 1D 32
Meadow La. Stoke 7B 40
Meadow Pl. Stoke 5C 42
Meadow Rd. B'stn 5C 46
Meadow Rd. Brn E 5G 23
Meadow Rd. Stoke 6B 22
Meadow Side. Knyp 4A 14
Meadowside. Sav G 5J 49
Meadowside. Stoke 7A 40
Meadowside Av. A'ly 3D 24
Meadowside La. Sch G 3E 12
Meadows Rd. Kid 2C 20
Meadows, The. Cong 4F 9
Meadows, The. End 2K 23
Meadows, The. Kid 2C 20
Meadows, The. Stoke 4G 35
Meadow Stile Cvn. Site.
Brn L 4K 13
Meadow St. New 6C 26
Meadow St. Stoke 3G 29
Meadows Way. Bid 3B 14
Meadowview. Stoke 1D 28
Meadow Way. Chu L 5H 11
Meads Rd. Als 6E 10
Mead, The. Stoke 7A 40
Meaford Dri. Stoke 4D 40
Meaford Rd. B'stn & Knen 6C 46
Meakin Av. New 3E 38
Meakin Clo. C'dle 5F 45
Meakin Clo. Cong 6K 9
Meakins Row. Stoke 1E 40
Medina Way. Kid 1E 20
Medway Dri. Bid 1C 14
Medway Pl. New 2E 38
Medway Wlk. Stoke 7K 21
Meerbrook Clo. Stoke 2A 46
Meere Clo. Stoke 1D 28
Mega Bowl. 1K 33 (3A 4)
Megacre. 3H 25
Megacre. Big E 2H 25
Meigh Rd. Ash B & Werr 2B 36
Meigh St. Stoke 1B 34 (3G 5)
Meiklejohn Pl. Stoke 5K 21
Meir. 5B 42
Meir Hay. 2J 41
Meirhay Rd. Stoke 4J 41
Meir Heath. 2B 48
Meir Rd. Stoke 5K 41
Meir St. Stoke 7G 21
Meir Vw. Stoke 4B 42
Melbourne St. Stoke 1J 41
Melchester Gro. Stoke 5K 41
Melfont St. Stoke 1H 27
Meliden Way. Stoke 7J 33
Mellard St. A'ly 3E 24
Mellard St. New 3D 32 (1B 6)

A-Z Stoke 65

Mellors Bank—Nelson Pl.

Mellors Bank. *Mow C* 4G **13**
Mellor St. *Pac* 2J **21**
Melrose Av. *Meir H* 3B **48**
Melrose Av. *New* 1D **38**
Melrose Av. *S Grn* 5C **28**
Melrose Pl. *Leek* 4C **16**
Melstone Av. *Stoke* 1J **27**
Melton Clo. *Cong* 4B **8**
Melton Dri. *Cong* 4B **8**
Melville Ct. *New* 5F **39**
Melville Rd. *Stoke* 4K **41**
Melville St. *Stoke* 2D **34** (5H **5**)
Melvyn Cres. *New* 5F **27**
Menai Dri. *Knyp* 4C **14**
Menai Gro. *Stoke* 1H **41**
Mendip Grn. *Stoke* 3F **29**
Mendip Pl. *New* 2B **32**
Menzies Ho. *Stoke* 6A **42**
Mercer St. *Stoke* 5G **41**
Mercia Cres. *Stoke* 6K **27**
Mercury Pl. *Stoke* 3C **28**
Mere Ct. *Als* 6E **10**
Merelake. **3G 19**
Merelake Rd. *Tal P* 2F **19**
Merelake Way. *Als* 1G **19**
Meremore Dri. *New* 2A **26**
Mereside Av. *Cong* 5D **8**
Merevale Av. *Stoke* 3F **35**
Meriden Rd. *New* 4F **39**
Merino Clo. *Stoke* 6H **41**
Merlin Clo. *Stoke* 3K **21**
Merlin Grn. *Mad* 2B **30**
Merlin Way. *Kid* 7G **13**
Merrial St. *New* 4E **32** (3D **6**)
Merrick St. *Stoke* 7C **28**
Merrion Dri. *Stoke* 2A **28**
Mersey Rd. *New* 3D **38**
Mersey St. *Stoke* 1A **34** (4D **4**)
Merthyr Gro. *Knyp* 4D **14**
Merton St. *Stoke* 2H **41**
Metcalfe Rd. *Stoke* 1K **27**
Metro Bus. Pk. *Stoke* 2K **33** (4B **4**)
Mews Clo. *Stoke* 3F **35**
Mews, The. *New* 1G **33**
Michael Clo. *Stoke* 3C **42**
Michaels Clo. *New* 5F **27**
Michigan Gro. *Stoke* 6A **40**
Micklea La. *Long* 7A **16**
Mickleby Way. *Stoke* 7D **42**
Middle Cross St. *Stoke* 2H **41**
Middlefield Rd. *Stoke* 5J **35**
Middle La. *Cong* 3K **9**
Middle Madeley. **6A 30**
Middleport. **5J 27**
Middleton Clo. *Stoke* 1D **28**
Midfield Clo. *Gil H* 2H **15**
Midhurst Clo. *Pac* 3J **21**
Midway Dri. *B Bri* 1F **49**
Midway, The. *New* 5E **32** (4C **6**)
Midwinter Ct. *Stoke* 6H **27**
Milan Dri. *New* 7B **32**
Milborne Dri. *New* 1F **39**
Milburn Rd. *Stoke* 5A **28**
Milehouse La. *New* 1E **32**
Miles Bank. *Stoke* 3F **5**
Miles Green. **4F 25**
Miles Grn. Rd. *Big E* 4F **25**
Milford Av. *Werr* 1C **36**
Milford Rd. *New* 6D **32** (6B **6**)
Milford St. *Stoke* 1E **40**
Milgreen Av. *Stoke* 5C **28**
Milk St. *Cong* 4F **9**
Milk St. *Leek* 2G **17**
Millbank Pl. *New* 4C **32**
Millbank St. *Stoke* 3H **41**
Millbridge Clo. *Stoke* 1C **48**
Millbrook Gro. *Stoke* 3F **29**
Millbrook Way. *C'dle* 4H **45**
Mill Clo. *Cav* 3D **42**
Mill Ct. *Stoke* 7H **39**
Millend. **6D 18**
Mill End La. *Big E* 6D **18**
Millennium Way. *High B* 2C **26**
Millers La. *Stoke* 3F **29**
Miller St. *New* 4F **33** (2F **7**)
Millers Vw. *C'dle* 4J **45**
Millers Vw. *Kid* 2D **20**
Millers Wharf. *Rode H* 3G **11**
Millett Rd. *Stoke* 2F **35**
Millfield Cres. *Stoke* 3F **29**
Mill Fields. *Cong* 4F **9**
Mill Grn. *Cong* 4F **9**
Mill Gro. *C'dle* 4H **45**
Mill Gro. *Tal* 2A **20**
Mill Hayes Rd. *Knyp* 7B **14**
Mill Hayes Rd. *Stoke* 3H **27**
Mill Hill Cres. *Stoke* 7K **21**
Mill Ho. Dri. *C'dle* 5H **45**
Millicent St. *Stoke* 7D **34**
Mill La. *Mad* 6A **30**
Mill La. *Sch G* 3D **12**
Millmead. *Rode H* 3G **11**
Mill Ri. *Kid* 2D **20**
Millrise Rd. *Stoke* 3F **29**
Mill Rd. *C'dle* 4H **45**
Millstone Av. *Tal* 2B **20**
Mill Stream Clo. *C'dle* 4H **45**
Mill St. *Cong* 3H **9**
(Buxton Rd.)
Mill St. *Cong* 4F **9**
(Swan Bank)
Mill St. *Leek* 3E **16**
Mill St. *New* 4A **32**
Milltown Way. *Leek* 5H **17**
Mill Vw. *Stoke* 5C **22**
Millward Rd. *Stoke* 2H **35**
Millwaters. *C'dle* 4H **45**
Milner Ter. *Leek* 2H **17**
Milnes Clo. *Stoke* 4F **41**
Milton. **3G 29**
Milton Cres. *Tal* 3K **19**
Milton M. Als *7E* ***10***
(off Crewe Rd.)
Milton Rd. *Stoke* 5C **28**
Milton St. *Stoke* 2A **34** (5C **4**)
Milvale St. *Stoke* 5H **27**
Milverton Pl. *Stoke* 3F **41**
Milward Gro. *Stoke* 1A **48**
Minard Gro. *Stoke* 2B **42**
Minden Gro. *Stoke* 4C **28**
Mineal Rd. *Stoke* 6J **35**
Minerva Clo. *Knyp* 5A **14**
Minerva Rd. *Stoke* 7E **34**
Minfield Clo. *Kid* 3D **20**
Minshall Ct. Stoke *1B* ***40***
(off Minshall St.)
Minshall St. *Stoke* 1B **40**
Minster St. *Stoke* 3A **28**
Minton Clo. *C'dle* 5G **45**
Minton Clo. *Cong* 6K **9**
Minton Pl. *New* 7G **27**
Minton St. *New* 7G **27**
Minton St. *Stoke* 5H **33**
Miranda Gro. *Stoke* 3C **28**
Mistley Wlk. *Stoke* 4F **21**
Mitchell Av. *Tal* 2A **20**
Mitchell Dri. *Tal* 2A **20**
Mitchell Memorial Youth Cen. & Theatre. **2B 34 (4E 5)**
Mitchell St. *Stoke* 3J **27**
Moat La. *A'ly* 2B **24**
Moat, The. *Stoke* 2B **42**
Mobberley. **6G 45**
Mobberley Rd. *Stoke* 3F **21**
Moddershall Oaks. *Knen* 7A **48**
Moffat Gro. *Stoke* 6K **35**
Moffatt Way. *New* 3G **31**
Mollatts Clo. *Leek* 7C **16**
Mollatts Wood Rd. *Leek* 7C **16**
Mollison Rd. *Stoke* 6B **42**
Monaco Pl. *New* 6B **32**
Monkhouse. **2F 45**
Monkhouse. *C'dle* 3G **45**
Monkleigh Clo. *Stoke* 2A **46**
Monks Clo. *New* 7F **33**
Monkton Clo. *Stoke* 5F **41**
Monmouth Pl. *New* 2G **39**
Monsal Gro. *Stoke* 7E **28**
Montfort Pl. *New* 7E **32**
Montgomery Ct. *New* 4D **32** (2A **6**)
Montgomery Pl. *Stoke* 4C **42**
Montrose St. *Stoke* 1E **40**
Monty Pl. *Stoke* 1G **41**
Monument Rd. *Tal P* 5A **20**
Monument Vw. *Big E* 2G **25**
Monument Vw. *Mad H* 5B **30**
Monyash Clo. *Stoke* 7D **42**
Monyash Dri. *Leek* 4H **17**
Moody St. *Cong* 5F **9**
Moor Clo. *Bid* 1D **14**
Moorcroft Av. *New* 3E **38**
Moorcroft Clo. *C'dle* 5F **45**
Moorcroft Mus. **5A 28**
Moore St. *Stoke* 5K **27**
Moorfield Av. *Bid* 2B **14**
Moorfields. *Leek* 4G **17**
Moor Green. **6H 43**
Moorhead Dri. *Bag* 7K **23**
Moorhouse Av. *Als* 6E **10**
Moorhouse St. *Leek* 4G **17**
Moorings. *Cong* 6G **9**
Moorland Av. *Werr* 1C **36**
Moorland Clo. *Werr* 1C **36**
Moorland Rd. *Bid* 1C **14**
Moorland Rd. *Leek* 4J **17**
Moorland Rd. *Mow C* 3G **13**
Moorland Rd. *Stoke* 4K **27**
Moorlands Ct. *Bid* 2C **14**
Moorland Vw. *Stoke* 1B **28**
Moorland Wlk. C'dle *3G* ***45***
(off High St.)
Moor La. *C'dle* 2J **45**
Moorside Rd. *Werr* 1E **36**
Moorson Av. *Sch G* 2C **12**
Moor St. *Cong* 5G **9**
Moorsyde Rd. *Stoke* 1H **39**
Moorthorne Cres. *New* 6D **26**
Moorview Gdns. *Har* 5H **13**
Moran Gro. *Stoke* 5H **27**
Moran Rd. *New* 3C **32** (1A **6**)
Moresby Clo. *Stoke* 3G **29**
Moreton Av. *New* 6G **39**
Moreton Clo. *Kid* 3E **20**
Moreton Clo. *Werr* 3C **36**
Moreton Dri. *Als* 7D **10**
Moreton Ho. *New* 1G **33**
Moreton Pde. *New* 1G **33**
Morgan Way. *Stoke* 5K **21**
Morley Dri. *Cong* 6J **9**
Morley St. *Leek* 4E **16**
Morley St. *Stoke* 2A **34** (4D **4**)
Morningside. *Mad* 2B **30**
Mornington Rd. *Stoke* 4C **28**
Morpeth St. *Stoke* 3H **41**
Morris Sq. *New* 7G **27**
Morston Dri. *New* 4E **38**
Mortimer Pl. *Stoke* 2A **42**
Morton St. *Stoke* 5H **27**
Morville Clo. *Stoke* 6D **34**
Mosedale Av. *Stoke* 6A **42**
Moss Clo. *Werr* 1C **36**
Mossfield Cres. *Kid* 1E **20**
Mossfield Dri. *Bid* 3D **14**
Mossfield Rd. *Stoke* 6H **35**
Moss Fields. *Als* 7B **10**
Moss Grn. Rd. *Stoke* 6J **35**
Moss Gro. *New* 1A **26**
Moss Hill. **6J 23**
Moss Hill. *Stoc B* 6J **23**
Mossland Rd. *Stoke* 1H **41**
Moss La. *C'dle* 5J **45**
Moss La. *Cong* 1G **9**
Moss La. *Mad* 2A **30**
Moss La. *Sch G* 6B **12**
Moss La. *Spot A* 7D **48**
Mossley. **7K 9**
Mossley Ct. *Cong* 7H **9**
Mossley Gth. Clo. *Cong* 6J **9**
Moss Pk. Av. *Werr* 1B **36**
Moss Pl. *Kid* 7E **12**
Moss Ri. *New* 5F **39**
Moss Rd. *Cong* 7H **9**
Moss Side. *Stoke* 4D **28**
Moss St. *Stoke* 6D **22**
Moss Way. *Als* 7B **10**
Moston Ct. Cong *4H* ***9***
(off Brunswick St.)
Moston St. *Stoke* 7C **28**
Mostyn Clo. *Knyp* 4D **14**
Mott Pl. *Stoke* 4H **27**
Moulton Rd. *Stoke* 2G **41**
Mounfield Pl. *Stoke* 7C **34**
Mount Av. *Stoke* 6J **33**
Mountbatten Way. *Cong* 4F **9**
Mount Clo. *Werr* 1D **36**
Mountford St. *Stoke* 3J **27**
Mount Pl. *For* 7H **43**
Mount Pleasant. **1C 40**
(Fenton)
Mount Pleasant. **4E 12**
(Mow Cop)
Mount Pleasant. *C'dle* 3F **45**
Mount Pleasant. *Ches* 6B **26**
Mount Pleasant. *Cong* 5G **9**
Mount Pleasant. *Kid* 2D **20**
Mount Pleasant. *Leek* 3F **17**
Mount Pleasant. *New* 5F **33** (4F **7**)
Mount Pleasant. *Stoke* 2A **34** (5C **4**)
Mt. Pleasant Dri. Leek *3F* ***17***
(off Mount Pleasant)
Mt. Pleasant Rd. *Sch G* 3E **12**
Mount Rd. *B Bri* 7H **43**
Mount Rd. *Kid* 2D **20**
Mount Rd. *Leek* 3J **17**
Mountside Gdns. *Leek* 3J **17**
Mountsorrel Clo. *Stoke* 1B **46**
Mount St. *New* 6B **26**
Mount St. *Stoke* 7C **28** (1H **5**)
Mount, The. *Cong* 5C **8**
Mount, The. *Kid* 2D **20**
Mount, The. *New* 6B **26**
Mount, The. *Sch G* 3B **12**
Mousley St. *Stoke* 4H **27**
Mowbray Wlk. *Stoke* 4E **28**
Mow Cop. **3G 13**
Mow Cop. **3G 13**
Mow Cop Rd. *Mow C* 5F **13**
Mow La. *Mow C & Gil H* 1K **13**
Mow La. *Sch G & Mow C* 5D **12**
Moxley Av. *Stoke* 5C **28**
Mulberry Pl. *New* 4B **26**
Mulberry St. *Stoke* 2C **34** (4H **5**)
Mulgrave St. *Stoke* 7A **28** (1C **4**)
Mullberry Way. *Leek* 5H **17**
Mulliner Clo. *Stoke* 2J **35**
Munro St. *Stoke* 1K **39**
Munster Ter. *Stoke* 1J **39**
Murhall St. *Stoke* 4H **27**
Murray St. *Stoke* 4F **21**
Mustang Clo. *Stoke* 7F **21**
Myatt St. *Stoke* 7C **28** (1H **5**)
Mynors St. *Stoke* 1C **34** (2H **5**)
Myott Av. *New* 6D **32** (5B **6**)
Myrtle Av. *Stoke* 3C **42**

N

Nabbs Clo. *Kid* 1E **20**
Nabbswood Rd. *Kid* 1E **20**
Nab Hill Av. *Leek* 3D **16**
Nab Hill Ct. *Leek* 3D **16**
Nantwich Rd. *A'ly* 3A **24**
Napier Gdns. *Kid* 1D **20**
Napier St. *Stoke* 7C **34**
Naples Dri. *New* 7C **32**
Narvik Cres. *Stoke* 2B **28**
Naseby Rd. *Cong* 4C **8**
Nashe Dri. *Stoke* 4E **40**
Nash Peake St. *Stoke* 1F **27**
Nash St. *New* 3B **32**
Nathan Clo. *Stoke* 3E **42**
Navigation Rd. *Stoke* 5J **27**
Navigation St. *Stoke* 5H **27**
Naylor St. *Stoke* 6J **21**
Naylor Yd. Leek *3F* ***17***
(off Mount Pleasant)
Neale Pl. *Stoke* 7G **29**
Neath Clo. *Stoke* 3J **41**
Neath Pl. *Stoke* 7H **35**
Nellan Cres. *Stoke* 3C **28**
Nelson Bank. *Stoke* 4D **20**
Nelson Bldgs. *Kid* 2D **20**
Nelson Gro. *Als* 1G **19**
Nelson Ind. Est. *Tal* 2K **19**
Nelson Pl. *New* 4F **33** (3E **7**)

66 A-Z Stoke

Nelson Pl. *Stoke* 2C **34** (4H **5**)
Nelson Rd. *Stoke* 5H **33**
Nelson St. *Cong* 5F **9**
Nelson St. *Leek* 2G **17**
Nelson St. *New* 7F **27**
Nelson St. *Stoke* 1C **40**
Nephew St. *Stoke* 4H **27**
Neptune Gro. *Stoke* 6E **28**
Ness Gro. *C'dle* 1H **45**
Nethercote Pl. *Stoke* 5J **35**
Netherset Hey La. *Mad* 7A **30**
Netherton Gro. *Stoke* 2G **29**
Netley Pl. *Stoke* 7D **40**
Nevada La. *Hot I* 4A **28**
Neville St. *Stoke* 2J **39**
Nevin Av. *Knyp* 5C **14**
Newark Gro. *Stoke* 4F **21**
New Av. *Dray* 1K **49**
Newbold Cl. *Cong* 4H **9**
. . . . (off Herbert St.)
Newborough Clo. *Stoke* 6D **28**
Newburn Gro. *Stoke* 6A **40**
Newbury Gro. *Stoke* 7D **40**
Newby Ct. *Cong* 6C **8**
Newcastle Bus. Cen. *P East* . .4D **26**
Newcastle Crematorium.
. . . . *New* 5F **27**
Newcastle La. *Stoke* 7G **33**
Newcastle Rd. *A'bry & Cong* . . .7C **8**
Newcastle Rd. *Leek* 6D **16**
Newcastle Rd.
. . . . *Mad & Mad H* 1B **30**
Newcastle Rd. *New* 6F **39**
Newcastle Rd. *Stoke* 7G **33**
Newcastle Rd. *Tal* 3A **20**
Newcastle St. *New* 3K **31**
Newcastle St. *Stoke* 4G **27**
Newcastle-under-Lyme.
. . . . .4E **32** (3D **6**)
New Century St. *Stoke*
. . . . .1A **34** (3C **4**)
Newchapel. 1H **21**
New Chapel Ct. *Stoke* 7G **21**
Newchapel Observatory. . . .1H **21**
Newchapel Rd. *Kid* 7E **12**
New Clo. Av. *For* 6J **43**
Newcomen Gro. *Stoke* 6J **35**
Newcroft St. *New* 7F **27**
Newcrofts Wlk. *Stoke* 5C **22**
Newfield. 7F **21**
Newfield St. *Stoke* 7G **21**
Newfield Trad. Est. *Stoke* 6G **21**
Newfold Cres. *Brn E* 3G **23**
Newford Cres. *Stoke* 3E **28**
New Forest Ind. Est. *Stoke*
. . . . .7C **28** (1F **5**)
New Haden Rd. *C'dle* 4E **44**
New Hall Rd. *Stoke* 4J **41**
New Hall St. *Stoke* 1B **34** (2E **5**)
Newhaven Gro. *Stoke* 2A **46**
New Hayes Rd. *Stoke* 7H **21**
Newhouse Ct. *Stoke* 7G **29**
Newhouse Rd. *Stoke* 7G **29**
Newington Gro. *Stoke* 2B **46**
New Inn La. *Stoke* 5J **39**
New King St. *A'ly* 3D **24**
New Kingsway. *W Coy* 2B **42**
Newlands Clo. *New* 1E **38**
Newlands St. *Stoke* 4A **34**
New La. *Brn E* 2G **23**
New Leek La. *Bid* 2F **15**
Newleigh St. *Stoke* 3G **29**
Newlyn Av. *Cong* 7H **9**
Newman Clo. *Cong* 4D **8**
Newmarket Way. *C'dle* 1H **45**
Newmill St. *Stoke* 3F **29**
Newmount Rd. *Stoke* 1G **41**
New Pk. Gdns. *Stoke* 2B **46**
Newpool. 4A **14**
Newpool Cotts. *Bid* 5A **14**
Newpool Rd. *Knyp* 4K **13**
Newpool Ter. *Brn L* 5A **14**
Newport Gro. *New* 2B **26**
Newport La. *Stoke* 4H **27**
Newport St. *Stoke* 4H **27**
Newquay Ct. *Cong* 7G **9**

New Rd. *Big E* 2E **24**
New Rd. *Dil* 3K **43**
New Rd. *Mad* 1B **30**
New Rd. *Stoke* 2A **36**
New Row. *Mad H* 5B **30**
Newshaw Wlk. *Stoke*
. . . . .1C **34** (3H **5**)
Newstead. 7C **40**
Newstead Rd. *Stoke* 7G **29**
Newstead Trad. Est. *Stoke* 7C **40**
New St. *Bid M* 4E **14**
New St. *Cong* 5G **9**
New St. *Leek* 3G **17**
New St. *New* 7G **27**
New St. *Stoke* 4J **27**
New St. Cotts. *Hav* 1J **9**
Newton Ct. *Werr* 1B **36**
Newton Pl. *Cong* 5H **9**
Newton Rd. *New* 7E **26**
Newton St. *Stoke* 3H **33**
Newtown. *N'cpl* 1H **21**
New Victoria Theatre, The.
. . . . .3G **33** (1G **7**)
Niall Rd. *Stoke* 5J **39**
Nicholas Gro. *Leek* 5C **16**
Nicholas St. *Stoke* 4J **27**
Nicholls St. *Stoke* 1A **40**
Nicholson Way. *Leek* 3E **16**
Nidderdale Clo. *Cong* 2J **9**
Nightingale Way. *Als* 7C **10**
Nile St. *Stoke* 4K **27**
Noblett Rd. *Stoke* 5D **28**
Norbury Av. *Stoke* 3G **29**
Norbury Dri. *Cong* 3G **9**
Norfolk Clo. *New* 4E **38**
Norfolk Gro. *Bid* 1B **14**
Norfolk St. *Cong* 3G **9**
Norfolk Rd. *Kid* 1C **20**
Norfolk St. *Stoke* 3A **34**
Normacot. 4J **41**
Normacot Grange Rd.
. . . . *Stoke* 7A **42**
Normacot Rd. *Stoke* 3H **41**
. . . . (Millbank St.)
Normacot Rd. *Stoke* 4J **41**
. . . . (Queensberry Rd.)
Norman Av. *Stoke* 1J **27**
Normandy Gro. *Stoke* 2F **29**
Norman Gro. *New* 3G **33**
Normanton Gro. *Stoke* 7J **35**
Norris Rd. *Stoke* 1J **27**
Northam Rd. *Stoke* 6C **28**
North Av. *Leek* 4E **16**
Northcliffe. *Leek* 3E **16**
. . . . (off Belle Vue Rd.)
Northcote Av. *Stoke* 5K **33**
Northcote Ct. *New* 4F **33** (2F **7**)
Northcote Pl. *New* 4F **33** (2F **7**)
Northcote St. *Stoke* 4A **34**
Northesk Pl. *New* 1D **38**
Northfield Dri. *Bid* 2K **15**
Northfleet St. *Stoke* 2F **35**
Northgate Clo. *Stoke* 5J **39**
Northolme Gdns. *Als* 6D **10**
North Pl. *Stoke* 6G **29**
North Wlk. *Stoke* 5C **42**
N. West Ter. *Stoke* 3B **28**
Northwood. 1D **34**
. . . . (Stoke-on-Trent)
Northwood. 4F **39**
. . . . (Trentham)
Northwood Clo. *New* 4G **39**

Northwood Ct. *Stoke* 3H **5**
Northwood Grn. *Stoke* 1D **34**
Northwood La. *New* 4F **39**
Northwood Pk. Rd. *Stoke*
. . . . .7C **28** (1H **5**)
. . . . (in two parts)
Northwood Stadium. 1D **34**
Norton Av. *Stoke* 1K **27**
Norton Cres. *Stoke* 4C **28**
Norton Dri. *Stoke* 3C **28**
Norton Green. 6E **22**
Norton Hall Clo. *Stoke* 1D **28**
Norton Ind. Est. *Stoke* 2D **28**
Norton-in-the-Moors. 7D **22**
Norton La. *Stoke* 7D **22**
Norton St. *Stoke* 3G **29**
Norwich Pl. *New* 1F **39**
Norwich Rd. *Stoke* 3J **35**
Novi La. *Leek* 2H **17**
No. 1 Rd. N. *Rad G* 2A **18**
No. 1 Rd. S. *Rad G* 2A **18**
No. 2 Rd. N. *Rad G* 2A **18**
No. 2 Rd. S. *Rad G* 2A **18**
Nunn's Clo. *Stoke* 1D **42**
Nunn St. *Leek* 3E **16**
Nursery Av. *Stoc B* 1H **29**
Nursery Clo. Brn E 4G **23**
. . . . (off High La.)
Nursery Clo. *C'dle* 3F **45**
Nursery Clo. *Tal* 2A **20**
Nursery Dri. *Gil H* 2H **15**
Nursery La. *Cong* 5G **9**
Nursery La. *Stoc B* 1H **29**
Nursery Rd. *Als* 7A **10**
Nursery Rd. *Sch G* 5B **12**
Nursery St. *Stoke* 1K **39**
Nutbrook Av. *Stoke* 1B **40**
Nyewood Av. *Stoke* 1J **41**

Ogden Rd. *Stoke* 2B **34** (5F **5**)
Ogmore Gro. *Stoke* 6B **42**
O'Hare Pl. *Leek* 2H **17**
Ohio Gro. *Hot I* 4A **28**
Oldacres Rd. *Stoke* 2A **46**
Old Butt La. *Tal* 1K **19**
Old Chapel Clo. *K'le* 5F **31**
Oldcott Cres. *Kid* 3F **21**
Oldcott Dri. *Kid* 3F **21**
Oldcourt St. *Stoke* 1G **27**
Oldfield Av. *Stoke* 6C **22**
Oldfield Ind. Est. *Stoke* 2E **40**
Oldfield St. *Stoke* 1F **41**
Old Hall Dri. *New* 4C **8**
Old Hall St. *Stoke* 1B **34** (4F **5**)
Oldham St. *Join I* 3C **34** (6H **5**)
Oldhill Clo. *Tal P* 6B **20**
Old La. *Brn E* 2F **23**
Old Man of Mow, The. 2G **13**
. . . . (National Trust)
Oldmill St. *Stoke* 6B **34**
Old Rd. *B'stn* 4B **46**
Old Rd. *Big E* 1F **25**
Old Rd. *Knvn* 7H **47**
Old School Clo. *Kid* 2D **20**
Old Town Rd. *Stoke* . . .7B **28** (1F **5**)
Old Tramway. *Stoke* 1E **40**
Oldway Pl. *Stoke* 1H **41**
Old Wharf Pl. *Stoke* 3D **34**
Old Whieldon Rd. *Stoke* 7B **34**
Olive Gro. *New* 3A **26**
Oliver Lodge Ho. Stoke 6K **33**
. . . . (off Epworth St.)
Oliver Rd. *Stoke* 6H **33**
Olof Palme Gro. *Stoke* 4H **41**
Omega Way. *Stoke* 6K **39**
Onsetter Rd. *Stoke* 6J **35**
Onslow Dri. *New* 4E **26**
Ontario Clo. *Stoke* 6K **39**
Opal Rd. *Stoke* 1D **40**
Orb St. *Stoke* 2B **34** (4E **5**)
Orchard Cl. *Als* 6F **11**
Orchard Cres. *Tal* 2A **20**
Orchard Gdns. *Leek* 3D **16**
Orchard Pl. *B'stn* 6C **46**
Orchard Ri. *B Bri* 7F **43**
Orchards, The. *Stoke* 2D **40**
Orchard St. *New* 7F **27**
Orchard, The. *Brn E* 3F **23**
Orchard Way. *Cong* 4C **8**
Orchid Gro. *Stoke* 4H **33**
Orford Rd. *End* 2K **23**
Orford St. *New* 5G **27**
Orford Way. *Stoke* 6D **40**
Orgreaves Clo. *New* 4E **26**
Orgreave St. *Stoke* 5K **27**
Oriel St. *Stoke* 6K **33**
Orion Ct. *New* 5C **32** (5A **6**)
Orion St. *Stoke* 3B **28**
Orkney Av. *Pac* 3J **21**
Orlestone Pl. *Stoke* 4K **21**
Orme Rd. *Knyp* 5C **14**
Orme Rd. *New* 4C **32** (3A **6**)
Orme St. *Stoke* 4H **27**
Ormonde St. *Stoke* 1E **40**
Orpheus Gro. *Stoke* 6E **28**
Orton Rd. *New* 3D **32**
Orwell Dri. *Stoke* 1A **42**
Orwell Pl. *New* 2E **38**
Osborne Rd. *Stoke* 5H **33**
Osborne St. *Leek* 3H **17**
Osborne St. *Stoke* 6D **28**
Osprey Av. *Stoke* 7B **42**
Osprey Vw. *Kid* 7G **13**
Ostend Pl. *New* 6C **32**
Oswald Av. *Stoke* 1B **42**
Oulton Dri. *Cong* 4B **8**
Oulton Rd. *C'dle* 3J **45**
Oulton Rd. *Stoke* 4A **22**
Outclough Rd. *B Frd* 1A **22**
Outlook, The. *Stoke* 1A **28**
Oval, The. *Stoke* 4F **41**
Oval, The. *Werr* 1F **37**
Overdale Pl. *Leek* 4C **16**
Overhouse St. *Stoke* 3J **27**
Overland Dri. *Brn E* 3F **23**

Oversley Rd. Stoke	4K 21
Over The Hill. Bid M	1F 15
Overton Bank. Leek	3F 17
(off Mill St.)	
Overton Clo. Cong	4E 8
Overton Clo. L'tn	4F 41
Overwood Pl. Stoke	4J 21
Owen Gro. Stoke	3K 27
Oxford.	3K 21
Oxford Av. Stoke	5C 28
Oxford Cres. Stoke	6K 33
Oxford Rd. New	2G 33
Oxford Rd. Stoke	4A 22
Oxford St. Stoke	5K 33
Oxhay Ct. New	2F 33
Oxhay Vw. New	2F 33
Ox-Hey Cres. Bid	1C 14
Ox-Hey Dri. Bid	2J 15

P

Pacific Rd. Stoke	7K 39
Packett St. Stoke	2G 41
Pack Horse La. Stoke	4J 27
Packmoor.	2J 21
Paddock Cotts. Stoke	7K 39
Paddock Ri. Stoke	7K 39
Paddocks Grn. Cong	7H 9
Paddock, The.	4G 45
Paddock, The. Has G	1A 10
Padgbury Clo. Cong	6C 8
Padgbury La. Cong	5B 8
Padlowe St. Stoke	3H 27
Padston Dri. Als	7C 10
Padstow Way. Stoke	2A 46
Padworth St. Stoke	3B 42
Page St. Stoke	1B 34 (2E 5)
Paisley Clo. Stoke	5K 35
Paladin Av. Stoke	2C 42
Palatine Dri. New	6A 26
Pall Mall. Stoke	2B 34 (3E 5)
Palmers Grn. Stoke	5G 33 (4G 7)
Palmerston St. Join l	3C 34 (6G 5)
Palmerston St. New	7F 27
Palmerston Way. Bid	2C 14
Palmer St. Stoke	2J 41
Palmers Way. New	5G 33 (4G 7)
Palomino Clo. Stoke	6H 41
Pandora Gro. Stoke	6E 28
Panturner Rd. Stoke	6J 35
Parade, The. New	4K 31
Paradise St. New	4D 6
Paradise St. Stoke	1G 27
Paragon Av. New	3E 38
Paragon Clo. C'dle	5F 45
Paragon St. Stoke	3J 41
Paramount Bus. Pk. Stoke	4K 27
Paris Av. New	6B 32
Parish Clo. Als	6C 10
Park Av. C'dle	4H 45
Park Av. Kid	3B 26
Park Av. New	7F 27
Park Av. Werr	1E 36
Park Av. W Coy	1B 42
Park Av. W. New	7E 26
Park Bank. Cong	5H 9
Park Clo. Mad	5A 30
Park Ct. Ches	5B 26
Park Dri. B'stn	6B 46
Park Dri. C'dle	2F 45
Park Dri. Stoke	7H 39
Park Dri. Werr	1D 36
Park End.	7B 18
Park End. For	6J 43
Parker Jervis Rd. Stoke	2A 42
Parker St. Leek	3H 17
Parker St. Stoke	1A 34 (4D 4)
Parker Way. Cong	4C 8
Pk. Farm Vw. Stoke	4G 21
Parkfield Rd. Stoke	5H 41
Parkfields. End	2K 23
Parkfields Clo. B'stn	6B 46
Parkfields Clo. New	3H 31
Pk. Hall Av. Stoke	2B 42
Pk. Hall Bus. Village. Stoke	1K 41
Parkhall Country Pk.	6A 36

Pk. Hall Cres. Stoke	2B 42
Pk. Hall Ind. Est. Stoke	2H 27
Pk. Hall Rd. Stoke	7K 35
(in two parts)	
Pk. Hall St. Stoke	2H 41
Parkhead Cres. Stoke	3B 42
Parkhead Dri. Stoke	2B 42
Parkhouse Ind. Est. E. New	3C 26
Parkhouse Ind. Est. W. New	4C 26
Parkhouse Rd. E. P East	3C 26
Parkhouse Rd. W. New	3B 26
Parkhouse St. Stoke	3A 34 (6C 4)
Parklands. Kid	2E 20
Parklands, The. Bid M	1G 15
Parklands, The. Cong	5J 9
Park La. A'ly	6B 18
Park La. C'dle	2F 45
Park La. Cong	5G 9
Park La. End	1K 23
Park La. Knyp	4B 14
Park La. Stoke	1E 40
Park La. Clo. C'dle	3F 45
Parkleigh. Cong	5H 9
Park Pl. Stoke	7D 34
Park Rd. But	4B 38
Park Rd. Cong	4G 9
Park Rd. Leek	2E 16
Park Rd. Sil	4J 31
(in two parts)	
Park Rd. Stoke	3K 27
Park Rd. Werr	1D 36
Parkside. Mad	6A 30
Parkside. Stoke	7A 40
(Trentham)	
Parkside. Stoke	2A 42
(Weston Coyney)	
Parkside Cres. End	1K 23
Parkside Dri. New	2G 33
Parkside Gro. New	2G 33
Parkstone Av. New	5F 33 (5F 7)
Park St. Cong	5G 9
(Kinsey St.)	
Park St. Cong	5G 9
(Moor St.)	
Park St. Stoke	7E 34
Park Ter. Leek	4H 17
Park Ter. Stoke	1H 27
Park Vw. B Bri	1F 49
Park Vw. Cong	4G 9
Pk. View St. Stoke	5G 41
Pk. View Rd. Kid	7D 12
Park Way. For	6H 43
Parkway. Tren	7H 39
Parkway, The. New	7E 32
Parkway, The. Stoke	3B 34
Parkwood Av. Stoke	6J 39
Parliament Row. Stoke	1B 34 (3F 5)
Parliament Sq. Stoke	1B 34 (3F 5)
Parnell Sq. Cong	5J 9
Parrot's Drumble Nature Reserve.	6J 19
Parsonage St. Stoke	7G 21
Parson St. Cong	5E 8
Parton Gro. Stoke	2B 42
Partridge Clo. Cong	6G 9
Partridge Clo. Stoke	7B 42
Pastoral Clo. Mad	3B 30
Patch Mdw. C'dle	3E 44
Patefield Pl. B Frd	1A 22
Patterdale St. Stoke	1K 27
Pavilion Dri. Stoke	7K 27 (1A 4)
Pavilion Way. Cong	4E 8
Paxton St. Stoke	3C 34 (6G 5)
Paynter St. Stoke	1E 40
Peacehaven Gro. Stoke	2B 46
Peacock Hay.	7B 20
Peacock Hay Rd. Tal P	7B 20
Peacock Ho. Stoke	7J 39
Peacock La. New & Han	6D 38
Peacock Vw. Fen I	4E 34
Peak Dale Av. Stoke	4E 20
Peake St. New	2B 32
Peak Vw. Leek	4H 17
Pearl Gro. Stoke	6B 42

Pear Pl. Stoke	6J 35
Pear Tree Clo. B'stn	6C 46
Pear Tree Dri. Mad	1A 30
Pear Tree La. New	4A 26
Pear Tree Rd. Big E	3G 25
Peascroft Rd. Stoke	7C 22
Pebble Mill St. Stoke	2J 33
Peckforton Vw. Kid	4D 20
Peck Mill La. B Frd	2B 22
Pedley Ct. Stoke	6E 40
Pedley Gro. Stoke	3C 28
Peebles Grn. Stoke	3H 35
Peebles Rd. New	3G 31
Peel Ct. Kid	1D 20
(off Attwood St.)	
Peel Dri. A'bry	7D 8
Peel Hollow. A'ly	3B 24
Peel La. A'bry	7D 8
Peel St. Stoke	5H 41
(Dresden)	
Peel St. Stoke	4F 27
(Longport)	
Peel St. Wol	7F 27
Pegasus Gro. Stoke	3C 28
Peggy's Bank. Big E	4G 25
Pegroy Gro. Stoke	3C 28
Pelham St. Stoke	3C 34 (6G 5)
Pemberton Dri. Stoke	2B 48
Pembridge Rd. Stoke	7D 40
Pembroke Dri. New	6D 32 (6A 6)
Pembroke Rd. Stoke	3F 29
Penarth Gro. Stoke	7B 28 (1E 5)
Penarth Pl. New	6D 32 (6A 6)
Pendine Gro. Stoke	7G 35
Penfleet Av. Stoke	5B 42
Pengrove Clo. Stoke	3H 21
Penkhull.	6K 33
Penkhull Ct. Stoke	6K 33
Penkhull New Rd. Stoke	7J 33
Penkhull Ter. Stoke	6K 33
Penk Rd. For	7H 43
Penkville St. Stoke	1K 39
Penmark Gro. Stoke	6K 41
Penmere Dri. New	5F 39
Penmere Dri. Werr	2B 36
Pennell St. Stoke	1G 35
Pennine Way. Bid	2K 15
Pennine Way. New	2B 32
Pennington Clo. Stoke	4D 42
Pennyfields Av. Stoke	3G 27
Pennyfields Rd. N'cpl	1F 21
Penny La. Shop. Mall. C'dle	3G 45
Pennymore Clo. Stoke	6A 40
Penport Gro. Stoke	4F 41
Penrhyn Av. Stoke	3A 28
Penrith Clo. Stoke	2B 46
Penrith Ct. Cong	5C 8
Penrith Ct. New	7E 32
Pensford Gro. Stoke	7E 28
Pentland Gro. New	2B 32
Penton Pl. Stoke	7D 40
Penton Wlk. Stoke	7D 40
Pen y Bont Wlk. Knyp	4D 14
Pepper St. K'le	5F 31
Pepper St. New	4E 32 (4C 6)
Perceval St. Stoke	7D 28
Percival Dri. Stoc B	1H 29
Percy James Clo. Als	6F 11
Percy St. Stoke	1B 34 (3F 5)
Peregrine Gro. Stoke	7B 42
Perivale Clo. Stoke	6F 29
Perkins St. Stoke	4F 21
Perry Clo. Stoke	2C 34 (4G 5)
Perrymount Ct. Stoke	7J 33
Persia Wlk. Stoke	1G 27
Perth St. Stoke	1F 41
Perthy Gro. Stoke	7J 39
Perton Wood Vw. Stoke	3E 40
Petersfield Rd. Stoke	4K 21
Peterson Ho. Stoke	6A 42
Petrel Gro. Stoke	7C 42
Pevensey Gro. Stoke	7H 35
Philip La. Werr	1C 36
Philip St. Stoke	7D 34
Phillipson Way. Stoke	4C 28
Phipp Pl. Stoke	6C 40
Phoenix Clo. Kid	1F 21

Phoenix St. Stoke	1G 27
Picasso Ri. Stoke	1C 48
Piccadilly. Stoke	2B 34 (4E 5)
Piccadilly Arc. Stoke	1B 34 (3E 5)
Piccadilly St. Stoke	1G 27
Pickering Clo. Stoke	5F 41
Pickford Pl. Stoke	5A 42
Pickmere Clo. Stoke	1G 29
Pickwick Pl. Tal	1A 20
Pickwood Av. Leek	4H 17
Pickwood Clo. Leek	4H 17
Picton St. Leek	3E 16
Picton St. Stoke	2C 34 (4H 5)
Pidduck St. Stoke	5H 27
Pierce St. Stoke	1G 27
Piggott Gro. Stoke	2F 35
Pikemere Rd. Als	5C 10
Pilkington Av. New	7D 32
Pillar Clo. Stoke	6J 35
Pilsbury St. New	6G 27
Pilsden Pl. Stoke	7D 42
Pine Clo. Tal	4A 20
Pine Ct. Als	6F 11
Pine Ct. B Bri	7E 42
Pinehurst Clo. New	3E 38
Pine Rd. Stoke	2B 40
Pine Tree Dri. B Bri	7E 42
Pinewood Cres. Stoke	4C 42
Pinewood Gro. B Bri	1H 49
Pinewood Gro. New	3B 26
Pinfold Av. Stoke	7C 22
Pinhoe Pl. Stoke	3K 41
Pinnox St. Stoke	2H 27
Pioneer Pl. Stoke	1B 28
(off Brammer St.)	
Pippins, The. New	3F 39
Pireford Pl. New	3D 26
Pirehill Rd. New	3E 26
Pirie Clo. Cong	3J 9
Pirie Rd. Cong	2J 9
Pitcairn St. Stoke	1H 27
Pitcher La. Leek	4J 17
Pitfield Av. New	3D 26
Pitfield House.	3F 33 (1F 7)
(Arts Cen.)	
Pitgreen La. New	6F 27
Pit La. Tal P	5K 19
Pitlea Pl. Stoke	7H 35
Pitsford St. Stoke	4J 41
Pitts Hill.	6H 21
Pitts Hill Bank. Stoke	6J 21
Pitt St. E. Stoke	4K 27
Pitt St. W. Stoke	5K 27
Plainfield Gro. Stoke	5J 35
Plaisaunce, The. New	7E 32
Plane Gro. New	3B 26
Plantation Pk. K'le	7K 31
Plantation Rd. Stoke	1C 46
Plant St. C'dle	3H 45
Plant St. Stoke	2H 41
Platts Av. End	5K 23
Pleasant St. Stoke	5J 27
Plex St. Stoke	1G 27
Plex, The. Als	6E 10
Pleydell St. Stoke	5E 28
Plough Cft. Als	7B 10
Plough St. Stoke	7C 28 (1G 5)
Plover Clo. Stoke	7B 42
Plover Dri. Bid	2D 14
Plover Fld. Mad	2A 30
Plumtree Gro. Stoke	6E 28
Plymouth Gro. New	5C 26
Pochard Clo. Stoke	2C 28
Podmore Av. Als B	6G 25
Podmore La. Halm	6E 24
(in two parts)	
Podmore St. Stoke	5K 27
Podmore Ter. Halm	6E 24
Pointon Gro. Stoke	6F 23
Polperro Way. Stoke	7B 42
Pomona Ri. Stoke	4C 28
Pool Dam. New	5E 32 (5C 6)
Poole Av. Stoke	2G 29
Poolend.	1C 16
Pooles Rd. Bid M	2G 15
Poolfield Clo. New	5C 32 (5A 6)
Poolfield Av. N. New	5D 32 (4A 6)

Poolfields—Riley Av.

Poolfields. 5D 32 (5B 6)
Poolfields Clo. New 5C 32
Poolfields Ct. Brn E 4H 23
Poolhill Clo. Stoke 4F 41
Poolside. Mad 2B 30
Poolside. New 4D 32 (3B 6)
Poolside. Sch G 3H 11
Poolside. Stoke 6E 40
Poolside Ct. Als 6F 11
Pool St. New 5D 32 (5B 6)
Pool St. Stoke 7G 35
Poplar Av. New 2D 32
Poplar Clo. B Bri 1H 49
Poplar Clo. Cong 3C 8
Poplar Clo. New 2D 32
Poplar Ct. New 2D 32
Poplar Dri. Als 1F 19
Poplar Dri. Kid 2D 20
Poplar Dri. Stoke 4D 40
Poplar Gro. New 4G 33 (2G 7)
Poplar Gro. Stoke 5F 41
Poppyfields. Als 7C 10
Porlock Gro. Stoke 1A 46
Porthill. 5F 27
Porthill Bank. New 6F 27
Porthill Grange. New 6F 27
Porthill Grn. New 6F 27
Porthill Rd. Stoke 5G 27
Portland Clo. B Bri 7E 42
Portland Dri. Bid 2J 15
Portland Dri. For 6J 43
Portland Dri. Sch G 4B 12
Portland Gro. New 3E 38
Portland M. New 6E 26
Portland Pl. B'stn 3E 46
Portland Rd. Stoke 2G 41
Portland St. Leek 3G 17
Portland St. Stoke 7A 28 (1C 4)
Portland St. N. Leek 3G 17
Portland St. S. Leek 3G 17
Port St. Stoke 5H 27
Port Va. Ct. Stoke 3K 27
Port Vale F.C. (Vale Pk.) 3K 27
Port Va. St. Stoke 5H 27
Post La. End 2K 23
Post Office Sq. Mad 3B 30
Post Office Ter. Ful 7F 49
Potteries Mus. & Art Gallery, The. 2B 34 (4E 5)
Potteries Shop. Cen. Stoke 1B 34 (2F 5)
Potteries Way. Stoke 7B 28 (1E 5) (in two parts)
Potters Barn, The. 1B 10
Potters Barn, The. Has G 1B 10
Potters End. Bid 1A 14
Poulson St. Stoke 6A 34
Pound Gdns. Stoke 7C 22
Poundsgate Gro. Stoke 6A 40
Povey Pl. New 3E 26
Powderham Clo. Stoke 3H 21
Powell St. Stoke 7A 28 (1C 4)
Power Gro. Stoke 2F 41
Powerleague Soccer Cen. 3C 40
Power Wash Trad. Est. Knyp 5A 14
Powy Dri. Kid 1E 20
Premier Gdns. Kid 1C 20
Prestbury Av. New 5E 38
Preston St. Stoke 4B 28
Pretoria Rd. Stoke 2K 33 (6A 4)
Priam Clo. New 3E 26
Price St. Stoke 3J 27
Priestley Dri. Stoke 2J 41
Priesty Ct. Cong 5F 9
Priesty Fields. Cong 5F 9
Prime St. Stoke 7D 28
Primitive St. Mow C 3F 13
Primrose Dell. Mad 2A 30
Primrose Gro. New 3F 33
Primrose Hill. Stoke 4K 39
Primrose Vale. 4J 9
Prince Charles Av. Leek 2J 17
Prince George St. C'dle 3G 45
Prince's Rd. Stoke 5J 33
Princess Av. A'ly 3E 24
Princess Av. Leek 1J 17
Princess Ct. Tal P 6A 20
Princess Dri. Stoke 3B 42
Princes Sq. Stoke 4G 27
Princess St. Bid 3C 14
Princess St. Cong 4F 9
Princess St. New 5F 33 (4F 7)
Princess St. Tal P 6A 20
Prince St. Leek 2G 17
Princetown Clo. Stoke 7B 42
Priorfield Clo. Stoke 2G 41
Priory Av. Leek 1H 17
Priory Clo. Cong 7K 9
Priory Ct. Stoke 7H 29
Priory Pl. Kid 7E 12
Priory Rd. New 6D 32 (6B 6)
Priory Rd. Stoke 6G 29
Priory, The. End 1K 23
Probyn Ct. Stoke 4H 41
Prospect Pl. Leek 4F 17
Prospect Rd. Leek 4H 17
Prospect St. Cong 5E 8
Prospect St. Stoke 6H 27
Prospect Ter. New 4D 32 (2B 6)
Providence Sq. Stoke 1G 5
Providence St. Stoke 7C 28
Provost Pl. Leek 2H 17
Pullman Ct. C'dle 4F 45
Pump Bank. K'le 6G 31
Pump St. Leek 2G 17
Pump St. New 5D 32 (5B 6)
Pump St. Stoke 6K 33
Purbeck St. Stoke 5A 28
Purser Cres. New 7E 26
Pyenest St. Stoke 3A 34

Q

Quabbs La. For 6K 43
Quadrangle, The. End 2K 23
Quadrant Rd. Stoke 1B 34 (2E 5)
Quadrant, The. Stoke 2F 5
Quail Gro. Stoke 7B 42
Quarry Av. Stoke 5J 33
Quarry Bank. 4G 31
Quarry Bank Rd. K'le 4G 31
Quarry Clo. Stoc B 1H 29
Quarry Clo. Werr 1B 36
Quarry Rd. Stoke 5J 33
Quarry Ter. Kid 2D 20
Quarry Wlk. Path. C'dle 6K 45
Quayside. Cong 6G 9
Queen Anne St. Stoke 5A 34
Queen Elizabeth II Ct. Stoke 7C 34
Queen Mary Rd. Stoke 5K 39
Queen Mary's Dri. B'stn 3D 46
Queens Av. Stoke 1H 27
Queensberry Rd. Stoke 4J 41
Queens Clo. B'stn 5E 46
Queens Ct. New 4F 33 (2E 7)
Queens Ct. Stoke 5G 41 (off Queen's Pk. Av.)
Queen's Dri. Bid 4C 14
Queens Dri. Leek 1J 17
Queens Gdns. Tal P 5A 20
Queensmead Rd. Stoke 7A 42
Queen's Pk. Av. Stoke 5G 41
Queen's Rd. Stoke 5J 33
Queens Row. B'stn 5E 46
Queen's Ter. Stoke 1D 34
Queen St. A'ly 3D 24
Queen St. C'dle 3H 45
Queen St. Ches 5B 26
Queen St. Cong 5E 8 (Booth St.)
Queen St. Cong 3H 9 (Havannah St.)
Queen St. Kid 1D 20
Queen St. Leek 3G 17
Queen St. New 6E 26 (Heaton Ter.)
Queen St. New 4F 33 (2E 7) (Nelson Pl.)
Queen St. Stoke 4J 27
Queens Wlk. Stoke 2C 42
Queensway. Als 5C 10
Queens Way. New 7E 32
Queensway Ct. Stoke 5B 42 (off Broadway)
Queensway Ind. Est. Stoke 4F 27
Quinta Rd. Cong 4C 8
Quintin Wlk. Stoke 2B 28
Quinton Gro. New 1E 32

R

Race Course. New 4K 31
Racecourse Rd. Stoke 2K 39
Rachel Gro. Stoke 7G 35
Radford Rd. Stoke 4J 33
Radley Way. Werr 2C 36
Radnor. 1A 8
Radnor Clo. Cong 4D 8
Radnor Pk. Trad. Est. Cong 3C 8
Radstone Ri. New 3E 38
Radway Green. 2A 18
Radway Grn. Rd. Rad G 3A 18
Radway Green Sports & Social Club. 6F 11
Raglan St. Stoke 7C 34
Raglan Wlk. Stoke 7C 34 (off Raglan St.)
Railton Av. Stoke 5F 41
Railway Cotts. Brn L 6A 14
Railway Cotts. Cong 6J 9
Railway Cotts. Stoke 3B 40
Railway Ct. End 2K 23
Railway Enterprise Cen. Stoke 4K 33
Railway Pas. Stoke 2H 41
Railway St. Stoke 2H 27
Railway Ter. B Bri 7F 43
Railway Ter. Stoke 3H 41
Rainford Clo. Pac 2J 21
Rainham Gro. Stoke 3K 21
Rakeway. 5J 45
Rakeway Rd. C'dle 5H 45
Ralph Dri. Stoke 4D 28
Ramage Gro. Stoke 5J 41
Ramsay Clo. B'stn 3D 46
Ramsey Rd. New 3D 32
Ramsey St. Stoke 1B 40
Ramshaw Gro. Stoke 7J 35
Ramshaw Vw. Leek 1H 17
Randel La. Stoke 3E 20
Ranelagh St. Stoke 2B 34 (5E 5)
Rangemore Ter. New 2G 33
Ransome Pl. Stoke 2K 41
Ranworth Clo. New 4E 38
Rathbone Av. New 2G 33
Rathbone St. Stoke 1H 27
Rattigan Dri. Stoke 2A 42
Ratton St. Stoke 1C 34 (2G 5)
Ravenna Way. Stoke 1K 41
Ravenscliffe. 6D 20
Ravenscliffe. New 5F 27 (off First Av.)
Ravenscliffe Rd. Kid 3D 20
Ravens Clo. Big E 1F 25
Ravensdale. 2F 27
Ravenside Retail Pk. Stoke 5C 34
Raven's La. Big E 1G 25
Ravenswood Clo. New 3D 38
Rawle Clo. C'dle 3F 45
Rawlins St. Stoke 7D 28 (1H 5)
Rayleigh Way. Stoke 4J 35
Raymond Av. Stoke 5C 28
Raymond St. Stoke 3B 34 (6E 5)
Reade's La. Cong 7K 9
Reading Way. Stoke 3J 35
Reads Rd. Fen I 5E 34
Rebecca St. Stoke 5A 34
Recorder Gro. Stoke 5A 22
Recreation Rd. Stoke 4K 41
Rectory Gdns. Tal P 5A 20
Rectory Pas. Stoke 3A 34 (6D 4)
Rectory Rd. Stoke 3A 34 (6C 4)
Rectory St. Stoke 3A 34 (6C 4)
Rectory Vw. Tal P 5A 20
Red Bank. Stoke 5H 41
Redbridge Clo. Stoke 5J 39
Red Bull. 7A 12
Redcar Rd. Stoke 7K 39
Redfern Av. Cong 3H 9
Red Hall La. Halm 1C 30
Redheath Clo. New 3H 31
Redheath Cotts. New 3G 31
Redhills Rd. Stoke 4E 28
Red Ho. Cres. Stoke 3F 41
Redland Dri. Stoke 2J 35
Red La. L Oaks 2H 29
Red La. Mad 3B 30
Red Lion Clo. Tal 4A 20
Red Lion Pas. Stoke 2A 34 (5D 4)
Red Lion Sq. Ches 5B 26
Redman Gro. Stoke 5B 28
Redmine Clo. New 1D 32
Red Street. 1A 26
Redwing Dri. Bid 2D 14
Redwing Gro. Pac 2H 21
Redwood Pl. Stoke 5A 42
Reedbed Clo. Stoke 1B 28
Reedham Way. Stoke 3J 35
Reeves Av. New 1E 32
Reeves Av. Stoke 1K 27
Refinery St. New 5F 33 (5E 7)
Regency Clo. Tal P 6A 20
Regency Dri. Stoc B 7G 23
Regent Av. Stoke 1J 27
Regent Ct. New 6E 26
Regent Ho. B Frd 1A 22 (off Outclough Rd)
Regent Rd. Stoke 3B 34 (6E 5)
Regent St. Leek 3G 17
Regent St. Stoke 1J 39
Regent Theatre. 2B 34 (4E 5)
Reginald Mitchell Ct. Stoke 2C 34 (5G 5)
Reginald Mitchell Way. Stoke 7F 21
Reginald St. Stoke 4K 27
Regina St. Stoke 2C 28
Registry St. Stoke 5A 34
Reid St. Stoke 4H 27
Rembrandt Way. Stoke 1C 48
Remer St. Stoke 6A 28
Renard Way. Stoke 7C 42
Renfrew Clo. New 5C 32
Renfrew Pl. Stoke 5K 39
Renown Clo. Stoke 4E 34
Repington Rd. Stoke 4D 28
Repton Dri. New 1C 38
Reservoir Rd. Stoke 4K 41
Reynolds Av. New 6B 26
Reynolds Rd. Stoke 1K 27
Rhodes Ct. New 5F 27
Rhodes St. Stoke 6C 28
Rhondda Av. Stoke 5B 28
Rialto Pl. Stoke 1G 27
Ribble Clo. New 3E 38
Ribble Dri. Bid 1D 14
Ribble Ind. Est. Stoke 5H 27
Ribblesdale Av. Cong 2J 9
Ricardo St. Stoke 5G 41
Riceyman Rd. New 3E 26
Richards Av. Stoke 1J 27
Richardson Pl. Stoke 5A 22
Richmond Av. Stoke 5C 28
Richmond Gro. New 2G 33
Richmond Rd. Stoke 5J 39
Richmond St. Stoke 5K 33
Richmond Ter. Stoke 3A 34
Ridding Bank. Han 7E 38
Ridge Clo. B'stn 7B 46
Ridge Cres. Stoke 1A 48
Ridgefields. Bid M 1G 15
Ridgehill Dri. Mad H 6C 30
Ridgehouse Dri. Stoke 1K 33 (3A 4)
Ridge Rd. Stoke 5G 21
Ridge Wlk. Stoke 7A 42
Ridgeway. Brn E 3C 22
Ridgmont Rd. New 2C 38
Ridgway Dri. B Bri 7E 42
Ridgway Pl. New 6G 27
Ridgway Rd. Stoke 4B 34
Ridley St. Stoke 1B 40
Ridley Wlk. Stoke 1B 40
Rigby Rd. Kid 7E 12
Riley Av. Stoke 2A 28

A-Z Stoke 69

Riley St. N. *Stoke* 4H 27	Rookery La. *Stoke* 3J 39	Ruabon Clo. *Knyp* 4D 14
Riley St. S. *Stoke* 4J 27	Rookery Rd. *Kid* 7F 13	Rubens Way. *Stoke* 7C 42
Rileys Way. *Big E* 2G 25	Rookery, The. 7F 13	Rubian St. *Stoke* 7E 34
Rill St. *Stoke* 2G 41	Rookery, The. *New* 4K 31	Rudyard. 1A 16
Rimini Clo. *Stoke* 1K 41	Rope St. *Stoke* 4G 33 (3G 7)	Rudyard Gro. *New* 1F 33
Rindle, The. *C'dle* 3E 44	Rope Wlk. *Cong* 4F 9	Rudyard Rd. *Bid M* 1G 15
Ringland Clo. *Stoke* . .1C 34 (3H 5)	Roseacre. *New* 5C 32 (6A 6)	Rudyard Rd. *Rud* 1A 16
Ripon Av. *New* 5B 26	Roseacre Gro. *Stoke* 1A 48	Rudyard Way. *C'dle* 2J 45
Ripon Rd. *Stoke* 6E 40	Roseacre La. *B Bri* 1G 49	Rugby Clo. *New* 1C 38
Riseley Rd. *Stoke* 5G 33 (4H 7)	Rose Bank St. *Leek* 3G 17	Rugby Dri. *Stoke* 5G 41
Rists Ind. Est. *New* 1C 32	Rosebank Ter. *Leek* 3G 17	Runnymede Clo. *Stoke* 2G 35
Rists Rd. *New* 1C 32	(off Rose Bank St.)	Rupert St. *Bid* 2B 14
Rivendell La. *Leek* 7G 17	Roseberry Dri. *Mad* 1B 30	Rushcliffe Dri. *Stoke* 7B 42
Riverdale Dri. *Stoke* 3H 21	Roseberry St. *Stoke* 6J 21	Rushmoor Gro. *Stoke* 7C 42
Riverdane Rd. *Cong* 3G 9	Rosebery Clo. *Bid* 2D 14	Rushton. *New* 2C 38
Riverhead Clo. *Stoke* 6E 22	Rose Cotts. *Werr* 1K 23	Rushton Clo. *Brn E* 4G 23
River Lea M. *Mad* 2B 30	Rosehill Clo. *Stoke* 3G 29	Rushton Gro. *Stoke* 5K 27
Riverside Ct. *Stoke* 1E 34	Roseland Cres. *Stoke* 3G 29	Rushton Rd. *Stoke* 5K 27
Riverside Rd. *Stoke* 3H 39	Rosemary Pl. *Stoke* 5D 28	Rushton Way. *For* 6H 43
Riversmead. *New* 2E 38	Rosemary St. *New* 6C 26	Ruskin Clo. *Stoke* 2J 41
River St. *Cong* 4F 9	Rosendale Av. *New* 6C 26	Ruskin Rd. *Cong* 5E 8
Rivington Cres. *Stoke* 5K 21	Roseneath Pl. *Stoke* 3G 29	Rusper Clo. *Stoke* 6E 28
Rixdale Clo. *Stoke* 7B 28 (1E 5)	Rossall Av. *New* 1C 38	Ruston Av. *Stoke* 5A 22
Robert Heath St. *Stoke* 2B 28	Rose Tree Av. *Stoke* 4H 39	Rutherford Av. *New* 3E 38
Roberts Av. *New* 3D 32 (1B 6)	Rosevale Bus. Pk. *New* 4C 26	Rutherford Pl. *Stoke* 6H 33
Roberts Clo. *Als B* 6G 25	Rosevale Ct. *New* 4B 26	Ruthin Gro. *Knyp* 4D 14
Robertson Dri. *New* 2C 32	Rosevale La. *New* 4B 26	Ruthin Rd. *Stoke* 3H 35
Robertson Sq. *Stoke* 2H 39	Rosevale Rd. *P West* 3G 29	Rutland Clo. *Cong* 3G 9
Robert St. *Stoke* 7G 21	Rosevale St. *Stoke* 3G 29	Rutland Pl. *New* 2F 39
Robertville Rd. *Stoke* 2G 35	Rosevean Clo. *Stoke* . .7B 28 (1E 5)	Rutland Rd. *Kid* 1D 20
Robina Dri. *C'dle* 3H 45	Roseville Dri. *Cong* 7K 9	Rutland Rd. *Stoke* 2H 41
Robin Cft. *Stoke* 4J 27	Rosewood Av. *Stoc B* 7H 23	Rutland St. *Stoke* 7A 28 (1C 4)
Robin Hill. 2E 14	Rossall Av. *New* 1C 38	Ruxley Ct. *Stoke* 2F 35
Robin Hill. *Bid M* 3F 15	Ross Clo. *Stoke* 2B 42	Ruxley Rd. *Stoke* 2F 35
Robin Hill Gro. *Stoke* 1G 41	Rossett Gro. *Stoke* 3J 21	Rydal Ct. *Cong* 5C 8
Robinson Av. *Stoke* 4C 28	Rosslyn Rd. *Stoke* 4H 41	Rydale Way. *Cong* 7K 9
Robinson Ct. *Stoke* 6E 40	Rosy Bank. *Werr* 1H 29	Rydal Way. *Als* 5D 10
Robinson Rd. *Stoke* 6J 39	Rother Wlk. *Stoke* 7K 21	Rydal Way. *New* 2E 38
Robson St. *Stoke* 2A 34 (5D 4)	Rothesay Av. *New* 6C 32	Ryder Rd. *Stoke* 6B 42
Roche Av. *Leek* 1H 17	Rothesay Ct. *New* 6C 32	Rye Bank. *New* 4E 32 (3D 6)
Rochester Rd. *Stoke* 1G 41	Rothesay Ct. *Stoke* 4J 41	Rye Bank Cres. *New* . . .4F 33 (2D 6)
Rochford Clo. *Leek* 4D 16	Rothesay Rd. *Stoke* 4J 41	Ryebrook Gro. *Stoke* 5J 21
Rochford Way. *Stoke* 4J 35	Rothley Grn. *Stoke* 6E 40	Rye Clo. *Als* 7C 10
Rock End. 4E 14	Rothsay Av. *Stoke* 4C 28	Ryecroft. *New* 4E 32 (2C 6)
Rockfield Av. *L Oaks* 3J 29	Rothwell St. *Stoke* 7J 33	Ryecroft Rd. *Stoke* 1D 28
Rock House Dri. *B'stn* 6C 46	Rotterdam. *New* 4C 32 (3A 6)	**Rye Hills.** 4E 24
Rockhouse La. *Tal* 3K 19	Rotterdam Rd. *New* 4C 32	Rye Hills. *Big E* 3F 25
(in two parts)	**Rough Close.** 4K 47	Ryeland Clo. *Stoke* 6H 41
Rockingham Dri. *C'dle* 3J 45	**Roughcote.** 7D 36	Rylestone Clo. *Stoke* 7C 42
Rocklands. *New* 5F 27	Roughcote La. *Cav* 7D 36	
Rockside. *Mow C* 4F 13	Roughwood La.	
Rocks, The. *Brn E* 3G 23	*Has G & Chu L* 1B 10	**S**
Rode Ct. *Cong* 4H 9	Roundfields. *Stoc B* 1H 29	
Rode Hall. 3J 11	Roundway. *Stoke* 4D 40	**S**ackville St. *Stoke* . . .3H 33 (1H 7)
Rode Heath. 3G 11	Roundwell St. *Stoke* 1G 27	Saffron Clo. *Stoke* 1B 48
Rodehouse Clo. *Rode H* 3G 11	Rowanall Vw. *Leek* 5D 16	Sage Clo. *Stoke* 3B 34 (6F 5)
Rode, The. *Als* 6E 10	Rowan Clo. *Als* 7E 10	St Aidan's St. *Stoke* 7G 21
Rodgers Ct. Stoke 4F 21	Rowan Clo. *Bid M* 2G 15	St Andrews Cres. *Stoke* 5C 28
(off Rodgers St.)	Rowan Clo. *Chu L* 4D 10	St Andrews Dri. *Kid* 7F 13
Rodgers St. *Stoke* 3F 21	Rowan Clo. *Kid* 3D 20	St Andrew's Dri. *New*
Roebuck Shop. Cen., The.	Rowan Gro. *Stoke* 3D 40	. . . . .5C 32 (4A 6)
New 5E 32 (4D 6)	Rowan Pl. *New* 4B 26	St Andrews Gdns. *Als* 1F 19
Roebuck St. *Stoke* 5B 34	Rowhurst Clo. *Stoke*	St Andrews Sq. *Stoke* 6K 33
Roe La. *New* 2D 38	*Row I & New* 5K 25	St Anne's Va. *Brn E* 2G 23
Roe Pk. *Mow C* 1H 13	(in two parts)	St Ann St. *Stoke* 1C 34 (3H 5)
Roe St. *Cong* 5G 9	Rowhurst Clo. Ind. Est.	St Ann Wlk. *Stoke* 3H 5
Rogate Clo. *Stoke* 7G 35	*Row I* 5K 25	St Anthony's Dri. *New* 6C 32
Rogers Av. *New* 2C 32	Rowhurst Pl. *Stoke* 6B 22	St Bartholomews Clo.
Rogerstone Av. *Stoke* 7H 33	Rowland St. *Stoke* 5G 41	*Stoke* 7D 22
Rolfe Clo. *Stoke* 4K 39	Rowley Av. *New* 5B 26	St Bernard Pl. *Stoke* 7F 29
Roma Clo. *Stoke* 6J 41	Rownall Pl. *Stoke* 4B 42	St Bernard's Rd. *New* 3C 32
Roman Dri. *New* 7A 26	Rownall Rd. *Stoke* 4B 42	St Chads Rd. *Stoke* 1H 27
Romer Side. *Stoke* 5H 35	Rownall Rd. *Werr* 1E 36	St Chad's Ter. *New* 2A 26
Romford Pl. *Stoke* 7C 42	Roxburghe Av. *Stoke* 4J 41	St Christopher Av. *Stoke* 6H 33
Romney Av. *New* 6B 26	Royal Doulton Hall. *Stoke* 5B 34	St Clair St. *Stoke* 4H 41
Romney Gro. *Stoke* 6H 41	*Royal Doulton Vis. Cen.* 4K 27	St Davids Way. *Knyp* 4D 14
Romsey Clo. *Stoke* 5J 35	Royal St. *Stoke* 1F 41	St Dominic's Ct. *Stoke* 5K 33
Ronald St. *Stoke* 4H 41	Royal Wlk. *C'dle* 3G 45	St Edmund's Av. *New* 5G 27
(in two parts)	Royce Av. *Knyp* 5A 14	St Edward St. *Leek* 4F 17
Ronaldsway Dri. *New* 3D 32	Roycroft Clo. *New* 4E 26	St Gabriels St. *Als* 7D 10
Ronald Wlk. *Stoke* 4H 41	Royden Av. *Stoke* 1E 34	St Georges Av. *End* 5K 23
Ronson Av. *Stoke* 2H 39	Roylance St. *Stoke* 1G 27	St Georges Av. *Stoke* 7K 21
Rood Hill. *Cong* 4F 9	Royle Pk. *Cong* 4F 9	St Georges Av. N. *New* 7E 26
Rood La. *Cong* 4F 9	Royle St. *Cong* 4F 9	St George's Av. S. *New* 7E 26
Rookery Av. *New* 5F 41	Royston Wlk. *Stoke* 3H 41	St George's Av. W. *New* 7E 26
Rookery Ct. *Stoke* 3H 39	Royville Pl. *Stoke* 4C 28	St Georges Cres. *Stoke* 5K 39
Rookery Cres. *C'wll* 5K 49		St George's Rd. *New*

	. . . . .5D 32 (4A 6)
St Giles Rd. *New* 3C 32	
St Gregorys Rd. *Stoke* 3F 41	
St Helier Clo. *New* 3C 38	
St James Av. *Cong* 5E 8	
St James Ct. *A'ly* 2E 24	
St James Ct. *Bid* 1K 15	
St James Ct. *Cong* 5E 8	
St James Pl. *Stoke* 5K 39	
St James St. *Stoke* 2A 34 (5D 4)	
St John's Av. *New* 1F 33	
St John's Av. *Stoke* 2H 39	
St Johns Pl. *Bid* 3C 14	
St John's Pl. *New* 3C 32	
St John's Rd. *Bid* 4B 14	
St John's Rd. *Cong* 3H 9	
St John's Sq. *Stoke* 4J 27	
St John St. *Stoke* 7C 28 (1G 5)	
St John's Wood. *Kid* 2C 20	
St Joseph St. *Stoke* 4F 21	
St Lucy's Dri. *New* 5F 27	
St Luke's Clo. *New* 3J 31	
St Luke's Ct. *Stoke* 4G 5	
St Luke St. *Stoke* 2C 34 (4H 5)	
St Margaret's Av. *New* 7G 27	
St Margaret's Dri. *Stoke* 4D 28	
St Margarets Gro. *Stoke* 3D 40	
St Mark's Clo. *Stoke* . .3A 34 (6D 4)	
St Mark's St. *Stoke* . . .3A 34 (6D 4)	
St Martin's La. *Stoke* 3H 41	
St Martin's Rd. *New* . . .5C 32 (4A 6)	
St Martin's Rd. *Tal P* 5B 20	
St Mary's Clo. *Als* 5D 10	
St Mary's Ct. *Cong* 5C 8	
St Mary's Dri. *New* 5D 32 (4A 6)	
St Mary's Rd. *New* 7G 27	
St Mary's Rd. *Stoke* 1J 41	
St Matthew St. *Stoke* 7E 34	
St Michael's Cotts. *Hul W* 1D 8	
St Michael's Ho. *Stoke* 5J 21	
St Michael's Rd. *New* 2E 32	
St Michael's Rd. *Stoke* 6J 21	
St Nicholas Av. *Stoke* 1D 28	
St Patrick's Dri. *New* 5C 32	
St Pauls Ct. Stoke 4H 27	
(off St Pauls St.)	
St Paul's Ct. *Stoke* 4E 40	
St Paul's Rd. *New* 4D 32 (3A 6)	
St Pauls St. *Stoke* 4H 27	
St Peters Clo. *Stoke* 6A 34	
St Peters La. *B Bri* 7H 43	
St Peters Rd. *Cong* 6G 9	
St Peter's Wlk. *Stoke* 6K 27	
St Saviours St. *Tal* 2A 20	
St Stephens Ct. Bid 1C 14	
(off Thames Dri.)	
St Stephens Ct. Cong 4H 9	
(off Herbert St.)	
St Thomas Pl. *Stoke* 7J 33	
St Thomas St. *Mow C* 3G 13	
St Vincent Pl. *New* 3B 32	
Salcombe Rd. *Stoke* 5C 28	
Salem St. *Stoke* 2J 33 (5A 4)	
Salford Pl. *Cong* 4G 9	
Salisbury Av. *Stoke* 3B 34	
Salisbury Clo. *Mad* 6A 30	
Salisbury St. *Leek* 3F 17	
Salisbury St. *Stoke* 1H 27	
Salkeld Pl. *Stoke* 6A 22	
Salop Gro. *New* 2F 39	
Salop Pl. *Kid* 7D 12	
Saltdean Clo. *Stoke* 4K 41	
Salters Clo. *Werr* 2C 36	
Salters La. *Werr & Stoke* 2C 36	
Salt La. *Has G & Chu L* 1A 10	
Sampson St. *Stoke* 1A 34 (2D 4)	
Samuel St. *Pac* 2J 21	

Sancton Grn.—Southfields

Sancton Grn. *Stoke* 4H **27**
Sandbach Rd. *Chu L* 4E **10**
Sandbach Rd. *Cong* 5A **8**
Sandbach Rd. *Rode H* 1E **10**
Sandbach Rd. *Stoke* 5A **28**
Sandbach Rd. N. *Als* 6D **10**
Sandbach Rd. S. *Als* 7E **10**
Sandcrest Pl. *Stoke* 5A **42**
Sandcrest Wlk. *Stoke* 5A **42**
Sanderson Pl. *New* 6E **26**
Sandford Hill. **1H** 41
Sandford St. *New* 4B **26**
Sandford St. *Stoke* 1H **41**
Sandgate St. *Stoke* 3J **41**
Sandhurst Av. *Stoke* 5A **42**
Sandhurst Clo. *New* 7F **27**
Sandhurst Pl. *Stoke* 6A **42**
Sandiway Pl. *Stoke* 6D **28**
Sandon Av. *New* 1D **38**
Sandon Clo. *C'wll* 5K **49**
Sandon Ct. *Stoke* 7A **42**
Sandon Old Rd. *Stoke* 7A **42**
Sandon Rd. *C'wll* 5K **49**
Sandon Rd. *Stoke* 7A **42**
Sandon St. *Leek* 5F **17**
Sandon St. *Stoke* 2K **33** (4B **4**)
Sandown Clo. *C'dle* 1H **45**
Sandown Pl. *Stoke* 2H **29**
Sandpiper Ct. *Kid* 1F **21**
Sandra Clo. *Stoke* 2K **27**
Sandringham Cres. *Stoke* 5K **39**
Sandsdown Clo. *Bid* 1B **14**
Sandside Rd. *Als* 7C **10**
Sands La. *Stoke* 7F **15**
Sands Rd. *Har* 4H **13**
Sandwell Pl. *Stoke* 6K **41**
Sandwick Cres. *Stoke* 6E **28**
Sandwood Cres. *Stoke* 1H **41**
Sandy Brook Clo. *Leek* 6G **17**
Sandybrook La. *Leek* 7G **17**
Sandyfield Rd. *Stoke* 7D **28**
Sandyford. **5G** 21
Sandy Hill. *Werr* 1D **36**
Sandylands Cres. *Chu L* 5G **11**
Sandy La. *Brn E* 3G **23**
Sandy La. *Cong* 3A **8**
(Holmes Chapel Rd.)
Sandy La. *Cong* 5D **8**
(Newcastle Rd.)
Sandy La. *New* 3F **33** (1G **7**)
Sandy La. *Stoke* 2H **29**
Sandy La. M. *Cong* 2E **8**
Sandy Rd. *Gil H* 2H **15**
Sandy Rd. *Stoke* 4G **21**
Sangster La. *Stoke* 2C **28**
Sant St. *Stoke* 4H **27**
Saplings, The. *New* 3F **39**
Saracen Way. *Stoke* 5B **42**
Sargeant Av. *Stoke* 5K **21**
Sark Clo. *New* 2B **38**
Sark Pl. *Stoke* 7J **35**
Sarraine Ind. Pk. *C'dle* 4E **44**
Sarver La. *Dil* 2K **43**
Saturn Rd. *Stoke* 3B **28**
Saunders Rd. *New* 1E **32**
Saverley Green. **5J** 49
Saverley Grn. Rd. *Ful* 7G **49**
Sawpit Yd. *Mad* 6A **30**
Sawyer Dri. *Bid* 1B **14**
Scarlett St. *New* 5E **32** (4D **6**)
Scarratt Clo. *For* 6J **43**
Scarratt Dri. *For* 7J **43**
Sceptre St. *Stoke* 2B **34** (5E **5**)
Scholar Green. **4B** 12
School Clo. *Big E* 3H **25**
School Clo. *Dil* 1A **44**
School Clo. *Leek* 5D **16**
School La. *A'bry* 7D **8**
School La. *Bid M* 1G **15**
School La. *Cav & Stoke* 3E **42**
School La. *Long* 6A **16**
School La. *Stoke* 6E **40**
School Rd. *Bag* 2K **29**
School Rd. *Stoke* 7F **29**
School St. *Ches* 6C **26**
School St. *Leek* 3F **17**
School St. *New* 4F **33** (3E **7**)
School St. *Stoke* 3H **39**
Scot Hay. **2E** 30
Scot Hay Rd. *Als B* 1F **31**
Scot Hay Rd. *Sil* 2F **31**
Scotia Bus. Pk. *Stoke* 2H **27**
Scotia Rd. *Stoke* 1H **27**
Scott Clo. *Rode H* 2F **11**
Scott Lidgett Ind. Est.
Stoke 5G **27**
Scott Lidgett Rd. *Stoke* 5G **27**
Scott Rd. *Stoke* 6J **21**
Scott St. *New* 4F **33** (3E **7**)
Scragg St. *Pac* 3J **21**
Scrimshaw Dri. *Stoke* 1B **28**
Scrivener Rd. *Stoke* 4J **33**
Seabridge. **3C** 38
Seabridge La. *New* 2B **38**
Seabridge Rd. *New* 6D **32** (6B **6**)
Seaford St. *Stoke* 4A **34**
Seagrave Pl. *New* 7D **32**
Seagrave St. *New* 4F **33** (3F **7**)
Seaton Clo. *Stoke* 6K **41**
Sebring Av. *Stoke* 6K **41**
Second Av. *Kid* 2B **20**
Second Av. *New* 5F **27**
Second Av. *Stoke* 1J **35**
Sedbergh Clo. *New* 2C **38**
Seddon Ct. *Stoke* 3H **5**
Seddon Rd. *Stoke* 6A **42**
Sedgley Wlk. *Stoke* 2H **41**
Seedfields Rd. *Stoke* 3D **40**
Sefton Av. *Cong* 6J **9**
Sefton Av. *Stoke* 5D **28**
Sefton Rd. *Stoke* 4K **41**
Sefton St. *Stoke* 2K **33** (4B **4**)
Selborne Rd. *Leek* 5F **17**
Selbourne Dri. *Stoke* 4J **21**
Selby Clo. *New* 1D **38**
Selby St. *Stoke* 1C **42**
Selby Wlk. *Stoke* 7D **40**
Selwood Clo. *Stoke* 5J **41**
Selworthy Rd. *Stoke* 6F **23**
Selwyn St. *Stoke* 7A **34**
Semper Clo. *Cong* 3J **9**
Settle Gro. *Stoke* 7B **42**
Seven Arches Way. *Stoke* 6B **34**
Sevenoaks Gro. *Stoke* 1C **48**
Severn Clo. *Bid* 2D **14**
Severn Clo. *Cong* 6H **9**
Severn Dri. *New* 3E **38**
Severn St. *Stoke* 7A **28**
Seymour St. *Stoke* 2D **34** (4H **5**)
Shackleton Dri. *Stoke* 7F **21**
Shackson Clo. *Stoke* 3B **34**
Shady Gro. *Als* 6E **10**
Shaftesbury Av. *Stoke* 2K **27**
Shakerley Av. *Cong* 4H **9**
Shakespeare Clo. *Kid* 3C **20**
Shakespeare Clo. *Stoke* 2F **29**
Shakespeare Ct. *Bid* 3B **14**
Shaldon Av. *Stoc B* 7H **23**
Shallowford Ct. *Stoke*
2K **33** (5B **4**)
Shannon Ct. Stoke *4F* ***21***
(off Shannon Dri.)
Shannon Dri. *Stoke* 4E **20**
Shardlow Clo. *Stoke* 7F **35**
Sharman Clo. *Stoke* 6J **33**
Sharron Dri. *Leek* 4J **17**
Shaw Pl. *Leek* 3H **17**
Shawport Av. *New* 4D **26**
Shaw St. *Bid* 3B **14**
Shaw St. *New* 4E **32** (2C **6**)
Shaw St. *Stoke* 7A **28** (1B **4**)
Sheaf Pas. *Stoke* 3H **41**
Sheaf St. *Stoke* 3A **34** (6D **4**)
Shearer St. *Stoke* 3A **34**
Sheep Mkt. *Leek* 3F **17**
Sheepwash. *Cav* 6F **37**
Shefford Rd. *New* 3C **38**
Shelburne St. *Stoke* 1K **39**
Sheldon Av. *Cong* 6J **9**
Sheldon Gro. *New* 6C **26**
Sheldrake Gro. *Stoke* 7G **35**
Shelford Rd. *Stoke* 5G **21**
Shelley Clo. *Kid* 3D **20**
Shelley Clo. *Rode H* 2F **11**
Shelley Dri. *C'dle* 4F **45**
Shelley Rd. *Stoke* 6G **29**
Shelsley Rd. *C'dle* 2J **45**
Shelton. **4A** 34
Shelton Farm Rd.
Stoke 3A **34** (6D **4**)
Shelton New Rd.
Stoke 4G **33** (3G **7**)
Shelton Old Rd. *Stoke* 5K **33**
Shelton Pool. 4A 34
Shemilt Cres. *Stoke* 1B **28**
Shendon Ct. *New* 5D **26**
Shenfield Grn. *Stoke* 3J **35**
Shenton St. *Stoke* 1J **41**
Shepherd St. *Bid* 3B **14**
Shepley Gro. *Stoke* 7D **40**
Sheppard St. *Stoke* 7K **33**
Sherborne Clo. *Stoke* 7D **40**
Sherborne Dri. *New* 1D **38**
Sheridan Gdns. *Stoke* 4E **40**
Sheriden Way. *New* 3B **32**
Sheringham Pl. *New* 1G **33**
Sherratt Clo. *Cong* 5G **9**
Sherratt St. *Stoke* 1B **28**
Sherwin Rd. *Stoke* 1J **27**
Sherwood Rd. *Stoke* 7A **42**
Shetland Rd. *Stoke* 3E **40**
Shillingford Dri. *Stoke* 6A **40**
Shilton Clo. *Stoke* 1J **39**
Shinwell Gro. *Stoke* 6B **42**
Shipley Pl. *Stoke* 2B **28**
Shirburn Rd. *Leek* 3H **17**
Shirburn Ter. *Leek* 4H **17**
Shirebrook Clo. *Stoke* 7D **40**
Shirley Av. *Werr* 1C **36**
Shirley Rd. *Stoke* 3B **34** (6E **5**)
Shirley St. *Leek* 4E **16**
Shirley St. *Stoke* 4G **27**
Shoobridge St. *Leek* 4G **17**
Shop La. *Cong* 6G **9**
Short Bambury St. *Stoke* 7J **35**
Short St. *Stoke* 3H **41**
Shorwell Gro. *Stoke* 3H **21**
Shotsfield Pl. *Stoke* 3F **29**
Shotsfield St. *Stoke* 3F **29**
Showan Av. *New* 2G **33**
Shraleybrook. **4B** 24
Shraleybrook Rd.
A'ly & Halm 4B **24**
Shrewsbury Dri. *New* 2B **26**
Shugborough Clo. *Werr* 3B **36**
Shutlanehead. **5A** 38
Sidcot Pl. *Stoke* 5C **28**
Sideway. **3A** 40
Sideway. *Stoke* 3A **40**
Sideway Rd. *Stoke* 2A **40**
Sidings Pl. *Stoke* 2G **41**
Sidings, The. *C'dle* 4G **45**
Sidmouth Av. *New* 4F **33** (2E **7**)
Silk St. *Cong* 5F **9**
Silk St. *Leek* 3F **17**
Sillitoe Pl. *Stoke* 7K **33**
Silsden Gro. *Stoke* 4D **42**
Silver Clo. *Bid* 2B **14**
Silverdale. **3K** 31
Silverdale. *New* 3K **31**
Silverdale Bus. Pk. *Sil* 4A **32**
Silverdale Pk. New *3K* ***31***
(off Silverdale)
Silverdale Rd. *New* 4A **32** (2A **6**)
Silverdale Rd. *Wol* 7F **27**
Silverdale St. *New* 2B **32**
Silvergate Ct. *Cong* 7G **9**
Silvermine Clo. *Kid* 1E **20**
Silver Ridge. *B'stn* 7B **46**
Silverstone Av. *C'dle* 2H **45**
Silverstone Cres. *Stoke* 3H **21**
Silver St. *C'dle* 1H **45**
Silver St. *Cong* 5G **9**
Silver St. *Stoke* 7D **22**
Silverton Clo. *New* 4D **26**
Silverwood. *Kid* 2E **20**
Simister Ct. Stoke *1G* ***27***
(off Wesley St.)
Simonburn Av. *Stoke* 6H **33**
Simon Pl. *Stoke* 4A **34**
Simpson St. *New* 7E **26**
Simpson St. *Stoke* 3C **34**
Sinclair Av. *Als* 7C **10**
Sir Stanley Matthews Sports Cen.
5B 34
Siskin Pl. *Stoke* 7C **42**
Sitwell Gro. *Stoke* 2J **41**
Skellern Av. *Stoke* 1B **28**
Skellern St. *Tal* 1A **20**
Skipacre Av. *Stoke* 3C **28**
Skye Clo. *Stoke* 3K **41**
Slacken La. *Tal* 1A **20**
Slaidburn Gro. *Stoke* 7E **28**
Slaney St. *New* 6F **33** (6F **7**)
Slapton Clo. *Stoke* 4E **34**
Slater St. *Bid* 3B **14**
Slater St. *Stoke* 5H **27**
Sleeve, The. *Leek* 5D **16**
Sleigh Gro. *Leek* 4F **17**
Slindon Clo. *New* 3A **26**
Slippery La. *Stoke* 2A **34** (4D **4**)
Sloane Way. *Stoke* 7G **35**
Smallthorne. **2A** 28
Smallwood Clo. *New* 3A **26**
Smallwood Ct. Cong *4H* ***9***
(off Brunswick St.)
Smallwood Gro. *Stoke* 6E **28**
Smith Child St. *Stoke* 7G **21**
Smith Clo. *Als* 6C **10**
Smithfield Cen., The. *Leek* 4G **17**
Smithfield Ct. *Stoke* 6E **5**
Smithfield Ct. Stoke *1K* ***33*** *(3A* ***4****)*
(off Marina Way)
Smithpool Rd. *Stoke* 1B **40**
Smiths Bldgs. Stoke *5B* ***42***
(off Weston Rd.)
Smiths Pas. *Stoke* 1F **41**
Smith St. *Stoke* 2H **41**
Smithyfield Rd. *Stoke* 7C **22**
Smithy Gro. *Has G* 1A **10**
Smithy La. *Bid* 2J **15**
Smithy La. *C'dle* 6G **45**
Smithy La. *Hul W* 1D **8**
Smithy La. *Stoke* 3H **41**
Smokies Way. *Bid* 1B **14**
Sneyd Av. *Leek* 4F **17**
Sneyd Av. *New* 6C **32**
Sneyd Cres. *New* 6C **32**
Sneyd Green. **5C** 28
Sneyd Hill. *Stoke* 4A **28**
Sneyd Hill Trad. Est. *Stoke* 3A **28**
Sneyd Ind. Est. *Stoke* 4A **28**
Sneyd Pl. *Stoke* 5F **21**
Sneyd St. *Leek* 4F **17**
Sneyd St. *Stoke* 6A **28**
Sneyd Ter. *New* 3J **31**
Sneyd Wood Vw. *Stoke* 5B **28**
Snowden Way. *Stoke* 4C **42**
Snow Hill. *Stoke* 3A **34** (6D **4**)
Soames Cres. *Stoke* 7G **35**
Solly Cres. *Cong* 5C **8**
Solway Gro. *Stoke* 2K **41**
Somerford Ct. Cong *4H* ***9***
(off Brunswick St.)
Somerley Rd. *Stoke* 6E **28**
Somerset Av. *Kid* 1C **20**
Somerset Clo. *Cong* 3F **9**
Somerset Rd. *Stoke* 1D **34**
Somerton Rd. *Werr* 2B **36**
Somerton Way. *Stoke* 1J **41**
Somerville Av. *New* 2G **33**
Sonnet, The. *C'dle* 4F **45**
Sophia Way. *New* 4E **26**
Sorrel Clo. *Stoke* 2F **35**
Sorrento Clo. *Stoke* 2K **41**
Souldern Way. *Stoke* 2J **41**
Southall Way. *Stoke* 4F **35**
Southampton St. *Stoke*
7C **28** (1G **5**)
S. Bank Gro. *Cong* 5H **9**
Southbank St. *Leek* 4G **17**
Southborough Cres. *Stoke* 7A **22**
South Clo. *Als* 6B **10**
Southdown Clo. *Stoke* 6H **41**
Southern Ct. *Stoke* 6K **33**
Southern Way. *Stoke* 3C **28**
Southfields. Leek *4G* ***17***
(off Westfields)

A-Z Stoke 71

Southgate Av. Stoke 1B 46
Southlands. New 7F 27
Southlands Av. Stoke 5G 41
Southlands Clo. Leek 3D 16
Southlands Rd. Cong 6J 9
Southlow. 1G 37
Southlowe Av. Werr 1F 37
Southlowe Rd. Werr 1F 37
South Moorlands Leisure Cen.
.........4H 45
South Pl. Stoke 5C 22
South Rd. Stoke 7G 29
South St. Cong 4F 9
South St. Mow C 4E 12
South St. Stoke 5C 22
South Ter. New 7F 27
South Ter. New 1K 39
South Vw. Bid 2B 14
South Vw. Stoke 3A 48
South Vw. Cotts. Chu L 5G 11
South Wlk. Stoke 5C 42
S. Wolfe St. Stoke 6A 34
Spalding Pl. Stoke 5K 35
Sparch Av. New 1F 33
Sparch Gro. New 1F 33
Sparch Hollow. New 1F 33
Spark St. Stoke 6K 33
Spark Ter. Stoke 6K 33
Sparrow Butts Gro. Kid 1F 21
Sparrow St. Stoke 2C 28
Sparrow Ter. New 6E 26
Spa St. Stoke 5B 28
Speakman St. Stoke 4J 41
Spedding Rd. Fen I 5D 34
Spedding Way. Bid 2D 14
Speedwall St. Stoke 1H 41
Speedwell Rd. P East 3C 26
Spencer Av. End 5K 23
Spencer Av. Leek 4F 17
Spencer Clo. Als 6A 10
Spencer Pl. New 6B 26
Spencer Rd. Stoke 5B 34
Spencroft Rd. New 7C 26
Spens St. Stoke 4J 27
Spey Dri. Kid 1F 21
Spindle St. Cong 4G 9
Spinney Clo. End 3K 23
Spinney, The. Chu L 6B 12
Spinney, The. Mad H 5B 30
Spinney, The. New 4F 39
Spire Clo. Stoke 1D 28
Spitfire Way. Stoke 7F 21
Spode Clo. C'dle 4F 45
Spode Gro. New 3E 38
Spode Mus. & Vis. Cen. 4A 34
Spode St. Stoke 1A 40
Spoutfield Rd. Stoke 4J 33
Spout Hollow. Tal P 5A 20
Spout La. L Oaks 3H 29
Spragg Ho. La. Stoke 1D 28
Spragg St. Cong 4G 9
Spratslade Dri. Stoke 4G 41
Spring Bank. Sch G 2D 12
Spring Clo. Rode H 2F 11
Spring Cres. Brn E 4H 23
Springcroft. B Bri 1G 49
Springfield Clo. New 6C 26
Springfield Ct. Leek 3H 17
Springfield Cres. Stoke 4G 41
Springfield Dri. Cong 4F 9
Springfield Dri. For 6H 43
Springfield Dri. Kid 3A 20
Springfield Dri. Leek 3H 17
Springfield Gro. Bid 3C 14
Springfield Rd. Bid 3C 14
Springfield Rd. Leek 4H 17
Springfields. 1H 39
Springfields. B Bri 1F 49
Springfields Pk. Stoke 1H 39
Springfields Rd. Stoke 7H 33
Spring Garden Rd. Stoke 4G 41
Spring Gdns. For 6J 43
Spring Gdns. Leek 4E 16
Springhead Clo. Tal P 5A 20

Springpool. K'le 7K 31
Spring Rd. Stoke 4K 41
Springside Pl. Stoke 7D 40
Spring St. Stoke 4G 33 (3G 7)
Spring Vw. Brn E 4H 23
Springwood. 3K 25
Springwood Rd. New 4K 25
Sprink Bank Rd. Stoke 6K 21
Sprinkwood Gro. Stoke 3B 42
Sproston Rd. Stoke 6J 21
Spruce Gro. Rode H 3G 11
Spur St. Stoke 3C 34 (6H 5)
Square, The. Cav 4F 43
Square, The. New 7D 32
Square, The. Stoke 4C 42
Squires Vw. Stoke 6B 34
Squirrel Hayes Av. Knyp 4D 14
Squirrels, The. New 3F 39
Stadium Ct. Stoke 6K 27
Stadmorslow La. Har 6J 13
Stafford Av. New 1F 39
Stafford Cres. New 2F 39
Stafford La. Stoke 1B 34 (3F 5)
Staffordshire University. 5A 34
Stafford St. New 5E 32 (4D 6)
Stafford St. Stoke 1B 34 (3E 5)
Stallington. 3E 48
Stallington Clo. B Bri 3E 48
Stallington Gdns. B Bri 1G 49
Stallington Rd. Stoke & Ful 5C 48
Stamer St. Stoke 7A 34
Standard St. Stoke 7C 34
Standersfoot Pl. Stoke 5A 22
Standon Av. New 2K 25
Stanfield. 2J 27
Stanfield Cres. C'dle 5G 45
Stanfield Rd. Stoke 3K 27
Stanfield St. Stoke 7J 35
Stanhope St. Stoke 3A 34 (6C 4)
Stanier St. New 4D 32 (3B 6)
Stanier St. Stoke 7D 34
Stanley Ct. Als 6D 10
Stanley Dri. New 3K 25
Stanley Grn. Stoke 2F 29
Stanley Gro. New 3G 33 (1H 7)
Stanley Gro. Stoke 2G 29
Stanley Matthews Way.
Stoke 3B 40
Stanley Moor. 7K 23
Stanley Moss. 5K 23
Stanley Moss La. Stoke 6K 23
Stanley Moss Rd. Stoc B 6K 23
Stanley Rd. Gil H 2H 15
Stanley Rd. New 3G 33
Stanley Rd. Stoc B 7J 23
Stanley Rd. Stoke 5H 33 (4H 7)
Stanley St. Bid 2B 14
Stanley St. Leek 4F 17
Stanley St. Stoke 7H 21
Stansgate Pl. Stoke 7A 28 (1C 4)
Stansmore Rd. Stoke 4C 42
Stanton Clo. New 3C 32
Stanton Rd. Stoke 5B 42
Stanway Av. Stoke 5B 28
Stapleton Cres. Stoke 5F 41
Star & Garter Rd. Stoke 5K 41
Starling Clo. Kid 7G 13
Starwood Rd. Stoke 6K 41
Statham St. Stoke 2A 34 (5D 4)
Station Bri. Rd. Stoke 1D 40
Station Cres. Stoke 2C 28
Station Dri. K'le 5E 30
Station Gro. Stoke 3F 29
Station Rd. Als 7D 10
Station Rd. B'stn 6C 46
Station Rd. Bid 3C 14
(in two parts)
Station Rd. C'dle 4G 45
Station Rd. End 2K 23
Station Rd. Halm 5E 24
Station Rd. K'le 5D 30
(in two parts)
Station Rd. Kid 2C 20
Station Rd. Mad 3B 30
Station Rd. Mow C 2E 12
Station Rd. N'cpl 2H 21
Station Rd. Sch G & Mor 3B 12

Station Rd. Sil 3J 31
Station Rd. Stoke 5A 34
Station St. Leek 4E 16
Station St. Stoke 5G 27
Station Vw. Stoke 5B 42
Station Walks. Halm 5E 24
Station Walks. New 4E 32 (2D 6)
(in two parts)
Station Yd. Cong 6J 9
Staveley Clo. Stoke 2F 35
Staveley Pl. New 4H 31
Stedman St. Stoke 7C 28
Steele Av. Stoke 2A 28
Steel St. Stoke 1K 39
Stellar St. Stoke 3B 28
Stephens Way. Big E 2G 25
Step Row. Leek 4F 17
(off Cornhill St.)
Sterndale Dri. New 3E 38
Sterndale Dri. Stoke 7G 35
Stevenson Rd. Stoke 1F 35
Steventon Pl. Stoke 4J 27
Stewart Ct. Stoke 4J 35
Stewart St. Stoke 7C 34
Stile Clo. Brn L 5A 14
Stirling Clo. Stoke 6K 35
Stirling Ho. Stoke 5K 27
(off Bleak Pl.)
Stirling St. Stoke 4K 27
Stockfield Rd. Stoke 7A 42
Stockholm Gro. Stoke 5E 28
Stockton Brook. 6J 23
Stockwell Gro. Stoke 3J 41
Stockwell St. Leek 3F 17
Stockwell Vs. Leek 3F 17
Stockwood Rd. New 2C 38
Stoke Bus. Pk. Stoke 7B 34
Stoke City F.C. (Britannia Stadium)
.........3B 40
Stoke Gymnastics Cen. 4H 27
Stoke Old Rd. Stoke 4G 33 (3H 7)
Stoke-on-Trent. 1B 34 (3F 5)
Stoke-on-Trent Repertory Theatre.
.........4C 34
Stoke-on-Trent Ski Cen.
.........7J 27 (1A 4)
STOKE-ON-TRENT STATION.
RAIL 5A 34
Stoke Recreation Cen. 7A 34
Stoke Rd. Stoke 4A 34
Stokesay Dri. C'dle 3J 45
Stokesay Gro. Stoke 5K 27
Stoke-upon-Trent. 6A 34
Stone Bank Rd. Kid 3D 20
Stone Chair La. Sch G 2B 12
Stonehaven Gro. Stoke 3C 34
Stonehouse Cres. Werr 2C 36
Stonehouse La. Brn E 2F 23
Stone House Rd. Werr 2C 36
Stonehouses. 1J 49
Stoneleigh Rd. Stoke 6K 21
Stone Rd. R'gh C 5K 47
Stone Rd. Stoke 3H 39
Stone Rd. T'sor 5A 46
Stone St. Stoke 6K 33
(in two parts)
Stonewall Ind. Est. New 3A 32
Stonewall Pl. New 3A 32
Stonewood Clo. Stoke 3H 39
Stoneycroft. Stoke 2G 29
Stoneyfields. Bid M 2G 15
Stoneyfields Av. Stoke 2G 29
Stoneyfields Ct. New 3G 33 (1G 7)
Stoney La. End 4K 23
Stonor St. Stoke 6K 27
Stony La. A'bry 6E 8
Stopsley Clo. Cong 3B 8
Stormont Clo. Stoke 2B 28
Stowford Gro. Stoke 6A 40
Stradbroke Dri. Stoke 5F 41
Strand Clo. Stoke 3F 35
Strand Pas. Stoke 2G 41
(off Strand, The)
Strand, The. Stoke 3G 41
Strangman St. Leek 4F 17
Stranraer Clo. Stoke 2C 42

Stratford Av. New 2G 33
Stratford Clo. For 6H 43
Stratford Clo. Stoke 3E 28
Stratheden Rd. Stoke 2A 28
St. Anthony's Ct. Stoke 1A 40
Street La. Rode H 1G 11
Stretton Rd. New 3G 31
Stringer Ct. Stoke 1G 27
Stringer St. Bid 2B 14
Stroma Clo. Stoke 5J 27
Stross Av. Stoke 6J 21
Stroud Clo. Stoke 7C 42
Stuart Av. Dray 1K 49
Stuart Av. Stoke 7K 39
Stuart Gro. New 1F 33
Stuart Rd. Stoke 3C 34 (6H 5)
Stubbsfield Rd. New 6F 33 (6F 7)
Stubbs Ga. New 5F 33 (5E 7)
Stubbs La. Stoke 2C 34 (5G 5)
Stubbs St. New 5E 32 (4D 6)
Stubbs St. Stoke 4H 27
Stubbs' Walks. New 5F 33 (4F 7)
Sturgess St. Stoke 7K 33
Sudbourne Clo. Stoke 3H 21
Sudbury Pl. New 4E 38
Sudgrove Pl. Stoke 7C 42
Sudlow St. Stoke 5A 28
Suffolk Clo. Cong 3F 9
Suffolk Clo. New 2G 39
Suffolk Rd. Stoke 6H 41
Summerbank Rd. Stoke 7G 21
Summerfield. Kid 2E 20
Summerhill Dri. New 3A 26
Summer Row. Stoke 4G 41
Summer St. Stoke 1K 39
Summerville Rd. Stoke 3H 39
Sunbury Clo. Stoke 1B 46
Sundorne Pl. Stoke 3G 35
Sunningdale Clo. Stoke 1A 28
Sunningdale Gro. New 4A 26
Sunny Bank. Stoke 6H 27
Sunnybank Ct. Stoke 1K 27
Sunnycroft Av. Stoke 5F 41
Sunnyfield Oval. Stoke 3H 29
Sunnyhills Rd. Leek 6E 16
Sunny Hollow. New 2F 33
Sunnyside. Als 6B 10
Sunnyside Av. Stoke 1J 27
Sunridge Clo. Stoke 2G 29
Sun St. C'dle 3H 45
Sun St. Stoke 3K 33 (6B 4)
Sunwell Gdns. C'dle 3H 45
Surrey Dri. Cong 3G 9
Surrey Rd. Kid 1D 20
Surtees Gro. Stoke 1G 41
Sussex Dri. Kid 1C 20
Sussex Pl. Cong 2G 9
Sussex Pl. Stoke 5J 41
Sutherland Av. Stoke 5G 41
Sutherland Cres. B Bri 7F 43
Sutherland Dri. New 1C 38
Sutherland Rd. Long 7B 16
Sutherland Rd. Stoke 3H 41
Sutherland St. Stoke 7B 34
Sutton Dri. Stoke 2J 39
Sutton Pl. Stoke 6A 22
Sutton St. Ches 6B 26
Swaffham Way. Stoke 3J 35
Swainsley Clo. Stoke 5K 27
Swaledale Av. Cong 2J 9
Swallow Clo. Kid 1D 20
Swallow Clo. Stoke 7B 42
Swallow Cft. Leek 6D 16
Swallow Dri. Als 7C 10
Swallowmore Vw. Tal 3K 19
Swallow Wlk. Bid 3C 14
Swanage Clo. Stoke 7C 42
Swan Bank. 5B 30
Swan Bank. Cong 5F 9
Swan Bank. Mad H 5B 30
Swan Bank. Tal 4A 20
Swan Clo. Tal 3A 20
Swanland Gro. Stoke 2J 41
Swan La. Stoke 3H 39
Swan Sq. Stoke 4J 27
Swan St. Cong 5F 9
Swan St. Stoke 5K 33

Swanton Pl. *Stoke* 7J **39**
Swaythling Gro. *Stoke* 4J **35**
Swettenham Clo. *Als* 7D **10**
Swift Clo. *Kid* 1E **20**
Swift Dri. *Bid* 2D **14**
Swift Ho. *Stoke* 2E **5**
Swift Pl. *Stoke* 1A **42**
Swinburne Clo. *Stoke* 4E **40**
Swingle Hill Rd. *Stoke* 3E **40**
Swithin Dri. *Stoke* 7G **35**
Sycamore Av. *Als* 1F **19**
Sycamore Av. *Cong* 3B **8**
Sycamore Av. *Rode H* 3G **11**
Sycamore Clo. *Bid* 2K **15**
Sycamore Clo. *Kid* 3B **20**
Sycamore Clo. *Stoke* 2B **48**
Sycamore Gdns. Stoke 4G **27**
(off Station St.)
Sycamore Gro. *New* 2G **33**
Sycamore Gro. *Stoke* 3D **40**
Sydenham Pl. *Stoke* 5J **35**
Sydney St. *New* 3G **33**
Sylvan Gro. *Stoke* 3H **39**
Sylvester St. *Stoke* 4K **27**
Sytch Rd. *Brn E* 4G **23**

T

Talbot St. *Leek* 4G **17**
Talbot St. *Stoke* 3C **34** (6G **5**)
Talke .4K **19**
Talke Pits 6A **20**
Talke Rd. *Als* 7F **11**
Talke Rd. *High B* 7B **20**
Talke Rd. *P East & New* 4C **26**
Talke Rd. *Red S & Tal P* 1A **26**
Tall Ash Av. *Cong* 3J **9**
Tallis Gro. *Stoke* 7E **28**
Tally Clo. *Stoke* 6J **35**
Talsarn Gro. *Stoke* 1B **46**
Tamar Clo. *Cong* 6H **9**
Tamar Gro. *C'dle* 5H **45**
Tamar Rd. *Kid* 1E **20**
Tame Clo. *Bid* 1C **14**
Tame Wlk. *Stoke* 2B **42**
Tanners Rd. *Stoke* 5G **27**
Tanner St. *Cong* 5G **9**
Tansey Clo. *Stoke* 2F **35**
Tape St. *C'dle* 3G **45**
Tara Gro. *Stoke* 1F **29**
Target Clo. *Tal P* 5B **22**
Tarleton Rd. *Stoke* 1D **34** (3H **5**)
Tarporley Gro. *Stoke* 1H **39**
Tarragon Dri. *Stoke* 1B **48**
Tarvin Gro. *Stoke* 5J **21**
Tasman Sq. *Stoke* 7D **28**
Tatton Clo. *Als* 7D **10**
Tatton Clo. *Leek* 4C **16**
Tatton St. *Stoke* 4H **41**
Taunton Pl. *New* 5C **26**
Taunton Way. *Stoke* 3J **35**
Taurus Gro. *Stoke* 5J **21**
Tavistock Cres. *New* 1D **38**
Tavistock Pl. *Stoke* 4H **33** (2H **7**)
Tawney Clo. *Kid* 1E **20**
Tawney Cres. *Stoke* 3C **42**
Tay Clo. *Bid* 1D **14**
Tay Clo. *C'dle* 1H **45**
Tay Clo. *Stoke* 1H **41**
Taylor Av. *New* 1F **33**
Taylor Rd. *Stoke* 6G **29**
Taylor St. *New* 1F **33**
Taylor St. *Stoke* 4F **21**
Taynton Clo. *Stoke* 3K **21**
Teal Vw. *Stoke* 2C **28**
Teanford 7G **45**
Tean Rd. *C'dle* 5G **45**
Telford Clo. *Cong* 6J **9**
Telford Clo. *Kid* 3B **20**
Telford Way. *Stoke* 7K **21**
Tellwright Gro. *New* 5D **26**
Tellwright St. Stoke 3K **27**
Temperance Pl. Stoke 4G **21**
(off Willoughby St.)
Templar Cres. *New* 6E **26**
Templar Ter. *New* 6E **26**

Temple St. *Stoke* 7C **34**
Templeton Av. *Stoke* 5H **35**
Tenbury Grn. *Stoke* 4H **35**
Tenby Gro. *New* 5C **26**
Tennant Pl. *New* 5E **26**
Tennyson Av. *Kid* 3D **20**
Tennyson Clo. *C'dle* 4E **44**
Tennyson Clo. *Rode H* 2F **11**
Tennyson Gdns. *Stoke* 4E **40**
Tercel Gro. *Stoke* 7B **42**
Terence Wlk. *B Frd* 1A **22**
Tern Av. *Kid* 1F **21**
Tern Clo. *Bid* 2D **14**
Terrace, The. *C'dle* 3G **45**
Terrington Dri. *New* 4E **38**
Terry Clo. *Stoke* 3C **42**
Terson Way. *Stoke* 2A **42**
Tetton Ct. *Cong* 4H **9**
Tewkesbury Gro. *Stoke* 1F **35**
Tewson Gro. *Stoke* 5B **28**
Thackeray Dri. *Stoke* 4F **41**
Thames Clo. *Cong* 6H **9**
Thames Dri. *Bid* 1C **14**
Thames Dri. *C'dle* 5H **45**
Thames Rd. *New* 3D **38**
Thanet Gro. *Stoke* 3F **41**
Thatcham Grn. *Stoke* 7D **40**
Thatcher Gro. *Bid* 2A **14**
Thelma Av. *Brn E* 4G **23**
Theodore Rd. *Stoke* 2G **35**
Theresa Clo. *Stoke* 4K **39**
Third Av. *Kid* 2B **20**
Third Av. *Stoke* 1J **35**
Thirlmere Ct. *Cong* 5C **8**
Thirlmere Gro. *Stoke* 3K **41**
Thirlmere Pl. *New* 1E **38**
Thirsk Pl. *New* 3H **31**
Thistleberry Av. *New* . . .6C **32** (6A **6**)
Thistleberry Ho. *New* 5C **32**
Thistleberry Vs. *New* . . .5D **32** (5A **6**)
Thistles, The. *New* 6C **32**
Thistley Hough. *Stoke* 7J **33**
Thomas Av. *New* 1D **32**
Thomas Clo. *Als* 6F **11**
Thomas St. *Bid* 1C **14**
Thomas St. *Cong* 4G **9**
Thomas St. *Leek* 3E **16**
Thomas St. *Pac* 2J **21**
Thomas St. *Tal* 3A **20**
Thompstone Av. *New* 2C **32**
Thorley Dri. *C'dle* 4J **45**
Thornburrow Dri.
   Stoke 6H **33**
Thorncliffe Rd. *Thor* 2J **17**
Thorncliffe Vw. *Leek* 1J **17**
Thorncliff Gro. *Stoke* 7D **28**
Thorne Pl. *Stoke* 3C **42**
Thorneycroft Av. *Stoke* 2A **28**
Thornfield Av. *Leek* 4J **17**
Thornham Clo. *New* 4E **38**
Thornham Grn. *Stoke* 4H **35**
Thornhill Dri. *Mad* 1B **30**
Thornhill Rd. *Leek* 5D **16**
Thornhill Rd. *Stoke* 5K **35**
Thornley Rd. *Stoke* 1J **27**
Thornton Rd. *Stoke* 5B **34**
Thorpe Grn. *Stoke* 7E **40**
Thorpe Ri. *C'dle* 1H **45**
Three Fields Clo. *Cong* 4C **8**
Three Mile La. *K'le* 7F **31**
Thurlwood 2G **11**
Thurlwood Dri. *Stoke* 2E **28**
Thursfield Av. *Kid* 7F **13**
Thursfield Pl. *Stoke* 7C **22**
Thursfield Wlk. *Stoke* 6C **22**
Thurston Way. *Stoke* 5H **35**
Thyme Gro. *Stoke* 1C **48**
Tibb St. *Big E* 2G **25**
Tiber Dri. *New* 7A **26**
Tickhill La. *Dil* 1G **43**
Tidebrook Pl. *Stoke* 4H **21**
Tideswell Rd. *Stoke* 1H **41**
Tidnock Av. *Cong* 2G **9**
Tierney St. *Stoke* 7C **28** (1H **5**)
Tilbrook Clo. *Stoke* 5H **35**
Tilehurst Pl. *Stoke* 5D **40**

Tilery La. *Stoke* 5C **40**
   (in two parts)
Tilewright Clo. *Kid* 1E **20**
Tillet Grn. *Stoke* 3C **42**
Till Wlk. *Stoke* 7J **35**
Tilson Av. *Stoke* 6J **33**
Tilstone Clo. *Kid* 3D **20**
Timble Clo. *Stoke* 5H **35**
Times Sq. *Stoke* 2G **41**
   (off Market St.)
Timmis St. *Stoke* 2K **33** (5B **4**)
Timor Gro. *Stoke* 6A **40**
Timothy Clo. *Stoke* 7H **35**
Tintagel Pl. *Stoke* 5J **35**
Tintern Pl. *New* 5C **26**
Tintern St. *Stoke* 2D **34** (4H **5**)
Tipping Av. *Stoke* 5C **42**
Tirley St. *Stoke* 1D **40**
Tissington Pl. *Stoke* 7D **42**
Tittensor 6A **46**
Tittensor Rd. *New* 1F **39**
Tittensor Rd. *T'sor & B'stn* . . .7A **46**
Titterton St. *Stoke* 7B **34**
Tittesworth Av. *Leek* 2H **17**
Tiverton Rd. *Stoke* 4H **35**
Toft End Rd. *New* 3E **26**
Tolkien Way. *Stoke* 5K **33**
Toll Bar Rd. *Werr* 1E **36**
Tollgate Clo. *Tal* 3K **19**
Tollgate Ct. *Stoke* 6E **40**
Tomfields. *Big E* 4G **25**
Tomlinson St. *Stoke* 4G **27**
Tommy's La. *Cong* 3H **9**
Tonbridge Av. *Stoke* 7A **22**
Toney Pl. *Stoke* 2E **34**
Tongue La. *Brn E* 3D **22**
Tontine Sq. *Stoke* 1B **34** (3F **5**)
Tontines, The. *Stoke* 3F **5**
Tontine St. *Stoke* 1B **34** (3F **5**)
   (in two parts)
Tony Waddington Pl. *Stoke* . . .2B **40**
Top Chapel La. *Brn E* 2G **23**
Top Heath's Row. *Brn E* 3G **23**
Top Sta. Rd. *Mow C* 3F **13**
Topham Pl. *Stoke* 2F **35**
Torres Wlk. *Stoke* 7D **28**
Torridon Clo. *Stoke* 1B **46**
Tor St. *Stoke* 5C **28**
Torville Dri. *Bid* 2D **14**
Total Fitness 7G **33**
Tourist Info. Cen.
   (Congleton)
Tourist Info. Cen. 3F **17**
   (Leek)
Tourist Info. Cen. 4E **32** (3D **6**)
   (Newcastle-under-Lyme)
Tourist Info. Cen. 1B **34** (2F **5**)
   (Stoke-on-Trent)
Tower Clo. *Brn L* 4A **14**
Tower Hill Ct. *Cong* 4D **8**
Tower Hill Rd.
   Mow C & Brn L 2H **13**
Tower Sq. *Stoke* 1G **27**
Townend 7F **49**
Town End. *C'dle* 3F **45**
Townend. *Ful* 7F **49**
Townfield Clo. *Tal* 1A **20**
Townsend 2G **35**
Townsend La. *Sch G* 2H **11**
Townsend Pl. *Stoke* 2G **35**
Townsend Rd. *Cong* 5G **9**
Trade St. *Stoke* 6A **34**
Trafalgar Ct. *Stoke* 5K **27**
   (off Waterloo St.)
Trafalgar Rd. *Stoke* 5H **33**
Trafalgar St. *Stoke* 7B **28** (1E **5**)
Trafford Clo. *Leek* 4J **17**
Transport La. *Stoke* 3G **41**
Tranter Rd. *Stoke* 6G **29**
Travers Ct. *Stoke* 7C **34**
Travers St. *Stoke* 5H **27**
Trecastle Gro. *Stoke* 5K **41**
Tregaron Ct. *Ash B* 2B **36**
Tregenna Clo. *Stoke* 7B **42**
Tregew Pl. *New* 3A **32**
Tregowan Clo. *Stoke* 1A **28**

Trent Clo. *C'dle* 5H **45**
Trentfields Rd. *Stoke* 2F **29**
Trent Gro. *Bid* 4C **14**
Trent Gro. *New* 3D **38**
Trentham 7K **39**
Trentham Bus. Cen.
   Stoke 7C **40**
Trentham Ct. *Stoke* 7H **39**
Trentham Gardens &
   Pleasure Grounds 7H **39**
Trentham Gdns. Cvn. Pk.
   Stoke 7H **39**
Trentham Gdns. Clo.
   Stoke 7J **39**
Trentham Golf Course. 2A **46**
Trentham Gro. *New* 1F **33**
Trentham Lakes N. *Stoke* 4C **40**
Trentham Lakes S. *Stoke* 7C **40**
Trentham M. *Stoke* 7K **39**
Trentham Rd. *But* 6A **38**
Trentham Rd. *Hem H* 7B **40**
Trentley Dri. *Bid M* 2G **15**
Trentley Rd. *Stoke* 7J **39**
Trentmill Nature Pk. 3D **34**
Trentmill Rd. *Stoke* 3D **34** (6H **5**)
Trent Rd. *For* 6H **43**
Trentside Bus. Pk. *Stoke* 2A **40**
Trentside Rd. *Stoke* 6F **23**
Trent St. *Stoke* 2E **34**
Trent Ter. *Stoke* 6F **23**
Trent Vale. 3H **39**
Trent Valley Rd. *Stoke* 2J **39**
Trent Wlk. *Stoke* 3C **34** (6H **5**)
Trentway Clo. *Stoke* 2F **35**
Trevithick Clo. *Stoke* 6J **35**
Trevor Dri. *Cav* 3E **42**
Trimley Way. *Stoke* 3G **35**
Trimpos. *Dil* 1C **44**
Triner Pl. *Stoke* 7D **22**
Tring Clo. *Stoke* 5H **35**
Trinity Ct. *Cong* 6K **9**
Trinity Ct. *New* 4B **26**
Trinity Pde. Stoke 1B **34** (3E **5**)
   (off Trinity St.)
Trinity Pl. *Cong* 7K **9**
Trinity Pl. *Stoke* 1G **35**
Trinity St. *Stoke* 1A **34** (3D **4**)
Triton Wlk. *Stoke* 3C **28**
Troutbeck Av. *Cong* 5C **8**
Troutdale Clo. *Stoke* 6G **35**
Trowbridge Cres. *Stoke* 2H **35**
Trubshaw 7G **13**
Trubshaw Ct. *Kid* 7F **13**
Trubshawe Cross. *Stoke* 4G **27**
Trubshawe St. *Stoke* 4G **27**
Trubshaw Pl. *Kid* 7E **12**
Truro Clo. *Cong* 7G **9**
Truro Pl. *Stoke* 3G **35**
Tudor Clo. *Stoke* 7K **33**
Tudor Ct. *Ful* 6F **49**
Tudor Ct. *New* 6E **26**
Tudor Gro. *New* 1F **33**
Tudor Hollow. *Ful* 6F **49**
Tudor Rose Way. *Stoke* 2C **28**
Tudors, The. *Stoke* 7H **21**
Tudor Way. *Cong* 6F **9**
Tulip Gro. *New* 3F **33** (1E **7**)
Tulley Pl. *Stoke* 2F **35**
Tulsa Clo. *Stoke* 4F **35**
Tunbridge Dri. *New* 3G **31**
Tunnel Ter. *Stoke* 6E **20**
Tunnicliffe Clo. *Stoke* 3K **41**
Tunstall. 1H **27**
Tunstall Greenway. *Stoke* 7H **21**
   (Boulevard, The)
Tunstall Greenway. *Stoke* 6H **21**
   (Furlong Rd.)
Tunstall Pool. 1H **27**
Tunstall Rd. *Knyp & Bid* 5B **14**
Tunstall Rd. Ind. Est. *Knyp* . . .6A **14**
Tunstall Western By-Pass.
   Stoke 2E **26**
Turin Pl. *Stoke* 7B **32**
Turnberry Dri. *Stoke* 6J **39**
Turner Av. *Big E* 3H **25**
Turner Cres. *Stoke* 6B **26**
Turner St. *Stoke* 7C **28** (1H **5**)

Turnhill Gro. *New* 5E **26**
Turnhurst. 4J **21**
Turnhurst Rd. *Pac* 2J **21**
Turnlea Clo. *Knyp* 4A **14**
Turnock St. *Stoke* 1H **35**
Tuscan Clo. *C'dle* 5F **45**
Tuscan Ho. *Stoke* 4G **41**
Tuscan St. *Stoke* 2H **41**
Tuscan Way. *New* 6A **26**
Tutbury Gro. *Stoke* 2J **41**
Tweed Gro. *New* 2D **38**
Tweed St. *Stoke* 2D **40**
Twemlow St. *Stoke* 2K **33** (4B **4**)
Twigg St. *Stoke* 3G **35**
Twyning Grn. *Stoke* 7E **40**
Tyler Gro. *Stoke* 4H **27**
Tyndall Pl. *Stoke* 6H **33**
Tyneham Gro. *Stoke* 2F **29**
Tyne Way. *New* 2D **38**
Tynwald Grange. *New* 3D **32**
Tyrell Gro. *Stoke* 4E **28**
Tyson Grn. *Stoke* 5J **35**

U

Ubberley. 4H **35**
Ubberley Grn. *Stoke* 3H **35**
Ubberley Rd. *Stoke* 3G **35**
Uffington Pde. *Stoke* 4H **35**
Ufton Clo. *Stoke* 1E **46**
Ullswater Av. *Stoke* 4H **27**
Ullswater Dri. *C'dle* 2H **45**
Ullswater Rd. *Cong* 5B **8**
Ulster Ter. *Stoke* 1K **39**
Ulverston Rd. *Stoke* 7E **40**
Umberleigh Rd. *Stoke* 7D **40**
Under The Hill. *Bid M* 1F **15**
Underwood Rd. *New* 4G **31**
Unicorn Ind. Est. *Stoke* 4G **27**
Unicorn Pl. *Stoke* 6J **21**
Union Clo. *Cong* 4F **9**
Union Ct. *Stoke* 7B **28** (1E **5**)
Union St. *Leek* 3G **17**
Union St. *Cong* 4F **9**
Union St. *Stoke* 7B **28** (1E **5**)
Unity Av. *Stoke* 5C **28**
Unity Way. *Tal* 3A **20**
University of Keele. 6J **31**
Unwin St. *Stoke* 1A **28**
(in two parts)
Uplands Av. *Stoke* 5J **21**
Uplands Av. *Werr* 2B **36**
Uplands Cft. *Werr* 1B **36**
Uplands Dri. *Werr* 2B **36**
Uplands Rd. *Stoke* 5G **29**
Uplands, The. *Bid* 2K **15**
Uplands, The. *New* 3F **33** (1E **7**)
Up. Belgrave Rd. *Stoke* 5J **41**
Upper Cres. *Stoke* 5H **33** (5H **7**)
Up. Cross St. *Stoke* 2H **41**
Up. Furlong St. *Stoke* 7C **34**
Up. Hillchurch St. *Stoke*
. . . . .1C **34** (2G **5**)
Up. Huntbach St. *Stoke*
. . . . .1C **34** (2G **5**)
Up. Market Sq. *Stoke*
. . . . .1B **34** (3F **5**)
Up. Marsh. *New* 2G **33**
Up. Normacot Rd. *Stoke* 4J **41**
(Lwr. Spring Rd.)
Up. Normacot Rd. *Stoke* 4J **41**
(Uttoxeter Rd)
Urmston Pl. *Stoke* 7E **40**
Utterby Side. *Stoke* 5H **35**
Uttoxeter Rd. *B Bri* 6D **42**
Uttoxeter Rd. *Dray* 1K **49**
Uttoxeter Rd. *Stoke* 3H **41**

V

Vale Gdns. *Als* 6F **11**
Valentine Rd. *Kid* 2D **20**
Vale Pleasant. *New* 3K **31**
Valerian Way. *Stoke* 1B **48**
Vale St. *New* 4B **26**

Vale St. *Sil* 3J **31**
Vale St. *Stoke* 6A **34**
Vale Ter. *Cong* 5F **9**
Vale, The. Cong 5F **9**
(off Priesty Fields)
Vale Vw. *New* 5G **27**
Vale Wlk. *Cong* 5F **9**
Valley Clo. *Als* 7A **10**
Valley Dri. *Leek* 4C **16**
Valley Pk. Way. *Stoke* 3E **40**
Valley Rd. *W Coy* 3C **42**
Valley Vw. *Cong* 4E **8**
Varey Rd. *Eat T* 3H **9**
Vaudrey Cres. *Cong* 4H **9**
Venice Ct. *New* 6B **32**
Venn Pl. *Stoke* 3D **34**
Ventnor Gro. *Stoke* 1E **46**
Venton Clo. *Stoke* 7D **22**
Venture Way. Stoke 1B **28**
(off Bradeley Village)
Verney Way. *Stoke* 7E **40**
Vernon Av. *A'ly* 2D **24**
Vernon Av. *Cong* 7H **9**
Vernon Clo. *A'ly* 2E **24**
Vernon Rd. *Stoke* 5A **34**
Verona Gro. *Stoke* 1K **41**
Vessey Ter. *New* 5F **33** (5E **7**)
Vicarage Cres. *Cav* 3E **42**
Vicarage Cres. *New* 6F **33** (6F **7**)
Vicarage Cres. *T'sor* 6A **44**
Vicarage La. *B'stn* 5D **46**
Vicarage La. *Mad* 3B **30**
Vicarage La. *Stoke* 2H **39**
Vicarage Rd. *Leek* 3G **17**
Vicarage Rd. *Stoke* 5J **33**
Vichy Clo. *New* 6B **32**
Vickers Rd. *Stoke* 6K **21**
Victoria Av. *Halm* 5F **25**
Victoria Av. *Kid* 1C **20**
Victoria Av. *Stoke* 3B **34** (6E **5**)
Victoria Clo. *Sil* 3K **31**
Victoria Cotts. *Stoke* 4K **41**
Victoria Ct. Kid 1D **20**
(off Attwood St.)
Victoria Ct. *New* 2F **33**
Victoria Ct. Stoke 7D **34**
(off Beville St.)
Victoria Hall. 2B **34** (4F **5**)
Victoria Ind. Complex.
Stoke 1F **41**
Victoria Pk. Rd. *Stoke* 1H **27**
Victoria Pl. *New* 5B **26**
(Chesterton)
Victoria Pl. *New* 7G **27**
(Wollaston)
Victoria Pl. *Stoke* 7D **34**
(in two parts)
Victoria Pl. Link.
Stoke 1E **40**
Victoria Rd. *New* 5F **33** (4F **7**)
Victoria Rd. *Stoke* 4C **34**
Victoria Row. *Knyp* 6B **14**
Victoria Sq. *Stoke* 2A **34** (5D **4**)
Victoria St. *C'dle* 3H **45**
Victoria St. *Ches* 5B **26**
Victoria St. *Cong* 5F **9**
Victoria St. *Leek* 3H **17**
Victoria St. *New* 5F **33** (5E **7**)
Victoria St. *Sil* 3K **31**
Victoria St. *Stoke* 3G **33** (1H **7**)
Victory Clo. *C'dle* 2H **45**
Vienna Pl. *New* 7C **32**
Vienna Way. *Stoke* 1K **41**
Views, The. *N'cpl* 1H **21**
Viggars Pl. *New* 3C **32**
Viking Way. *Cong* 3D **8**
Villa Clo. *Bid* 3B **14**
Village, The. 1K **23**
Village, The. *K'le* 6G **31**
Villas, The. *Stoke* 1K **39**
Villa St. *Stoke* 1K **39**
Villiers St. *Stoke* 5G **41**
Vincent St. *Stoke* 7D **28**
Vine Bank Rd. *Kid* 1D **20**
Vinebank St. *Stoke* 7K **33**
Vine Row. *Stoke* 7K **33**
Viscount Wlk. *Stoke* 7B **42**

Vivian Rd. *Stoke* 7E **34**
Vowchurch Way. *Stoke* 4H **35**

W

Wade Av. *New* 6G **27**
Wadebridge Rd. *Stoke* 4G **35**
Wade Clo. *C'dle* 5G **45**
Wade St. *Stoke* 3A **28**
Wadham St. *Stoke* 6K **33**
Waggs Rd. *Cong* 6E **8**
Wagg St. *Cong* 5F **9**
Wain Av. *New* 5C **32**
Wain Av. *Stoke* 6D **22**
Wain Dri. *Stoke* 7H **33**
(in two parts)
Wain Lea. 6J **13**
Wain St. *Stoke* 3J **27**
Wainwood Ri. *Stoke* 1J **39**
Wainwright Wlk. *Stoke* 3G **5**
Wakefield Rd. *Stoke* 2J **39**
Walcot Gro. *Stoke* 4F **35**
Walfield Av. *Cong* 2F **9**
Walgrave Clo. *Cong* 4C **8**
Walkergreen Rd. *New* 2A **26**
Walker Rd. *Stoke* 7J **21**
Walkers La. *Sch G* 1J **11**
Walker St. *Stoke* 2G **27**
Walklate Av. *New* 2G **33**
Walks, The. *Leek* 4E **16**
Wallbridge Clo. *Leek* 5D **16**
Wallbridge Dri. *Leek* 4D **16**
Wallbridge Park. 5C **16**
Wallbridge Precinct. Leek 5D **16**
(off Wallbridge Dri.)
Waller Rd. *Ful* 7F **49**
Walley Dri. *Stoke* 5G **21**
Walley Pl. *Stoke* 5K **27**
Walley's Dri. *New* 3G **33** (1G **7**)
Walley St. *Bid* 1B **14**
Walley St. *Stoke* 5K **27**
Wall Hill Ct. *Leek* 5F **17**
(off Junction Rd.)
Wallhill La. *B'lw* 6A **8**
Wallis St. *Stoke* 7G **29**
Wallis St. *Stoke* 7E **34**
Wallis Way. *Stoke* 2F **29**
Wallmires La. *Werr* 4E **36**
Wallworth's Bank. *Cong* 5G **9**
Walmer Pl. *Stoke* 1G **41**
Walney Gro. *Stoke* 7B **28**
Walnut Gro. *New* 4A **26**
Walnut Ri. *Cong* 5D **8**
Walpole St. *Stoke* 1J **41**
Walsingham Gdns. *New* 4E **38**
Walton Cres. *Stoke* 1B **40**
Walton Gro. *Tal* 3K **19**
Walton Pl. *New* 6C **26**
Walton Rd. *Stoke* 3J **39**
Walton Way. *Tal* 3K **19**
Warburton Ct. Stoke 5K **27**
(off Warburton St.)
Warburton St. *Stoke* 5K **27**
Wardle Cres. *Leek* 5F **17**
Wardle La. *L Oaks* 3H **29**
Wardle St. *Stoke* 1H **27**
Ward Pl. *Stoke* 6A **22**
Warminster Pl. *Stoke* 3F **41**
Warmson Clo. *Stoke* 7H **35**
Warner St. *Stoke* 2B **34** (4E **5**)
Warren Pl. *Stoke* 4J **41**
Warren Rd. *Stoke* 5A **22**
Warren St. *Stoke* 4J **41**
Warrilow Heath Rd. *New* 3K **25**
Warrington Dri. *Leek* 4D **16**
Warrington Rd. *Stoke* 4C **34**
Warrington St. *Stoke* 7E **34**
Warsill Gro. *Stoke* 2J **41**
Warwick Av. *C'dle* 4F **45**
Warwick Av. *New* 2F **39**
Warwick Av. *Stoke* 5A **42**
Warwick Clo. *Kid* 7D **12**
Warwick Gro. *New* 2H **33**
Warwick St. *Bid* 3B **14**
Warwick St. *New* 5B **26**

Warwick St. *Stoke* 2K **33** (5B **4**)
Washerwall. 1B **36**
Washerwall La. *Werr* 1B **36**
Washerwall St. *Stoke* 5J **35**
Washington Clo. *Gil H* 2H **15**
Washington St. *Stoke* 1H **27**
Watchfield Clo. *Stoke* 5A **42**
Waterbeck Gro. *Stoke* 2B **46**
Waterdale Gro. *Stoke* 3K **41**
Waterfall Cotts. *Werr* 5J **23**
Watergate St. *Stoke* 2F **27**
Waterhays Village. 2K **25**
Waterhead Rd. *Stoke* 5A **42**
Watering Trough Bank.
Mad H 5C **30**
Waterloo Gro. *Kid* 1D **20**
Waterloo Rd. *Stoke* 4K **33** (1D **4**)
Waterloo St. *Leek* 4E **16**
Waterloo St. *Stoke* 2C **34** (4G **5**)
Waters Edge. *Stoke* 6C **28**
Waterside Clo. *Mad* 2B **30**
Waterside Dri. *Stoke* 7D **40**
Water St. *New* 4F **33** (3F **7**)
Water St. *Red S* 2A **26**
Water St. *Stoke* 1K **39**
Waterworld. 1J **33** (2A **4**)
Watery La. *Stoke* 5J **41**
Watford St. *Stoke* 5B **34**
Watkin St. *Stoke* 1C **40**
Watlands Av. *New* 7F **27**
Watlands Rd. *Big E* 2F **25**
Watlands Vw. *New* 7E **26**
Watson Rd. *Stoke* 2J **39**
Watson St. *Stoke* 5J **33**
Watt Pl. *C'dle* 3G **45**
Waveney Ct. *New* 2E **38**
Waveney Gro. *New* 2E **38**
Waveney Wlk. N. *Stoke* 7K **21**
Waveney Wlk. S. *Stoke* 7K **21**
Waverley Pl. *New* 2D **38**
Waverton Rd. *Stoke* 6K **35**
Wavertree Av. *Sch G* 3B **12**
Wayfield Gro. *Stoke* 5G **33** (5H **7**)
Wayside. *Als* 1G **19**
Wayside Av. *New* 1F **33**
Wayte St. *Stoke* 7A **28**
Weaver Clo. *Als* 7B **10**
Weaver Clo. *Bid* 1C **14**
Weaver Clo. *C'dle* 1H **45**
Weaver Pl. *New* 2E **38**
Weaver St. *Stoke* 1B **34** (3E **5**)
Webberley La. *Stoke* 3H **41**
Webb St. *Stoke* 3C **42**
Webster Av. *Stoke* 1K **41**
Webster St. *New* 5F **33** (5F **7**)
Wedgwood. 4C **46**
Wedgwood Av. *Big E* 3G **25**
Wedgwood Av. *New* 6C **32**
Wedgwood Ct. *Stoke* . . .2K **33** (4A **4**)
Wedgwood Dri. *B'stn* 4B **46**
Wedgwood La. *B'stn* 3D **46**
Wedgwood La. *Gil H* 2H **15**
(in two parts)
Wedgwood Pl. *Stoke* 4J **27**
Wedgwood Potteries Mus. &
Vis. Cen. 3C **46**
Wedgwood Rd. *C'dle* 5F **45**
Wedgwood Rd. *Stoke* 7E **34**
Wedgwood Rd. *Tal P* 4A **20**
Wedgwood's Monument. 1K **25**
WEDGWOOD STATION. RAIL
. . . . .4C **46**
Wedgwood St. *Stoke* 4J **27**
Wedgwood St. *Wol* 7G **27**
Weetman Clo. *Stoke* 4F **21**
Weighton Gro. *Stoke* 4K **35**
Weir Gro. *Kid* 1E **20**
Welbeck Pl. *Stoke* 7H **29**
Welby St. *Stoke* 1C **40**
Welch St. *Stoke* 6A **34**
Weldon Av. *Stoke* 2C **42**
Welland Gro. *New* 3D **38**
Wellbury Clo. *Stoke* 2B **46**
Weller St. *Stoke* 5J **33**
Wellesley St. *Stoke* 3A **34**
Wellfield Rd. *Stoke* 3G **35**
Wellington Clo. *Cong* 3F **9**

Wellington Ct. *Leek* 4F **17**
Wellington Ct. *Stoke* . . .1C **34** (3H **5**)
Wellington Rd. *Kid* 1D **20**
Wellington Rd. *Stoke*
. . . . .1C **34** (3H **5**)
Wellington St. *Leek* 3F **17**
Wellington St. *New* 7F **27**
Wellington St. *Stoke* . . .1C **34** (4H **5**)
Wellington Ter. *Stoke*
. . . . .2C **34** (4H **5**)
Well La. *Als* 7D **10**
Well La. *Gil H* 2H **15**
Wells Clo. *Bid* 2C **14**
Well St. *Bid* 2B **14**
Well St. *C'dle* 3H **45**
Well St. *For* 6H **43**
Well St. *Leek* 4G **17**
Well St. *Mow C* 3G **13**
Well St. *New* 5F **33** (4E **7**)
Well St. *Stoke* 2C **34** (4G **5**)
Welsh Clo. *Stoke* 5J **41**
Welsh Row. *Mow C* 3H **13**
Wem Gro. *New* 2B **26**
Wendling Clo. *Stoke* 4J **35**
Wendover Gro. *Stoke* 4G **35**
Wendy Clo. *Stoke* 4G **35**
Wenger Cres. *Stoke* 7J **39**
Wenham Dri. *Stoke* 7C **42**
Wenlock Clo. *New* 2B **26**
Wenlock Clo. *Stoke* 3A **22**
Wensleydale Av. *Cong* 2J **9**
Wensleydale Clo. *Stoke* 5C **28**
Wentworth Dri. *Kid* 7F **13**
Wentworth Gro. *Stoke* 5E **28**
Werburgh Dri. *Stoke* 7J **39**
Wereton. 3D **24**
Wereton Rd. *A'ly* 3E **24**
Werrington. 1D **36**
Werrington Rd. *Stoke* 2F **35**
Wesker Pl. *Stoke* 2A **42**
Wesley Av. *Als* 6E **10**
Wesley Ct. *Cong* 5F **9**
Wesley Gdns. *Kid* 1D **20**
Wesley Pl. *Halm* 5E **24**
Wesley Pl. *New* 5C **32** (4A **6**)
Wesley St. *Big E* 3H **25**
Wesley St. *B Bri* 7H **43**
Wesley St. *Stoke* 1G **27**
Wessex Dri. *Stoke* 6K **39**
Westacre. *Stoke* 2E **34**
West Av. *New* 3G **33** (1H **7**)
West Av. *Stoke* 5J **33**
West Av. *Tal* 3K **19**
W. Bank. *Stoke* 7K **33**
Westbourne Clo. *Leek* 3D **16**
Westbourne Dri. *Stoke* 6H **21**
Westbourne M. *Cong* 5D **8**
W. Brampton. *New* 4E **32** (2D **6**)
Westbury Cen., The. *New* 4F **39**
Westbury Clo. *Stoke* 7E **28**
Westbury Park. 4E **38**
Westbury Rd. *New* 3E **38**
Westcliffe. 4J **21**
Westcliffe. *Leek* 3E **16**
(off Alma St.)
Westcliffe Av. *New* 3D **38**
WESTCLIFFE HOSPITAL. . . .4J **21**
West Cres. *Stoke* 4D **28**
W. End Av. *Leek* 4E **16**
W. End Cotts. *Cong* 5E **8**
Westerby Dri. *Werr* 2B **36**
Westerham Clo. *Stoke* 7J **39**
Westfield Av. *A'ly* 2D **24**
Westfield Rd. *Mow C* 3F **13**
Westfield Rd. *Stoke* 2G **35**
Westfields. *Leek* 4G **17**
Westfields. *Stoke* . . . .
Westhead Wlk. *Stoke* . .2A **34** (5C **4**)
West Heath. 5D **8**
W. Heath Shop. Cen. *Cong* 4C **8**
Westholme Clo. *Cong* 4D **8**
Westlands. 1D **38**
Westlands. *Big E* 2G **25**
Westlands Av. *New* 6C **32** (6A **6**)
Westlands, The. *Cong* 5E **8**
Westland St. *Stoke* 6K **33**
Westmarsh Gro. *Stoke* 7K **21**

Westmill St. *Stoke* 3C **34**
Westminster Pl. *Stoke* 5K **39**
Westminster Rd. *Leek* 2H **17**
Westmorland Av. *Kid* 4C **20**
Westmorland Clo. *Stoke* 3K **21**
Weston Clo. *Ash B* 2B **36**
Weston Clo. *New* 2C **32**
Weston Ct. *Stoke* 2B **42**
Weston Coyney. 2C **42**
Weston Coyney Rd. *Stoke* 3J **41**
Weston Dri. *Stoke* 2B **42**
Westonfields Dri. *Stoke* 3K **41**
Weston Rd. *Stoke* 5B **42**
Weston St. *Leek* 3H **17**
Weston St. *Stoke* 7J **35**
Westonview Av. *Stoke* 7J **35**
West Pde. *Stoke* 1B **40**
Westport Greenway. *Stoke* 2H **27**
Westport Lake Rd. *Stoke* 3G **27**
Westport Rd. *Stoke* 3H **27**
W. Precinct. *Stoke* 2B **34** (4F **5**)
West Rd. *Cong* 4D **8**
Westsprink Cres. *Stoke* 4K **41**
West St. *Bid* 3B **14**
West St. *Cong* 4E **8**
West St. *Leek* 3F **17**
West St. *Mow C* 4E **8**
West St. *New* 5F **33** (4E **7**)
West St. *Port* 5G **27**
West St. *Sil* 4J **31**
West St. *Stoke* 1C **42**
West Ter. *Kid* 2D **20**
West Ter. *Stoke* 5A **22**
West Vw. *New* 7E **26**
West Vw. *R'gh C* 3A **48**
Westview Clo. *Leek* 3D **16**
Westville Dri. *Cong* 5C **8**
Westwood Ct. *Stoke* . . .1C **34** (3H **5**)
Westwood Gro. *Leek* 3E **16**
Westwood Heath Rd. *Leek* 4D **16**
Westwood Pk. Av. *Leek* 4C **16**
Westwood Pk. Dri. *Leek* 4C **16**
Westwood Rd. *Leek* 4D **16**
Westwood Rd. *New* 6G **27**
Westwood Rd. *Stoke* 4B **42**
Westwood Ter. Leek *3E 16*
(off Wellington St.)
Wetenhall Dri. *Leek* 4C **16**
Wetherby Clo. *C'dle* 1H **45**
Wetherby Clo. *New* 5B **26**
Wetherby Rd. *Stoke* 7A **40**
Wetley Av. *Werr* 1G **37**
Wetley Moor. 6K **29**
Weybourne Av. *Stoke* 1G **29**
Whalley Av. *Stoke* 6H **33**
Wharfdale Rd. *Cong* 2J **9**
Wharfe Clo. *Cong* 6H **9**
Wharfedale Wlk. *Stoke* 3F **41**
Wharf Pl. *Stoke* 6B **34**
Wharf Rd. *Bid* 2B **14**
Wharf St. *New* 4G **33** (3F **7**)
Wharf Ter. *Mad H* 5C **30**
Wharton St. *Stoke* 3B **28**
Wheatfields. *Stoke* 1B **28**
Wheatley Bank Cotts. *Stoke* 2F **35**
Wheatly Av. *Stoke* 7H **33**
Wheelock Clo. *Als* 7B **10**
Wheelock Way. *Kid* 1E **20**
Whetstone Rd. *Gil H* 2H **15**
Whieldon Cres. *Stoke* 1C **40**
Whieldon Ind. Est. *Stoke* 7B **34**
Whieldon Rd. *Stoke* 7B **34**
Whimple Side. *Stoke* 4G **35**
Whitaker Rd. *Stoke* 3D **40**
Whitbread Dri. *Bid* 2D **14**
Whitchurch Gro. *New* 2B **26**
Whitcliffe Pl. *Stoke* 3E **40**
Whitcombe Rd. *Stoke* 4B **42**
Whitebeam Clo. *New* 3A **26**
Whitehall Av. *Kid* 1C **20**
Whitehall Rd. *Kid* 1C **20**
Whitehaven Dri. *Stoke*
. . . . .7A **28** (1D **4**)
Whitehead Rd. *Stoke* 6A **22**
Whitehill. 7E **12**
Whitehill Ter. *Kid* 1E **20**

Whitehouse Rd. *New* 2E **32**
Whitehouse Rd. *Stoke* 7F **29**
Whitehouse Rd. N. *New* 1E **32**
Whitehurst La. *Dil* . . .6K **37** & 1A **44**
Whiteridge Rd. *Kid* 1D **20**
Whitesands Gro. *Stoke* 1C **48**
Whitestone Rd. *Stoke* 1C **48**
Whitethorn Av. *B'stn* 6C **46**
Whitethorn Way. *New* 3B **26**
Whitfield. 5C **22**
Whitfield Av. *New* 5D **32** (5A **6**)
Whitfield Greenway. *Stoke* 1J **27**
(Greenbank Rd.)
Whitfield Greenway. *Stoke* 6J **21**
(Roseberry St.)
Whitfield Rd. *Kid* 1E **20**
Whitfield Rd. *Stoke* 4C **22**
Whitfield St. *Leek* 5F **17**
Whitfield Vs. *Stoke* 5C **22**
Whitley Rd. *Stoke* 5C **22**
Whitmore Av. *Werr* 1C **36**
Whitmore Rd. *But & New* 5A **38**
Whitmore Rd. *New & Tren* 6E **38**
Whitmore St. *Stoke* 3K **33** (6B **4**)
Whitridge Gro. *Stoke* 5J **35**
Whittle Rd. *Stoke* 6C **42**
Whygate Gro. *Stoke* 6E **28**
Wickenstones Ct. Bid *3C 14*
(off Edgeley Rd.)
Widecombe Rd. *Stoke* 6E **28**
Wigmore Pl. *Stoke* 7H **35**
Wignall Rd. *Stoke* 5G **21**
Wilbraham Rd. *Cong* 4H **9**
Wilbraham's Wlk. *A'ly* 2E **24**
Wilbrahams Way. *Als* 6E **10**
Wild Goose Av. *Kid* 7G **13**
Wilding Rd. *Stoke* 5C **22**
Wileman Pl. *Stoke* 7D **34**
Wileman St. *Stoke* 7D **34**
Wilfred Pl. *Stoke* 5H **33**
Wilkinson St. *Stoke* 2G **27**
Wilks St. *Stoke* 7H **21**
Willatt Pl. *Stoke* 3F **29**
Willdale Gro. *Stoke* 7E **28**
Willeton St. *Stoke* 2F **35**
Willfield La. *Brn E* 4G **23**
William Av. *Bid* 3C **14**
William Av. *Stoke* 6D **42**
William Birch Ct. *Stoke* 4F **35**
William Birch Rd. *Stoke* 4F **35**
William Clo. *For* 7J **43**
William Clowes St. *Stoke* 4J **27**
William Coltman Way.
Stoke 6F **21**
William Fiske Ct. *Stoke* 2H **39**
William Rd. *Kid* 1D **20**
William Ruston Rd. *Stoke* 2C **28**
Williamson Av. *Stoke* 5C **22**
Williamson St. *Stoke* 2H **27**
William St. *Cong* 3J **9**
William St. *Stoke* 7D **34**
William Ter. *Stoke* 5A **22**
Willmer Cres. *Mow C* 4E **12**
Willott Hill Rd. *New* 3A **26**
Willoughby St. *Stoke* 4G **21**
Willow Clo. *Kid* 4D **20**
Willow Clo. *New* 3A **26**
Willow Ct. *Als* 6F **11**
Willowcroft Ri. *B Bri* 6D **42**
Willowcroft Way. *Har* 6H **13**
Willowdale Av. *Stoke* 1B **40**
Willow Gro. *Stoke* 4D **40**
Willow La. *Stoke* 4B **48**
Willowood Gro. *Stoke* 6D **42**
Willow Pl. *Bid M* 1G **15**
Willow Row. *Stoke* 5G **41**
Willows Dri. *Stoke* 3B **48**
Willows, The. *Leek* 4D **16**
Willow St. *Cong* 4G **9**
Willow Tree Gro. *Rode H* 3G **11**
Willow Way. *For* 6H **43**
Wilmot Clo. *New* 2C **32**
Wilmot Rd. *Stoke* 2C **32**
Wilmot Gro. *Stoke* 7H **35**
Wilson Rd. *Stoke* 5J **39**
Wilson St. *New* 4E **32** (2D **6**)
Wilson St. *Stoke* 2A **28**

Wilson Way. *Stoke* 4F **21**
Wilton Av. *Werr* 1G **37**
Wilton St. *New* 3D **32**
Wiltshire Dri. *Cong* 3G **9**
Wiltshire Gro. *New* 2F **39**
Wimberry Dri. *New* 3A **26**
Wimborne Av. *Stoke* 7E **40**
Winchester Av. *Stoke* 3H **35**
Winchester Dri. *New* 2C **38**
Windermere Rd. *Cong* 5C **8**
Windermere Rd. *New* 2E **38**
Windermere St. *Stoke* 7A **28**
Windermere Way. *C'dle* 2J **45**
Windmill Av. *Kid* 3D **20**
Windmill Clo. *R'gh C* 3A **48**
Windmill Hill. *R'gh C* 3A **48**
Windmill Vw. *Werr* 1C **34** (2G **5**)
Windmill Vw. *Werr* 1D **36**
Windrush Clo. *Stoke* 2B **46**
Windsmoor St. *Stoke* 1A **40**
Windsor Av. *Stoke* 4J **41**
Windsor Dri. *Als* 6A **10**
Windsor Dri. *Leek* 2J **17**
Windsor Pl. *Cong* 5H **9**
Windsor Rd. *Stoke* 5K **39**
Windsor St. *New* 4F **33** (3E **7**)
Windy Arbour. *C'dle* 2H **45**
Windycote La. *Dil* 3H **37**
Wingate Wlk. *Stoke* 7E **40**
Winghay Clo. *Kid* 1E **20**
Winghay Clo. *Stoke* 4F **27**
Winghay Gro. *Stoke* 6A **22**
Wingrove Av. *Stoke* 5J **41**
Winifred Gdns. *Stoke* 6D **40**
Winifred St. *Stoke* 7A **28** (1D **4**)
Winnipeg Clo. *Stoke* 6A **40**
Winpenny Rd. *P East* 4C **26**
Winsford Av. *Stoke* 4K **41**
Winslow Grn. *Stoke* 4H **35**
Winston Av. *Als* 6D **10**
Winston Pl. *Stoke* 2F **35**
Winston Ter. *New* 6F **27**
Winterbourne Gro. *Stoke* 3K **41**
Winterfield La. *Hul* 5C **36**
Winterside Clo. *New* 3A **26**
Wintonfield St. *Stoke* 6B **34**
Winton Sq. *Stoke* 5B **34**
Wise St. *Stoke* 5H **41**
Witchford Cres. *Stoke* 7E **40**
Witham Way. *Bid* 1D **14**
Withies Rd. *Stoke* 2H **39**
Withington Rd. *Stoke* 4K **21**
Withnell Grn. *Stoke* 4K **21**
Withysakes. 1E **36**
Withysakes Rd. *Werr* 1E **36**
Witney Wlk. *Stoke* 7E **40**
Woburn Clo. *Stoke* 2B **46**
Woburn Dri. *Cong* 7K **9**
Wolfe St. *Stoke* 7A **34**
Wolseley Rd. *New* 7E **26**
Wolseley Rd. *Stoke* 2J **39**
Wolstanholme Clo. *Cong* 6H **9**
Wolstanton. 7G **27**
Wolstanton Retail Pk. *New* 7G **27**
Wolstanton Rd. *New* 6C **26**
Wolstern Rd. *Stoke* 1J **41**
Woodall St. *Stoke* 7A **28**
Woodbank St. *Stoke* 4J **27**
Woodberry Av. *Stoke* 1H **39**
Woodberry Clo. Stoke *1J 39*
(off Woodberry Av.)
Woodbridge Rd. *New* 4E **38**
Woodcock La. *Mow C* 4F **13**
Wood Cotts. *Werr* 4K **23**
Woodcroft. 5D **16**
Woodcroft. *Big E* 3H **25**
Woodcroft Av. *Leek* 5E **16**
Woodcroft Rd. *Leek* 5E **16**
Wood Dri. *Als* 7B **10**
Woodend St. *Stoke* 7E **34**
Woodfield Ct. *Leek* 3H **17**
Woodgate Av. *Chu L* 5H **11**
Woodgate St. *Stoke* 5B **42**
Woodhall Pl. *New* 3G **31**
Woodhall Rd. *Kid* 7F **13**
Woodhead Rd. *Stoke* 5G **29**
Woodhead Yd. *C'dle* 1H **45**

Woodhouse La.
  Bid & Bid M 2J **15**
Woodhouse La. Brn E 5D **22**
Woodhouse St. Stoke 7A **34**
Wooding Dean Clo. Stoke 1J **41**
Woodkirk Clo. Stoke 3K **21**
Woodland Av. New 7F **27**
Woodland Av. Stoke 7E **22**
Woodland Clo. Leek 7G **17**
Woodland Ct. Als 5E **10**
Woodland Gro. Bur 2A **28**
Woodland Hills. Mad 4A **30**
Woodland Rd. Rode H 2F **11**
Woodlands. Stoke 7J **27**
Woodlands Av. Cong 3F **9**
Woodlands Av. Tal 1A **20**
Woodlands Gro. Stoke 3B **48**
Woodlands La. B Bri 2J **49**
Woodlands Rd. Stoke 2H **39**
Woodlands, The. Stoke 2H **39**
Woodland St. Bid 3C **14**
Woodland St. Stoke 1H **27**
Wood Lane. 3H **25**
Wood La. Cong 3K **9**
Woodman St. Stoke 3G **29**
Woodpark La. Stoke 1H **47**
Wood Pl. Stoke 4C **42**
Woodruff Clo. Pac 2J **21**
Woodshutts. 2B **20**
Woodshutts St. Tal 2A **20**
Woodside. Chu L 6B **12**
Woodside. Leek 6G **17**
Woodside. Mad 1B **30**
Woodside Av. Als 6F **11**
Woodside Av. Brn E 5G **23**
Woodside Av. Kid 2D **20**

Woodside Cres. New 4F **39**
Woodside Dri. Stoke 3B **48**
Woodside La. Leek 7D **16**
Woodside Pl. Stoke 3G **29**
Woodside Vs. Stoke 2J **41**
Woodstock. 4D **20**
Woodstock Clo. New 2F **33**
Woodstock Rd. Stoke 4D **20**
Woodstock St. Stoke 3E **20**
Woodstone Av. End 5K **23**
Wood St. Big E 1F **25**
Wood St. Cong 4F **9**
Wood St. Leek 4G **17**
Wood St. Mow C 3F **13**
Wood St. Stoke 2H **41**
Wood Ter. Stoke 3A **34** (6D **4**)
Woodvale Cres. End 3K **23**
Wood Vw. Big E 3H **25**
Woodville Pl. Stoke 4B **42**
Woodville Rd. Stoke 4B **42**
Woodville Ter. Stoke 4C **42**
Woodward St. Stoke 6C **28**
Woolaston Dri. Als 7E **10**
Woolliscroft Rd. Stoke 2G **35**
Woolliscroft Av. New 2G **33**
Woolrich St. Stoke 5H **27**
Woolridge Ct. Stoke 3C **28**
       (off Community Dri.)
Woolston Av. Cong 5H **9**
Worcester Clo. Tal 4A **20**
Worcester Pl. Stoke 3J **35**
Wordsworth Clo. C'dle 4F **45**
Wordsworth Way. Als 6E **10**
Worrall St. Cong 4G **9**
Worsley Dri. Cong 6K **9**

Worth Clo. Stoke 2J **41**
Worthing Pl. Stoke 3G **41**
Wraggs La. Bid M 1G **15**
Wrenbury Clo. New 3A **26**
Wrenbury Cres. Stoke 4G **35**
Wren Clo. Bid 2D **14**
Wren Vw. Stoke 4J **41**
Wrexham Clo. Bid 1C **14**
Wright Av. New 5C **26**
Wrighton Clo. Stoke 3E **34**
Wright St. Tal 2A **20**
Wroxham Way. New 4D **38**
Wulstan Dri. New 2F **33**
Wulstan Rd. Stoke 6K **27**
Wyatt St. Stoke 4F **21**
Wycliffe St. Stoke 4J **27**
Wye Clo. C'dle 5H **45**
Wye Rd. New 2D **38**
Wymondley Gro. Stoke 1A **46**
Wynbank Clo. Big E 4F **25**
Wyndham Rd. Stoke 7E **40**
Wynford Pl. Stoke 4G **35**
Wynstay Av. Werr 2B **36**
Wynstay Ct. New 5F **39**

Y

Yale St. Stoke 5H **27**
Yardley Pl. Stoke 1E **46**
Yardley St. Stoke 6E **22**
Yardley Wlk. Stoke 1E **46**
Yarmouth Wlk. Stoke 1J **41**
Yarnbrook Gro. Stoke 1C **28**
Yarnfield Clo. Stoke 4B **42**
Yateley Clo. Stoke 3G **35**

Yates St. Stoke 2A **34** (5D **4**)
Yaxley Ct. New 4E **38**
Yaxley Pl. Stoke 1E **46**
Yeaman St. Stoke 7A **34**
Yeldham Pl. Stoke 1E **46**
Yeovil Pl. Stoke 1E **46**
Yew Pl. New 4A **26**
Yew Tree Av. Stoke 4D **40**
Yew Tree Clo. L Oaks 3J **29**
Yew Tree Ct. Als 1F **19**
Yew Tree Ter. Kid 3D **20**
York Av. Ful 6F **49**
York Clo. For 6J **43**
York Clo. Gil H 2H **15**
York Clo. Tal P 4A **20**
York Pl. New 4E **32** (3D **6**)
York Rd. Stoke 3C **42**
York St. Leek 3G **17**
York St. New 5F **33** (3F **7**)
York St. Stoke 7A **28** (1D **4**)
Youlgreave Av. Stoke 3G **35**
Youlton Pl. Stoke 3G **35**
Younger St. Stoke 7C **34**
Young St. C'dle 4H **45**
Young St. Stoke 5J **21**
Yoxall Av. Stoke 5J **33**

Z

Zamenhof Gro. Stoke 3B **28**
Zennor Gro. Stoke 3G **35**
Zetland Pl. Stoke 1E **46**
Zetland Wlk. Stoke 1E **46**
Zion St. Stoke 4K **27**
Zodiac Dri. Stoke 4H **21**